IRELAND

A Rand McNally Pocket Guide

John and Shirley Harrison

Rand McNally & Company
Chicago New York San Francisco

The authors and publishers wish to thank Macmillan Publishers Limited for their permission to include six lines from the *Collected Poems of W. B. Yeats* (pp. 92 and 97); and McCullough Pigott, Dublin, for 'Galway Bay' (p. 84).

Cover photographs

Irish Tourist Board: Bunduff beach, Westport House, Bunratty Folk Park
Northern Ireland Tourist Board: Mournes (harvest), Portrush harbour

Photographs

Peter Baker
pp. 71, 83 (btm)

J. Allan Cash
pp. 35 (col. 1 mid.), 44 (btm), 50, 56, 61, 79, 110, 114

Irish Tourist Board
pp. 13, 27, 29, 32 (col. 1 top, col. 2 top, btm), 33 (col. 1 top, btm), 35 (btm), 44 (top, mid.), 53, 57, 58, 64 (col. 1 mid., btm), 65, 66, 67, 74, 75, 82, 83 (col. 1 top, col. 2 top), 84, 85, 88, 90, 97, 99, 102, 103, 121 (col. 2 top, btm), 124, 125

Northern Ireland Tourist Board
pp. 32/3 (background), 35 (top, col. 2 mid.), 37, 93, 96, 104, 106, 107, 111, 115, 116, 117 (top, btm), 118 (top, col. 1 btm), 119

Office of Public Works, Dublin
p. 49

Waterford Crystal Limited
p. 64 (top, col. 2 mid.)

Zefa
pp. 33 (col. 2 top), 70, 77, 89

Town plans

M. and R. Piggott

Illustration

pp. 6–7 Peter Joyce

First published 1982
Revised edition 1986

Published by Rand McNally & Company
Chicago New York San Francisco
Printed in Great Britain
Library of Congress Catalog Card Number 85-60796

SBN 0-528-84840-2

HOW TO USE THIS BOOK

The contents page of this book shows how the country is divided up into tourist regions. The book is in two sections; general information and gazetteer. The latter is arranged in tourist regions with an introduction and a regional map (detail below left). All the towns in the gazetteer are shown on the regional maps. There are also plans of three of the main towns (detail below right), with places to visit and leisure facilities indicated by symbols. Main roads, railways and airports are shown on the maps and plans.

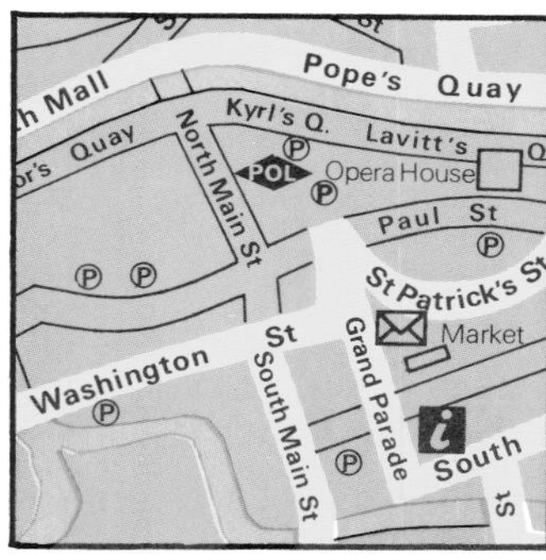

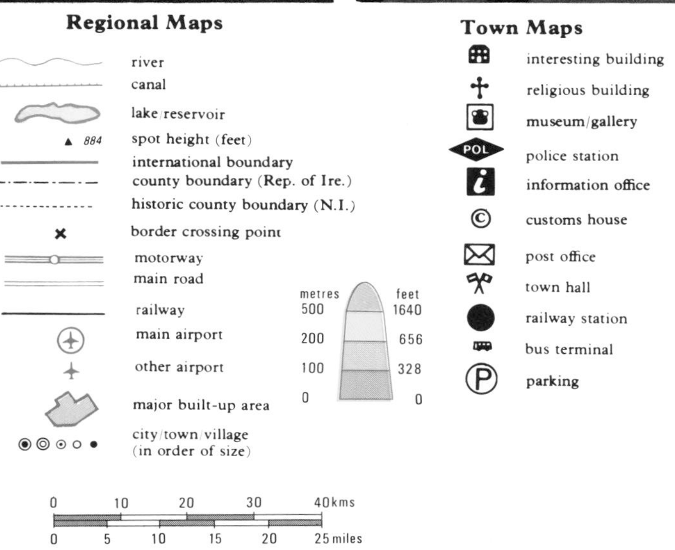

Every effort has been made to give you an up-to-date text but changes are constantly occurring and we will be grateful for any information about changes you may notice while travelling.

CONTENTS

Regions and Counties

1 Dublin City and the East
1 Dublin
2 Kildare
3 Louth
4 Meath
5 Wicklow

2 The South East
6 Carlow
7 Kilkenny
8 Tipperary (south)
9 Waterford
10 Wexford

3 The South West
11 Cork
12 Kerry

4 The Mid West
13 Clare
14 Limerick
15 Tipperary (north)

5 The West
16 Galway
17 Mayo

6 The Mid North
18 Fermanagh
19 Leitrim (north)
20 Sligo

7 The North West
21 Donegal
22 Londonderry
23 Tyrone

8 The North East
24 Antrim
25 Armagh
26 Down
27 Londonderry (east)

9 The Midlands
28 Cavan
29 Laois
30 Leitrim (south)
31 Longford
32 Monaghan
33 Offaly
34 Roscommon
35 Westmeath

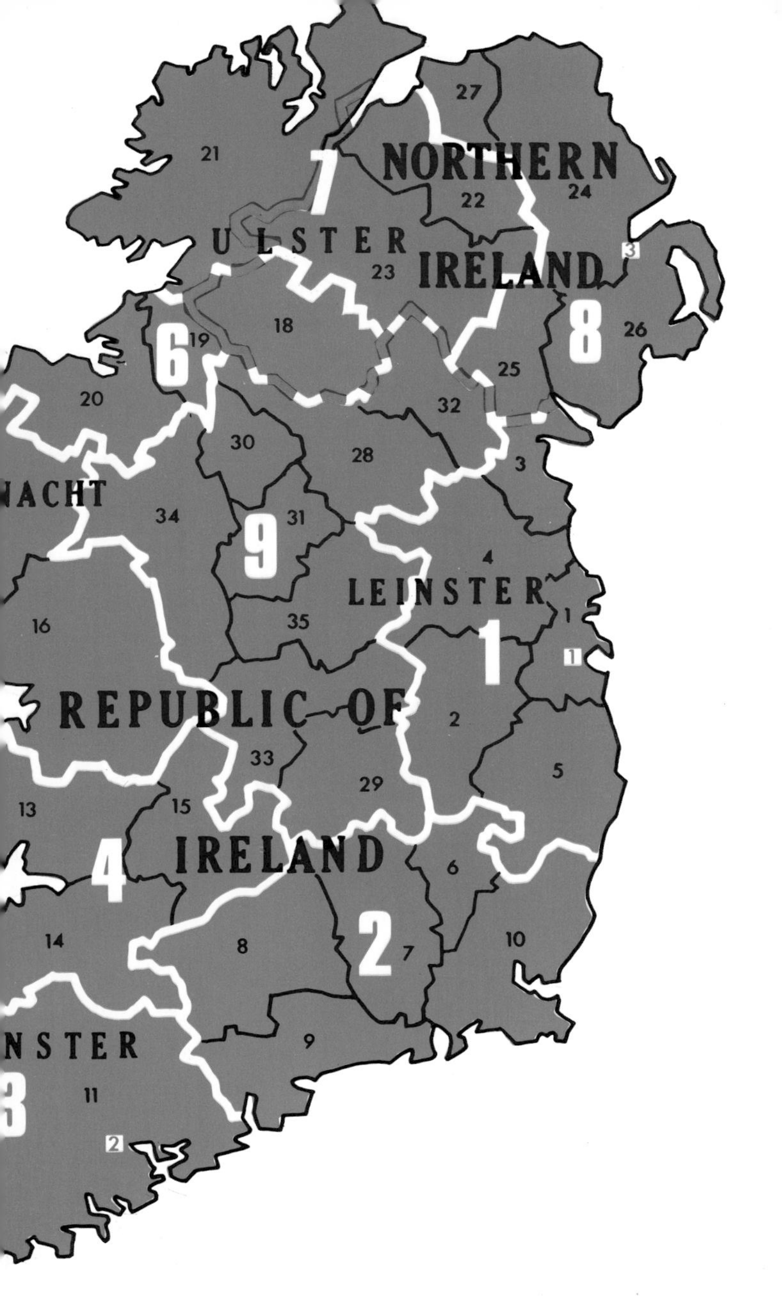

NORTHERN IRELAND
ULSTER
NACHT
LEINSTER
REPUBLIC OF IRELAND
NSTER
1
2
3
4
6
7
8
9
21
27
22
24
23
18
19
20
26
25
32
30
28
31
34
4
1
16
35
2
33
29
5
13
15
6
14
8
7
10
9
11

IRELAND

The British Isles is a group of islands on the north-west margin of the continent of Europe. The largest of these is Britain, the second largest, Ireland – the Emerald Isle, the Western Isle, Erin. The personality of the land and its people is largely due to its comparative size and position, cut off from its eastern neighbour and cut off by it. If it were larger, or out in mid-Atlantic, or if it were connected by land as Scotland and England are connected, it would be a very different country.

The Irish Sea, between Ireland and Britain, is on average 72km/45mi wide and at its narrowest, opposite Scotland, is only 18km/11mi wide; the Irish usually call this sea the 'channel'. The area of all Ireland is 84,421sq km/32,595sq mi, a little larger than Scotland; and the six counties of the north east, which are a separate political entity, are smaller than Yorkshire – only 14,139sq km/5459sq mi.

Being on the western edge of the British Isles – or the eastern edge of the Atlantic – the climate is wetter but more equable than Britain's. Snow is very rare, drought rarer. There's plenty of rain to keep the grass green and the rivers full, and it would be foolish to visit Ireland without a raincoat. But it's nearly always gentle rain, and not so much as the comedians would have you believe; it is unpredictable, however, so if your activities depend on the weather don't plan too far ahead. The Irish tolerance of the weather leads to their tolerance of the unaccountable weaknesses of their fellow humans.

Even if it is raining one day, it will be fine and clear the next – or perhaps the day after – and you can be sure that, 'You should have been here yesterday – not a cloud in the sky all day'. The cloud matters as much as the rain. Lying low over the mountains even in summer, it may seem sombre but so much more interesting than Mediterranean blue. Then, it can blow away in minutes for a quick burst of warm sunshine and a change of scene that keeps artists busy. The average temperature in January is 4°C, and in July and August 14-16°C; the sunniest months are May and June.

Ireland, in comparison with the European continent, looks rather like rural Britain. The resemblance is not just in the legacy of colonialism, but in the shapes of the fields and their hedges, the planting and the crops, gates and roads, the proportions of the windows in the square, slate-roofed houses. Only the far west, the poor wind-blown seaboard of white-washed cottages on bare hillsides, looks quite different. But on a closer inspection the resemblance fades – for a Briton, it's like looking at the world through a distorting lens, nothing is quite right. Even the things that seem most familiar – food, pubs, seaside resorts, landladies, clothes – suffer some distortion. It's a shift not of place but of time; the familiarity is with the Britain of thirty or even fifty years ago.

Indeed, here lies perhaps the greatest charm of Ireland not just for the British but for any visitor. The country has modern amenities but retains the simplicity of the rural countryside, something which has vanished from most other places. Even Northern Ireland, known as the industrialized part of the country, is for the most part solidly rural. In the south, which has been working hard to develop manufacturing industries, you have to look hard to find anything but agriculture and a life that takes agriculture as the norm (with the exception of Dublin). This quality may be due partly to the low density of population – there are now 3.5 million people in the Republic, making it the most thinly populated country in Europe after Norway and Sweden, with a density of only 46 per sq km/120 per sq mi. In Northern Ireland there are about $1\frac{1}{2}$ million people.

Nowhere in Ireland is more than 88km/55mi from the sea and yet the sea has played no great part in Irish life, except to bring invaders.

The influence of Britain is seen most strongly in the political partition of Ireland. The six counties of the north east constitute one province (the only province) of the United Kingdom of Great Britain and Northern Ireland, while the other 26 counties form the Republic of Ireland. The Republic claims sovereignty over the six counties but does not exercise it. Instead, the government of the Republic recognizes that Britain is at present the authority in Northern Ireland. Within Northern Ireland there is a continuing struggle between the nationalists, who are all Catholic and want the six counties to

become part of the Republic, and the Protestant majority who want to be no part of the Republic, preferably by maintaining the union with Britain. The politics and warfare of Northern Ireland leave it a place which you can visit and enjoy happily if you know what to expect.

You have to be prepared for the visual shock of seeing military checkpoints; concrete gun sites, barbed wire, armed soldiers in battledress at the border and in such places as Londonderry and Belfast. But once you get beyond these points and overcome this first impression you will be delighted you made the effort to meet the people and visit the country. Northern Ireland is different. Life there is more ordered and more down to earth. The people have coped with economic difficulties for far longer than the present recession in Britain. The problems of making a living are more important for almost all of them than 'the Troubles'. They have a refreshing 'let's get on with it' attitude. Paradoxically the countryside is quiet and peaceful, even in South Armagh and South Fermanagh where there is a timelessness which otherwise may be felt only in the more remote country lanes of the South of England.

The 32 counties of Ireland have been grouped historically into four provinces – Leinster in the south east, Munster in the south west, Connacht in the mid west, and Ulster in the north. This grouping is no longer used except in some sporting events, especially since Ulster has been split between Northern Ireland, which has become more 'British' in the sixty years since partition, and the three counties of Donegal, Cavan and Monaghan, which have become more 'Irish'.

For the purposes of describing Ireland for visitors, the country has been split into nine regions. These coincide with the seven regions into which the Irish Tourist Board has divided the Republic and with the natural groupings, older than partition, which are used in Northern Ireland. The order in which the areas are listed might be followed by those touring in Ireland, beginning in Dublin and proceeding south and west. **Dublin City and the East** includes the capital of the Republic with its historic buildings, shops, culture and conversation, plus beauty spots within easy reach for a day's outing – counties Dublin, Kildare, Louth, Meath and Wicklow. The sunny **South East,** with the longest history of settlement from England and the bravest history of resistance to England, is now the most prosperous part of Ireland – counties Carlow, Kilkenny, South Tipperary, Waterford and Wexford. The warm **South West** region contains the most famous scenic areas of Ireland – counties Cork and Kerry. The rich **Mid West** region, land of castles and dairies all within easy reach of Shannon airport – counties Clare, Limerick and north Tipperary. The bleak **West** region of Ireland, symbol of Gaelic Irishness with the beauty of Connemara – counties Galway and Mayo. The **Mid North** region is one of the most scenic in Ireland; Fermanagh is known for its lakes and Leitrim (north) has an international reputation as a coarse fishing region while Sligo, a county of lakes, forests and mountains is for lovers of nature. The **North West** is a combination of the empty wilds of Donegal and the rich lowlands of Londonderry and Tyrone. The **North East** covers the counties of Antrim, Armagh, Down and East Londonderry. The ninth grouping, called **The Midlands,** with its lakes and bogs covers the counties Cavan, Laois, Leitrim (south), Longford, Monaghan, Offaly, Roscommon and Westmeath.

The people of Ireland are descended from Gaelic settlers of two thousand years ago and immigrants from Britain over the past thousand years, the immigrants being absorbed by the Gaels little by little over the years. Most Irish, except those in the north who consciously look to Britain as their cultural origin, try to promote the Gaelic or Irish side of life for itself, but also to show they are not British. One national characteristic is the ability to live and let live, though this may sound strange in view of the intensity of rebellion shown in the past and the intermittent fighting going on today.

Irish people tend to be rather shy; the stereotype of the blustering Irish cop in American films is very hard to find. However, if you show any sign of friendliness, it's almost sure to be returned – just as it's easier to cope with the weather than to grumble, it's easier to be nice than nasty. Another stereotype you don't find is Paddy – the unreliable yokel, loveable if he weren't a menace. The Irish manage –

or muddle — in much the same way as anybody else, but they're not so concerned with an outward show of order.

Life is relaxed, slow-moving and easy-going. It really is, as the brochures say, the land where it's 'easy to take it easy'. There's probably more tolerance in most (but certainly not all) areas of conduct than anywhere else; people are polite but not formal, attentive but not pressing. To make up for the slow pace, life goes on very late at night, but also tends to start fairly late in the morning.

One stereotype which is lifelike is the 'talking Irishman' — the soft but clear melody of the accent, and the picturesque music of the words can still charm the birds off the trees; part of the trick is haziness where precision will do you no good. Graphic phrases, rooted partly in the Gaelic, flow easily. There's no shortage of 'blarney', talk which deceives without giving offence, especially for strangers. For the most part it's not really meant to deceive.

The gift for words comes out best in politics, and in the Irishman's attitude to politicians. With the music of those voices and the inspiring rhetoric which flows so easily, there may be no need for clear-cut proposals. The Irish know this, and treat their politicians with respectful contempt.

A less attractive side to the Irish character is the sense of grievance, but there's no grudge to go with it.

Ireland, or at least the Republic, is moving into the late 20th century with cautious industrialization and a countryman's desire for change. Exports are still mainly agricultural, and the biggest single export is one brand of stout. Around Shannon and along the east coast industry is increasing, but most industry is still related to food processing. Along with this, there is continuous drift from the land — Dublin already contains nearly one third of the population of the Republic.

The Republic is very conscious of its role as a small but independent country. Here perhaps is one of the strongest motives for preserving independence when tempted to 'closer association' with Britain in return for a united Ireland. Within Britain the Republic would number only three and a half million people — five million if all 32 Irish counties were counted — out of a total of 54 million.

Over half the people of the Republic are under 25. This makes it a more lively, bustling country than the Ireland of tradition, but it also produces familiar problems — the alienation of youth and a growing crime rate (though still the lowest in western Europe). Emigration, which for nearly two centuries has been Ireland's answer to poverty and an increasing population, has virtually stopped and in fact immigrants are moving in. This is a sign of the prosperity that Ireland has enjoyed since entering the EEC; the Common Agricultural Policy could almost have been designed to help Irish farmers, and the Irish are natural entrepreneurs when the opportunity presents itself.

Recent years have seen a marked growth in the standard of living with increasing car and television ownership, and foreign holidays. The old Gaelic values, based on a very different way of life, are under heavier pressure than they were under British rule. The final result of breaking away from Britain into European prosperity could have been to anglicize Ireland more than occupation did; but the Irish have discovered the art of compromise and are incorporating their traditional values into the consumer society.

THE PAST

About ten thousand years ago Ireland was connected to Britain and continental Europe by land bridges. Certain plants and animals migrated to Ireland, but before all species had established themselves, the seas rose, forming the present islands. As a result, Ireland has poorer soils and less diverse wildlife; for example, the beech tree is foreign to Ireland and there are no snakes.

Around 5000 BC the first men appeared — they used canoes like the currachs that are still the most practical form of small boat in Ireland's far west — but at the same time the bogs were starting to form on the waterlogged central plain. Today when the peat is carted away to fuel the power stations, traces of Old Stone Age agriculture are found underneath. The people of the New Stone Age arrived at about the same time as in Britain, say 2000 BC, leaving the passage graves of the Boyne Valley (see Drogheda, p. 54), and after them came the bronze workers. Who those early people were and what they looked like we do not know, but if it is true that earlier races had a knowledge of magic forces in the earth which we have lost, and if it is true that there is a strain in the Irish temperament still in touch with this magic, then the origin of this strain is in the Bronze Age population. They were overwhelmed but not destroyed by the next migrants, the Celts.

The Celts began to arrive in Ireland around 300 BC, and they may still have been coming in when the first Saxon pirates began to appear off the Roman shores of Britain; but the Romans and Saxons never got as far as Ireland, and the Celts were able to settle down and develop in their own way. Their pastimes were much the same as Latin authors of the time described for Celts in other countries – 'music, witty conversation, and stealing each other's cattle' – and there was little change until the Flight of the Earls. Their social system was based on the *fine* or extended family, and gave rise to the tradition of hospitality and story-telling which survives in Ireland today. There were no landowners – the cultivated land belonged to the tribe, and was periodically redistributed so that everybody got a share of the good and the bad – and the chiefs were elected from certain families so they had no rights in the land except while they were chief. There was no law as we know it but there was a class of lawyers called *brehons*, men who knew the exact scale of fines and compensations for all the offences their age could imagine; the chiefs and provincial kings were not there to enforce the law, this was left to public opinion. All this guaranteed trouble when Celtic society clashed later with a law-giving, land-owning, hereditary aristocracy from across the channel.

The tribes were loosely grouped into five to eight confederacies or provinces which had provincial kings. In about AD 76 one king in Meath took the title High King because it was in his territory that the tribes met from time to time to try to settle their differences without fighting. Whether the establishing of the High Kingship means that there was in any sense a united Ireland may seem like an obscure question, but popular argument about the rights of a united Ireland today implies that we can answer the question. From the time of the High Kings all history in Ireland is seen through the eyes of parties to a struggle which is still going on, and it is not possible to summarize it without deciding for one side or the other.

Conversation in Ireland makes constant references to people and events in the past, so here's a list including some of those who are treated as familiarly as George Washington or William the Conqueror.

Saint Patrick was a Romanized, Welsh Christian who, after escaping from Irish pirates in Co. Antrim, and learning the faith of his time in a French monastery, returned to Ireland about AD 432 to organize the Christians there into dioceses; to do this, he had to convert the pagan kings. Since there were no towns his diocesan structure gradually broke down and was replaced by a Christianity based on monasteries. Monks from Ireland were prominent in carrying the faith back to Europe where it had been submerged by continuing pagan invasion.

The **Danes** were the last of the pagan invaders. As Vikings or Norsemen they swept up the river valleys of France, England and Ireland, pillaging the monasteries and then founding trade settlements which later became towns. In France they settled and became the French-speaking Normans; in England they were checked by Alfred the Great (the cake burner); and in Ireland they stayed in their towns; fighting and trading with the natives, intermarrying, becoming the Dano-Irish alongside the native Irish.

Brian Boru was a provincial Irish king (Munster) who then made himself High King. Unlike his predecessors, who had only a vague spiritual seniority, he was a political overlord, more akin to the feudal kings then emerging in Europe. He built schools, roads and bridges, and dispensed justice like a mediaeval king. He died in AD 1014 at Clontarf, leading an Irish army with some Danish allies against the Danish king and his Irish allies; their defeat prevented the establishment of a Danish central monarchy that could challenge his own.

The **Normans** claimed descent from the Danes who had settled in Normandy, and conquered England in the ten years from 1066. A hundred years later from their base in England they began the conquest of Ireland which was never to be completed. They built castles, introduced new farming techniques, and became Celtic chiefs, combining with or replacing the Celtic aristocracy. They quickly gave up Norman French in favour of Irish, and became 'more Irish than the Irish themselves'. A new society arose, Celtic in outlook but with some Norman ideas concerning warfare and property; it is called the Gaelic order and lasted until after 1600. As in England, some families trace their name and descent back to the Normans; but unlike England, many more are aware of descent from Celtic kings.

The **Pale** was a small region around Dublin, varying in size, which acknowledged the authority of the English crown. After the Saxons and the Normans settled in England, settlers were sent to Ireland to colonize existing towns, the Pale and the south east. In the towns there was an attempt (unsuccessful) at segregation, to stop the settlers from going native, but in the country they soon adopted native ways while in some cases retaining their English language. In the south east there grew up the first English-speaking Irish; only in the Pale did the settlers retain the outlook of their native land and allegiance to its rulers.

The Protestant **Reformation** was a movement, mainly in Germany and Scotland, to reform the teaching of the Catholic church in various doctrinal matters, and this involved, almost incidentally, denying the authority of the Pope. King Henry VIII of England was no doctrinal Protestant, but the idea of denying the authority of the Pope appealed to him so he made the Church of England half Protestant. He let the Irish parliament declare him King of Ireland, to show that he did not derive his rights there from the Pope, and dissolved the Irish monasteries as he had those in England, using their lands to buy the loyalty of the Gaelic chiefs. It was he who created the breach between Protestant ruler and Catholic subject which in later years prevented a merger between the two.

Plantation was the idea of Henry's daughter, Mary. She was a Catholic, and to prevent rebellion in the parts of Ireland that had accepted her father's reforms she cleared the land in Counties Laois and Offaly and settled 'loyal' colonists there. Within ten years they were Irish rebels. Her sister, the Protestant Elizabeth, was faced with rebellions by the Gaelic chiefs, which were put down with increasing severity, and the plantations were extended to Cork and other parts of Munster. These early plantations consisted of granting huge tracts of land to a few landowners, and left little mark on Ireland.

More significant was the plantation of Ulster, carried out after the Flight of the Earls. The Earls of Tyrone and Donegal had been defeated after years of rebellion, but were left in possession of their lands so the English crown could rule through them. They were Gaelic chiefs, but at the same time mediaeval English aristocrats and also Renaissance princes; when they realized they had no future except as figureheads, they just upped and went (1607). Their lands, or rather the lands of their people, were confiscated and parcelled out amongst settlers from Scotland and England (see p. 98). The settlers were much more numerous than in Laois and Munster, and the plantation has survived; every settler on the good lands was a Protestant, while all the Irish who were dispossessed and driven into the bad lands were Catholics.

Oliver Cromwell led the armies of Parliament which defeated the king in the English Civil War, and having executed the king he crossed to Ireland to sort out the civil war there. Eight years previously the Irish dispossessed by the plantation of Ulster, aware that the king was about to be otherwise engaged, had tried to recover their lands and massacred many of the English settlers, leaving the rest in a mood of siege from which they have never really recovered. After that the different groups left in Ireland by plantations, the Reformation, and earlier settlements, split and became involved in a many-sided war of impossible confusion. To show that a new order had arrived, Cromwell massacred the garrison of the first town to oppose him, Drogheda (p. 56), and went on to crush the rest. The lands of all those who could not prove they had supported Parliament were confiscated, and Catholics, even if they could prove they had been loyal, were forced to exchange their lands for bog in the barren wastes of Connacht.

The **Battle of the Boyne** was fought in 1690 between a Catholic and a Protestant claimant to the English throne (see Drogheda, p. 56). For the Irish, it was not a religious war but a chance to reverse the Cromwellian settlement. The Protestant victory has been celebrated every year since then, as a ritual to annoy Catholics rather than an act of thanksgiving.

The **Penal Laws** were passed after the Battle of the Boyne to exclude Catholics from public office, buying land, teaching, even holding Mass; but they did allow Catholics to pay rent and dream of revenge.

The **Ascendancy** was the name given to the Irish Protestants, mostly of English origin, who conformed to the established church (*ie* the Church of Ireland, neither Catholic nor Presbyterian) and who ran the country under the Penal Laws. They formed a distinct social class, a mixture of aristocrats, landed gentry, professionals and black sheep, not quite able to compete with their counterparts in England. So in the Irish context the antagonism felt by the landless for the rich was increased by difference of religion and even of race. The Ascendancy, later called the Anglo-Irish, could not feel secure. Not all Protestants belonged to the Ascendancy — there were Protestant tenants in the south, who got preferential treatment compared to their Catholic colleagues, and dissenters in the north, mainly Scots Presbyterians, who enjoyed traditional rights against the landowners.

The **American War of Independence** was seen as a refusal by the English and Ulster-Scots in the American colonies to accept rule from the 'mother country' — the colonists had become a nation. It created an opportunity and an example for the Ascendancy in Ireland to see that they too were colonials, ruled from Britain in the interest of Britain; in their view they were no longer Englishmen living abroad, but Irish. They threatened revolt, and were fobbed off with a parliament free to legislate without approval from London.

Wolfe Tone was a Protestant who believed in equality for Catholics and Protestants (the Penal Laws had almost fallen away by his time, 1790), the separation of Ireland from England and the creation of a Republic. He headed a rebellion with French Support but it was a fiasco and ended in a massacre of Protestant tenants by Catholic labourers, and a worse massacre of Catholic insurgents by British troops.

The **Union** of Ireland with Great Britain was the English response to Wolfe Tone's rebellion, and took place in 1801. The Prime Minister, Pitt, saw the Union as leading to a partnership of equals, at least to the extent that the union of Scotland with England had been an equal partnership a hundred years earlier, and he saw that the first step must be complete Catholic Emancipation. But he could not overcome the prejudices of his time – the ruling clique believed they had to govern Ireland, and kept a Lord Lieutenant in Dublin as though it were still a colony. So the Union was doomed to failure; in the next 115 years there was little but the fight for Irish independence.

The Year 1829 is remembered in Ireland as the year O'Connell forced the British government to permit Catholics to sit in parliament – the final step in Catholic emancipation. More significantly, it was the year of the Rainhill Trials in England, to find the best steam locomotive – an event which marks that Britain was about to become a rich industrial nation, while most of Ireland remained totally rural and poor. In the same year, the first mill for the mechanical spinning of flax was built in Belfast – the north east of Ireland was about to join Britain in the Industrial Revolution.

The **Famine** took place in the years 1845-49. From 1780 the population of Ireland had grown from under four million to nearly nine million; while the east of Ireland was raising cattle and grain to feed Britain, the west was growing potatoes to fatten people. In 1845 there was a partial failure of the potato crop, and the authorities coped rather well though the Prime Minister, Peel, was dismissed for his foresight in ordering supplies of grain. In 1846 the crop failed completely, and tens of thousands starved while the authorities did what they could. The harvest of 1847 was superb, and everybody but the Irish forgot Ireland. In 1848 the harvest failed again, and the following winter was the worst on record. The official figure for deaths by starvation was 20,000; the more likely figure is 800,000 dead of starvation and disease; about 700,000 people emigrated to Britain and a million to North America. By 1851 the population was down to 6½ million, and emigration from Ireland continued for another hundred years.

The revolutionary movement to break the Union and establish Irish independence began at the height of the famine, and continued until the Easter Rising of 1916. It merged, in the 1880s, with the Land War to strengthen the position of the rural peasantry against the landlords. For a time effort was diverted into the parliamentary fight, under Parnell, for Home Rule, *ie* partial self-government under the British Crown. Then, towards the end of the 19th century, a nationalist movement grew which coloured the political movements. Two important bodies were set up: the Gaelic Athletic Association of 1884 to encourage Celtic-Irish sports, and the Gaelic League of 1893 to promote the vanishing Celtic-Irish speech; and the literary movement of Yeats began to show that literature in English did not have to reflect English values but could be based on Celtic-Irish traditions. There was a growing feeling that Irish equated with Gaelic, and Gaelic with Catholic.

Kindness was the policy adopted by the British government at the turn of the century as the way to silence Irish agitation. Reforms and palliatives were rushed through which nearly worked. The landlords were bought out and Ireland became a nation of owner-occupiers; the co-operatives enriched farming in the more favoured areas, while the Congested Districts Board improved life in the infertile west; local government on the British pattern was set up; health and housing were tackled; catholic universities were set up. The right-wing government thought they were 'killing Home Rule by kindness', with a Marxist reliance on economic factors. What they were really engaged in was an attempt to make the Union work by letting Ireland develop to the same position as Britain. They were a hundred years too late but, even so, the policy nearly succeeded.

The **Easter Rising** took place on Easter Monday 1916; its moving spirit was Patrick Pearse. Pearse saw that the Irish people had almost swallowed the bait of the kindness policy – of 120,000 Irish volunteers, formed to fight against the king's troops, 110,000 had volunteered to fight for king and country in the 1914-18 war. With a blend of political realism and mystical insight Pearse envisaged a blood sacrifice as the only way to pull Ireland back from assimilation into British life. Many politicians know the value of a martyr, but Pearse was unusual in offering himself for martyrdom. He and his followers occupied some buildings in Dublin, proclaimed a Republic, were captured and 17 of them shot. The Rising was not intended to achieve anything militarily, but only to stir the Irish soul. In that it succeeded – after the war Irish Catholics rejected British rule completely.

The **Anglo-Irish War** was fought from 1919-21, an attempt to maintain British rule by force until peace could be established on British terms. It ended with a treaty by which the 26 Catholic counties became the Irish Free State, while the six counties of the north east were free to choose their future status and, inevitably, chose to maintain the Union as the Province of Northern Ireland.

The **Irish Civil War,** or the Troubles, was fought in 1922 between the majority who thought the treaty was a useful step towards a Republic of all Ireland, and the anti-treaty forces who insisted on an immediate Republic (partition seemed temporary, and unimportant at the time). The majority won. In 1937 the Free State became 'Eire' – a Republic in all but name – and then came the 1939-45 war. Eire stayed neutral; out of the war came a Britain with less confidence in its mission to rule, and an Ireland with more confidence in itself. In 1949 the 26 counties declared themselves a Republic, and the name of the state became the Republic of Ireland; the British government recognized this, but guaranteed that the province of Northern Ireland would remain part of the United Kingdom so long as that was the wish of the majority in the six counties.

When Britain joined the **European Economic Community** in 1973, Ireland was still so closely tied to Britain economically that it had to follow (fortunately this happened to be the Irish wish anyway). Within the community, the export-minded industries that were started in the Republic have flourished, and agriculture has become very prosperous, at least in comparison with the rural Ireland of even twenty years ago.

THE LANGUAGE

According to its constitution, the first language of the Republic is Irish; English is permitted as the second official language. Clearly, this is a legal fiction, for almost the only language spoken in Ireland is English, and if you want to hear Irish you must go looking for it. It is conceivable that this theoretical primacy of Irish could be scrapped in the interest of unity, but, even if it is, the spirit that put Irish in first place will remain, as an ideal to Nationalists and a source of suspicion to Protestants.

It is worth knowing about the status of the Irish language, if you're interested in Ireland. There is no need for the visitor to learn any of the language itself, though in the Republic many signs and official notices are in both languages. Just remember that over the toilets the words MNA is not a misspelling of men but is Irish for ladies.

The language is called *Ghaeilge,* the English form of which is Gaelic. However, 'Gaelic' usually means Scots Gaelic, and the correct English name for the language is Irish Gaelic.

Modern Irish is descended from a Celtic language that was brought to Ireland around 300 BC; it has changed enormously from that early Celtic, but less than say French has changed from Latin or English from Old Saxon. The Celtic languages were Indo-European as were the Latin and Germanic languages which displaced them everywhere but the western fringe of Europe. One Celtic language which became established in Britain is still spoken today as Welsh. A rather different form of Celtic became dominant in Ireland. The British form is sometimes called Brythonic while the Irish form is called Goidelic, and since a British 'q' sound appears as an Irish 'p' sound they are also called q-Celtic and p-Celtic.

This difference in language is often used to argue that the Irish are of a 'different' race and are therefore a separate nation. However, it is probable that Brythonic was spoken in Ireland, too; whether the Brythons got there first and were conquered by a later wave of Goidels, or vice versa, we cannot tell.

When the monks adapted the Latin alphabet for writing Irish, they used only 18 letters and made up their own rules for representing sound-changes that would not be noticed by a foreign ear but are part of the grammar of Irish. This has led to the impossible-looking clusters of letters you see in written Irish – Diarmaid Ui Suilleabhain and Dermot O'Sullevan are pronounced the same way. For ceremonial purposes the 18 characters are printed today in 'Gaelic' typeface which is based on the normal script used in the eighth century throughout north-west Europe.

For another thousand years Irish was the language of the chiefs and of the people of Ireland. Settlers speaking Norman-French or mediaeval English adopted Irish, and the decline did not begin until the early 17th century when the last native chiefs were forced to flee. By 1841 nearly half the people used Eng-

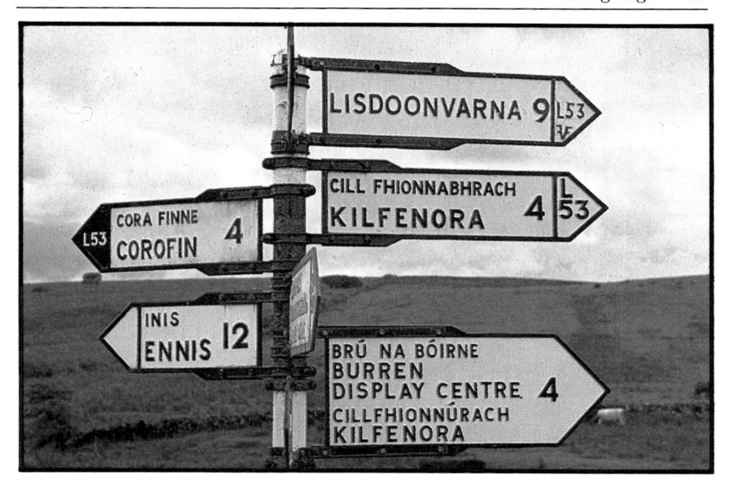

lish as their mother tongue. The famine speeded up the collapse of Irish – nearly all those who died or emigrated were Irish-speaking, and those who were left found that to get on at all they had to speak the language of the wealthy English. By the time of independence there were just a few pockets of country along the western seaboard where Irish was still spoken, and these were declared 'Gaeltacht'. Various forms of economic support are given to people in the Gaeltacht, to prevent decline in population and encourage the preservation of Irish.

According to census returns, 29% of the population (of the Republic) is Irishspeaking. This total is made up of 1% using Irish every day; 8% able to speak Irish as a learned language; and 20% who remember a bit of the Irish they learned at school, and would like to see an Irish-speaking Ireland. They may not be in sufficient numbers to form a community but there are more than enough to form an effective pressure group, encouraging successive Irish governments in their policy of support for the Irish language.

The most obvious evidence of the policy in action is road signs; destination signs are bilingual, with the name in Irish on top, in small characters, and the name in English underneath (see above). On buses and coaches, the destination boards are only in Irish. Official notices are put up in both Irish and English, though important notices may be in English only. Public announcements at airports and sometimes at bus stations are in Irish and English, and most national (not local) newspapers have a column in Irish. There are regular programmes in Irish on television, and a purely Irish radio station for the Gaeltacht. With these exceptions, you're not likely to come across much Irish.

Some Irish words that you will encounter in place names are: *Ar* or *Ard* – high; *Ath* – ford; *Bally* – inhabited place; *Ben* – peak; *Caher* – stone fort; *Clon* – meadow; *Drum* – hill; *Dun* – fort; *Ken* – head; *Kil* – church; *More* – great; *Muc* – pig; *Oughter* – upper; *Ros* – wood or promontory; *Slieve* – mountain; *Tra* – beach; *Tully* – hillock.

Irish is a compulsory subject at school and, throughout the Gaeltacht, there are summer Irish 'colleges'. Schools and community centres are used as centres for teaching Irish, while children and sometimes adults go to spend a few weeks with an Irish-speaking family, partly for a summer holiday and partly to experience, at first hand, their national culture. Attendance at Irish colleges is voluntary, yet the kids come in their thousands to learn what they call 'our native language'.

The motivation of those wanting to encourage Irish and even make it the real national language comes from the belief that the soul of a people is in its language; while the language lives, Irish culture and a distinctive Irish identity cannot die.

In making Irish the national language, one of the difficulties is to decide on the standard. In countries where a single dialect has emerged as the standard for a national tongue, it has been the speech of a ruling class or of the Court. Irish, however, is the language of a struggling peasantry, and there are three different dialects – Munster, spoken in Cork and Kerry; Connacht, spoken in Galway and Mayo; and Donegal, all equally correct. Nowadays the tendency is to let people speak Irish with their own local accent.

The only language in Northern Ireland is English. The settlers arrived from England or the Scottish Lowlands speaking a language that had been theirs for 20 generations; the majority of the Catholics are descendants of 're-immigrants'.

LEGEND AND LITERATURE

In Gaelic society the past was remembered and re-told by two kinds of court historian, the *filis* and the *bards*. Bards were an ancient Celtic order of poets who composed and often sang, usually to the accompaniment of a harp, verses celebrating the achievements of chiefs and warriors. St Patrick, who traditionally is supposed to have arrived in Ireland about AD 432 and who converted Ulster, Connacht and Munster to Christianity, was the first to appreciate the worth of the pagan morality, and following his directions their legends were recorded by monkish writers. In more modern Irish life the semi-professional storyteller, *shanachie*, kept alive the memory of the same legends and added some of his own, and his tales have been captured by folklore societies and tape recorders.

The tradition is not dead, and if you sit in a group and steer the conversation towards what the others remember hearing as children, you will hear the Irish gift for talk. Whether it's Finn MacCool, or what grandfather said to Parnell, or what father did to the Tans, the dead come alive. Local legends abound, but for these sophisticated times the speaker begins them with a little disclaimer, 'They do say . . .' Here are some of the main characters who turn up again and again – it may help to know who they are.

The Fomorians were sea-pirates who drove the first invaders, the sons of Nemed, out of Ireland; the Nemedians fled to Greece but came back under the name of Firbolg and occupied the whole land. Then the Tuatha De or De Dananns arrived from Spain (or Scythia, or Scotland); they took over, but let the Firbolg stay on as a subject race. The Tuatha De were gods but their spells were not sufficient to defeat the Milesians, who came from Egypt, the last invaders of Ireland. The Tuatha De still live underground, beneath the tumuli of the Boyne Valley; they were worshipped as gods by the Celts who claimed descent from the Milesians.

Hero of the northern Celts was Cuchulain, whose base was the Cooley Peninsula (see Dundalk, p. 57). Queen Maeve of Connacht summoned the armies of all Ireland to aid her capture the brown bull of Ulster while the men of Ulster were under a fairy spell, but Cuchulain fought the cattle raiders off single-handed for three months.

For the midland Celts the hero was Finn MacCool. He was the giant who built the Giant's Causeway to go and fight a Scottish giant, and formed Lough Neagh by scooping up a huge boulder and throwing it into the Irish Sea where it remains as the Isle of Man. Finn headed a militia called the Fianna, or Fenians, who defended Ireland from her enemies and protected the honour of her maidens; they invented Gaelic football. Finn was to marry Grania, daughter of Cormac son of Art (called Art the Lonely because he had no wife; Cormac was reared by a she-wolf), but when she saw how old Finn was, she ran off with a younger member of the Fianna called Dermot. Finn chased them and the places the couple stopped are marked by huge stone slabs mounted on pillars. Some call these Diarmaid and Grianna's beds, others call them Druids' altars, and still others call them dolmens. Finn later had a son called Oisin, or Ossian, who was a poet.

Early Irish literature consists of annals, genealogies and epics recalling the deeds of Cuchulain, Finn, *et al*; similar themes occur in European literature, *eg* the story of Tristan and Isolde, and in the Arthurian legends. Conditions in Ireland in more modern times did not encourage literature in Irish, though there have been modern writers of merit especially in short stories.

Writers in English have tended to come from the Anglo-Irish (with emphasis on the Irish), and modern Irish writers use English with no loss of nationality. Jonathan Swift (1667-1745) is chiefly remembered for *Gulliver's Travels*; Oliver Goldsmith (1728-74) *She Stoops to Conquer*; Sheridan (1751-1816) *The Rivals* and *School for Scandal*; Maria Edgeworth (1767-1849) *Castle Rackrent*; Thomas Moore (1779-1852) the poet, sentimentalized or satirized; George Moore (1852-1933) and George Russell (penname AE, 1867-1935) poets and novelists.

Later Irish writers are much better known, especially James Joyce (1882-1941) – *The Dubliners*, *Portrait*, *Ulysses* and *Finnegan's Wake*. The poet W.B. Yeats (see Sligo, p. 97) must be the greatest pure poet Ireland has produced;

his influence extended to the nationalist cause, stimulating those around him and particularly in the Abbey Theatre.

The other well-known names are all dramatists: Oscar Wilde and George Bernard Shaw left Ireland for England, to shock and succeed while John M. Synge and Sean O'Casey stayed at home to see Ireland bleed. After them came Brendan Behan, playing the universal Irishman, and Samuel Beckett. Seamus Heaney, a highly regarded poet today, was born near Londonderry in Northern Ireland.

FORMALITIES

Passports The United Kingdom (of Great Britain and Northern Ireland) and the Republic of Ireland constitute a 'common travel area', which means that they impose the same controls on immigration from outside the British Isles. Consequently, if you live in the British Isles or have already entered the country as a visitor, no passport need be shown when travelling between Great Britain and Ireland, or across the border between the Republic and Northern Ireland. (See below.) Evidence of identity may be asked for, and a passport is handy for this purpose. Citizens of the USA and other non-EEC countries must be able to show their passports when staying longer than three months.

Britain has fairly tough Anti-Terrorist laws. This sometimes leads to form-filling, particularly for air passengers, but most passengers leave and enter both countries without a glance from customs or immigration.

For entry into Ireland (or Britain) from outside the common travel area, a valid passport is needed. For citizens of the EEC, USA and British Commonwealth, no visa is needed.

When crossing the border between Northern Ireland and the Republic, there is no passport control. However, there may be a security check and you could be asked for evidence of identity, for which a driving licence is sufficient.

Driving A foreign visitor must hold a full driving licence to drive a car in the Republic, and a full licence or British provisional licence in Northern Ireland (See p. 20).

Health An existing reciprocal agreement means that British visitors to the Republic are entitled to free medical treatment. They will need the form E111 issued by the Department of Health and Social Security. As Northern Ireland is part of the UK, British visitors will get exactly the same treatment that they would at home. There are similar arrangements for visitors from other EEC countries. They should have brought with them the relevant form certifying that they are entitled to medical benefits in their own country, and need to contact the local Health Board (addresses in telephone directory) who will arrange for the treatment. Non-EEC visitors are in principle required to pay, though emergency hospital treatment and, by courtesy, emergency doctor's or dentist's treatment may be free. They are recommended to take out medical insurance valid for the Republic and Northern Ireland before leaving their home country.

Animals Both the United Kingdom and the Republic maintain a strict barrier against the importation of animals from outside the British Isles, because of the possible introduction of rabies. You can take in a pet, therefore, only if you are prepared to leave it (at your own expense) in quarantine for six months. Dogs and cats may be taken without restriction between Britain, Northern Ireland and the Republic, but not guinea pigs, rabbits, mice, monkeys and other animals which are high rabies risks.

CUSTOMS

The Customs authorities of the Republic issue a little green leaflet called 'Customs Guide' which details those goods on which duty is payable, those which are prohibited, and the allowances of duty-free personal goods. A similar leaflet is available from H.M. (*ie* British) Customs. These make complicated reading but in summary take it that import duty, value added tax and, on alcohol and tobacco, excise duty, are payable on everything except personal effects (clothing, camera, fishing rods, *etc*) and that firearms, meat and birds are prohibited. Irish Customs are more strict than most concerning books and pictures that could be considered offensive.

The Customs of both countries allow, as a concession not as a right, the import of certain amounts of excisable goods without payment of duty. (See table over.) The allowances of cigarettes and drinks are only for persons aged 17 or over.

British Customs permit each person to bring back the quantities listed in the column marked * (bought tax-paid in the Republic) or ** (bought in a duty-free shop).

US Customs permit duty-free $300 of goods per person, 1 US quart of liquor per person over the age of 18 (or 20, or 21 according to point of entry), and 100 cigars per person.

Duty-free allowances *subject to change*

			Bought duty free or outside EEC	Duty and tax paid in EEC
Tobacco	Double if you live outside Europe	Cigarettes	200	300
		or		
		Cigars *small*	100	150
		or		
		Cigars *large*	50	75
		or		
		Pipe tobacco	250 gm	400 gm
Alcohol		Spirits *over 38.8° proof*	1 litre	1½ litres
		or		
		Fortified or sparkling wine	2 litres	3 litres
		plus		
		Table wine	2 litres	4 litres
Perfume			50 gm	75 gm
Toilet water			250 cc	375 cc
Other goods			£28	£120

US customs permit duty-free $300 retail value of purchases per person, 1 quart of liquor per person over 21, and 100 cigars per person.

In travelling between Britain and the Republic, it is possible to buy duty-free goods on board ship or at the international airport. Duty-free goods for travellers to the USA can be bought at Shannon Airport.

There are of course no duty-free allowances, and no Customs, for travel between Britain and Northern Ireland since this is internal travel. There are also no allowances of duty-free goods when travelling between the Republic and Northern Ireland – air travellers have to bypass the duty-free shop. Tariffs are much the same on both sides of the border.

There are about 20 'approved' crossing points over the border (see maps) and a large number of 'unapproved' crossings (50 to 100). There is no regular check at unapproved crossings but the occasional security check. It is legal to cross at an unapproved crossing, but not encouraged.

CURRENCY

The unit of currency in the Republic is the punt (IR£) divided into denominations of IR£1, IR£5, IR£10, IR£20, IR£50 and IR£100 notes with six coins in use. These have values of ½p, 1p, 2p, 5p, 10p and 50p. One hundred pence make up one IR£. In value the Irish punt is usually close to the pound sterling but the two currencies are separate. The Irish punt is now linked with several other currencies as part of the European Monetary System.

From October 1984 visitors from the UK must use either traveller's cheques or Eurocheques: personal cheques are no longer accepted by Irish banks. The Central Bank of Ireland, the equivalent of the Bank of England, is considering introducing shortly a 20p coin which will be round in shape, not hexagonal like its British equivalent. The Republic is also considering the introduction of an IR£ coin.

In Northern Ireland the currency used is the pound sterling. Unlike England, Northern Ireland is not phasing out its £1 note.

Money from the Republic cannot be used freely in the north and should be changed into sterling. Sterling can be used in the Republic, but will be accepted at face value.

Credit cards are accepted in Ireland, in hotels, garages, by car hire companies and by shops that expect tourists. Dollar bills are accepted in most hotels and by car hire companies but for everyday use they should be changed in a bank.

In the Republic, banks are open Monday to Friday from 1000 to 1230 and 1330 to 1500 (1700 on Thursdays in Dublin); in provincial towns they stay open late on market day (once a week) usually until 1700. Banks in Northern Ireland are open Monday to Friday from 0930 to 1230 and from 1330 to 1530. Outside bank hours you can change money in a tourist information office at bank rate or in a hotel at discount.

HOW TO GET THERE

From North America

Scheduled air services to the Republic are offered by Aer Lingus and North West Orient. Aer Lingus flies from Boston and New York. North West Orient, which has a major network of starting airports, uses Boston and Minneapolis St Paul as its major gateways. International transatlantic flights begin or terminate at Shannon (flying time 7 hrs). Aer Lingus flights originate from or continue on to Dublin with a 45 minute stop at Shannon, though strictly speaking the Dublin/Shannon leg is an internal flight.

No direct scheduled service between Belfast and North America – use Dublin, Prestwick or London.

APEX fares entail some restriction on length of stay but offer a significant saving on the heavy cost of scheduled services.

Charter flights, as part of a package tour which includes hotel, cottage, car rental, coach tour or boat cruising, work out even cheaper than APEX fares; details from your travel agent, because the market is highly competitive and constantly changing.

From Europe

Irish Continental Line provides a car ferry service to Rosslare from Le Havre (3-5 departures a week, 21 hr crossing) and from Cherbourg (1-2 departures a week, 17 hr crossing) and to Cork from Le Havre (1 departure a week, $21\frac{1}{2}$ hrs crossing).

Aer Lingus in association with national carriers provides **scheduled flights** between Cork, Shannon and Dublin and Amsterdam, Brussels, Copenhagen, Dusseldorf, Frankfurt, Geneva, Hamburg, Jersey, Madrid, Milan, Munich, Paris, Rome and Zurich. British Midland Belfast/Paris, week days only.

From Britain

Car ferries: Stranraer/Larne ($2\frac{1}{4}$ hrs

Currency of the Republic of Ireland

crossing, up to 8 daily) Sealink; Cairnryan/Larne ($2\frac{1}{4}$ hrs crossing, 4 daily) Townsend Thoresen, Liverpool/Dublin (7-9 hrs crossing, 1 daily) B + I; Pembroke/Rosslare (4 hrs crossing, 2 daily) B + I; Fishguard/Rosslare ($3\frac{3}{4}$ hrs crossing, 2 daily) Sealink; Holyhead/Dun Laoghaire ($3\frac{1}{2}$ hrs crossing, up to 4 sailings daily, each way) Sealink; Holyhead/Dublin ($3\frac{1}{2}$ hrs crossing, 1 daily) B + I.

Different combinations of car passenger fares, reductions for returns, and the introduction of special promotional fares, make it difficult to compare tariffs, but in the end there's not much to choose between the prices. The notorious cattle-carriers of 20 years ago have gone, and the boats are reasonably comfortable today; it's worth paying the extra for first class, for one thing the piped music is much softer.

NB Stranraer and Cairnryan are both about two hours' driving from Glasgow; Liverpool, Holyhead, Fishguard and Pembroke are all about the same distance from London – Liverpool is motorway nearly all the way, while the road to Holyhead through North Wales can be very slow in summer if you're caught behind a caravan (trailer).

Direct flights between **Cork** and London (Heathrow and Gatwick), Manchester, Plymouth, Birmingham, Bristol, Exeter; between **Dublin** and London (Heathrow and Gatwick), Bristol, Birmingham, Blackpool, Cardiff, Castle Donington, Edinburgh, Glasgow, Leeds, Liverpool, Newcastle-on-Tyne; between **Belfast** and London (Heathrow), Liverpool and Glasgow; between Glasgow and **Londonderry.** The carriers are: British Airways and Aer Lingus, British Midland Airways, Brymon Airways, Dan Air, and Loganair. Loganair also flies to Belfast harbour from Edinburgh, Glasgow, Manchester and Blackpool. For addresses see p. 41/2.

Flights between Britain and the Republic count as international flights, open to price competition but subject to IATA; flights between Britain and Northern Ireland count as domestic flights, prices being subject to government regulation. However, disguised price competition in the form of promotional offers is on the increase.

New services In 1985 a Dublin/Holyhead helicopter service will be introduced. Details from Dublin City Helicopters, Holyhead (0407) 810880. There will also be a ferry service between Swansea and Cork. Details from Swansea Cork Kerry Car Ferries Ltd, Swansea (0792) 475495.

Travel times Rosslare is 163km/102mi from Dublin, Dun Laoghaire 12km/7mi; Larne is 33km/21mi from Belfast. Aldergrove Airport is 20km/12mi from Belfast city centre (Great Victoria Street Coach Station), about 30 mins in the bus. Dublin Airport is 10km/6mi from Dublin city centre; the airport bus starts from the bus station and takes 20 mins (subject to traffic delays) – every 20 mins weekdays, every 30 mins Sundays; a taxi from the bus station to Dublin Airport takes about 15 mins and costs about four times as much as the bus.

INTERNAL TRAVEL

Using public transport alone is not the easiest way to tour Ireland – services between main centres are adequate, but reliance on buses for out-of-the-way places demands planning, patience and careful study of the timetables. The advantage of public transport over a rented car is not only that it is cheaper, but it brings you into contact with other passengers – for the first half-hour you may sit in silence, but then the talk starts to flow.

Trains in Northern Ireland are operated by NIR (Northern Ireland Railways); coaches and buses by UTA (Ulster Transport Authority). In the Republic, trains, coaches and city buses are all operated by CIE (*Coras Iompair Eireann,* Irish Transport Authority). There are a few privately-operated bus services in the Republic, *eg* St Kevins, Waterford, but these are purely local and you can find them only by enquiring locally. For CIE, the main enquiry offices are at 59 Upper O'Connell Street and 35 Lower Abbey Street, Dublin (Tel: 787777 and 300777); for UTA, 10 Glengall Street, Belfast (Tel: 20011, and 20574 after 1800). Various freedom tickets are available from CIE, UTA and NIR giving unlimited travel for the set period. The Rail Rover, both in the Republic and in Northern Ireland, is hardly worthwhile because train services are so limited, but the Republic combined road-and-rail Rambler ticket is only slightly more expensive and good value. An Overlander ticket gives unlimited travel on trains, buses and coaches in both parts of Ireland. These tickets are obtainable from main enquiry offices.

If you intend to get around by public transport, do get the rail and bus timetables along with your Rover ticket. With a little planning you can get nearly everywhere without spending too long in a place of little interest.

Railways

In the Republic, most services radiate from Dublin, to Wexford and Rosslare, Waterford, Cork, Tralee, Limerick, Galway, Westport and Ballina, and Sligo. The only cross-country services are Limerick/Waterford, and radiating from Mallow to connect Limerick, Tralee and Cork. On longdistance trains there are 'super-standard' luxury cars, for which a supplement is payable. Seats can be reserved except at busy times. Bicycles may not be taken on trains. Children up to 15 years of age – half fare; below 5 – free. Day return tickets available at single fare on many services. Eurail Passes are accepted. Student passes can be validated at a CIE office for use in the Republic. Old age pensioners of the Republic are by law entitled to free rail and bus travel, and in practice if not by law old age pensioners from the UK get a similar concession. Main line trains in the Republic are smooth and punctual, with large picture windows. Restaurant car on some trains between Dublin and Cork, Limerick and Mallow. The suburban services of Dublin (Balbriggan and Howth to Greystones, now electrified) and Cork (Cork to Cobh) are called cattle trucks by the users, but this is a little unfair. The 'Radio Train' (Dublin/Killarney, and Dublin/Connemara) is for tourists in a hurry; running commentary and piped music.

The cross-border train is Belfast/Dublin via Portadown, Dundalk and Drogheda: 2½ hrs, five times a day in each direction; the timetable is the same in both directions. Cheap day returns; half-price day returns on Thursdays. Restaurant car on most trains.

The only other trains in Northern Ireland are Belfast to Antrim, Coleraine and Londonderry, to Larne, to Bangor; and Antrim to Lisburn.

Buses

CIE and UTA provide **sightseeing tours.** Many private operators, *eg* Joe Walsh, Pad Coach Tours, Dublin City and Shannonway Tours also provide coach tours usually combined with accommodation and, if you want it, travel from the UK. Details from the tourist boards or your travel agent. Plentiful day tours from the main towns offered in travel agents' windows in the high streets.

The **provincial bus services** cover the country comprehensively – the only notable gaps are in north-west Donegal and the Kerry Peninsula. However, the frequency of services to anywhere off the beaten track is poor. The standard timetables are leisurely but adhered to. **Express services,** connecting main centres (but generally not in competition with the trains), also stick to the timetable, and take about twice as long as a car (including a refreshment stop). Bus fares are almost the same as standard train fares, but there are no supplements for super-standard as on trains. The destination boards on CIE buses are in Irish, but timetables are in English. Ordinary inter-town buses will stop by the roadside if you raise your hand, but express buses will (normally) stop only at scheduled stops.

The major towns have adequate **local buses;** Dublin has an extensive network of frequent and late-running buses, covering both the inner city and far out into the suburbs. Usually crowded, and subject to traffic delays. City buses are supposed to collect passengers at bus stops only, but some drivers will open the door for you between stops or at traffic lights.

Taxis

Dublin, Cork and Galway have metered taxi cabs – fares as shown on the meter; tipping fairly modest, *eg* 10%. In other towns, a fare is quoted on booking. Don't use metered taxis for travel between towns, it's liable to be ten times the train fare; it is cheaper to rent a chauffeured car – address in the Golden Pages directory. For Belfast taxis – authorized and pirate – see p. 115; Dublin taxis see p. 51.

Car Rental

For self-drive car rental, see below.

Bicycles

Most of the country, except the mountains where there are no roads anyway, is flat and well-suited to bicycling. The country is small enough to get around most places by bike. Bicycle hire available in many towns; details obtainable from tourist enquiry offices, from advertisements in town guides published by local Junior Chamber of Commerce, or from TI Irish Raleigh Ltd, Broomhill Road, Tallaght, Dublin 24.

Hitch-hiking

Hitch-hiking is widely accepted and more commonplace than anywhere else in western Europe. The western seaboard and the main roads out of the ports are full of backpacking, young tourists, but elsewhere there are plenty of well-dressed, well-heeled, mature Irish who rightly take it for granted that they will get a lift of a few miles in a few minutes. It is not a source of embarrassment in Ireland to be without a car and hitching a lift.

Hitching is not as common in Northern Ireland as in the Republic.

Off-shore Islands

A regular steamer service from Galway pier to the Aran Islands takes around 3 hrs. There are also private boats to Rathlin Island from Ballycastle, to the Blaskets from Dunquin, and to Tory Island from Gortahork; these run at irregular intervals.

Aer Aran operates 20 minute long scheduled flights from Galway to the Aran Islands and to Dublin.

MOTORING

Car Rental

A list of approved rental firms ('car hirers') is available from Bord Failte and the NITB; the names and addresses of nearly all car hirers, including local garages, are in the classified telephone directories. Many rental firms have stands at Dublin and Shannon airports, with rather fewer at Cork and Belfast. The airlines offer a combined 'fly-drive' which is generally cheaper than flying and renting the car separately but not if you are willing to shop around; the sea carriers similarly offer 'sail-drive'. (Time Off Ltd [2a Chester Close, London SW1] package travel accommodation and car hire for roughly the full cost of separate travel and accommodation.)

The published tariffs of the different rental firms do not differ by more than 20%, but out-of-season or when trade is bad there can be a large variation in the discounts available. Enquire in the town offices for cut rates.

Most rental firms expect payment in advance for the anticipated length of the rental. The published rate includes third party insurance but not full insurance against damage to the car. For this you must either leave a heavy deposit (*eg* £200) or pay extra insurance as a collision damage waiver.

To rent a car you need a full, valid driving licence issued in your country of residence. The conditions of booking say the licence must be free of endorsements, but this may be waived. Prior arrangements are needed for car rental to a person under 23, and for large cars to a person under 25.

There is usually no extra charge if you want to pick up a car in one centre and leave it in another. However, special documentation is needed if you want to take a rented car across the border; an extra charge will normally be made.

Own Car (from the UK)

You must have a full driving licence to drive in the Republic, and you must have held a full driving licence for at least one year (or, after qualifying, put a red 'R' in the window for restricted) to drive in Northern Ireland. A British provisional licence is valid in N.I. but not in the Republic. It is advisable to take the vehicle registration document with you. British car insurance is valid in N.I. and in the Republic it is valid but only for the minimum cover required by the Irish Road Traffic Act; for full cover you need a Green Card from your insurers.

The AA in the Republic operates similarly to the AA in Britain, though there are fewer roadside patrols; membership of the AA is effective in the Republic and in Northern Ireland. For the RAC, pay the foreign travel fee which gives you rights to the Shamrock Service. (The Royal Irish Automobile Club is just a club and does not give the same privileges as membership of the RAC.)

Rules of the Road

Drive on the left. A leaflet summarizing Irish traffic signs is available at the port of entry into the Republic; the signs are generally the same as, or similar to, those in the UK, but mandatory signs are red while warning signs are yellow. There is a general speed limit of 88kph/55mph in the Republic, while the British limit of 112kph/70mph applies in Northern Ireland. Parking regulations are similar in N.I., Britain and the Republic, with yellow lines, traffic wardens and limited waiting, but the practice differs considerably. In the Republic it is normal, though possibly illegal to park anywhere that does not obviously cause obstruction — many cars look as though they have been simply abandoned. Parking in N.I. is more disciplined and subject to 'control zones'. Look out for 'No unattended vehicles' warnings — suspicious cars are sometimes detonated. It is obligatory in the Republic for drivers and front seat passengers to wear seat belts. It is also obligatory in Ireland as a whole for motor cyclists to wear helmets.

Fuel

Petrol (gasoline) is available in the Republic in three grades — normal, premium and super — corresponding exactly in octane rating to the two-star, three-star and four-star sold in the UK. Prices are, allowing for currency exchange, more expensive than in Britain. Filling stations are plentiful, and usually open till at least 2200; don't be shy of getting the proprietor from his house or the pub if a country filling station appears closed in the evening. Not all filling stations open before 0900; there are '24 hours-a-day, 7 days-a-week' filling stations in at least Cork, Dublin, Galway, Naas and Shannon/Ennis.

Alcohol

It is illegal to drive or be in charge of a car if the alcohol content of your blood exceeds: 80mg/ml in Northern Ireland, or 125mg/ml in the Republic. The traffic police of both parts of Ireland are armed with the Breathalyzer, and use it.

Road Conditions

Roads in Northern Ireland are built to the same specification as in Britain, and are often of a higher standard; roads in the Republic are built to a lower standard, but are quite adequate for the low volume of traffic. There is very little heavy goods vehicle traffic, and you can drive all day on country roads and never be held up except for a herd of cows being urged to or from pasture early in the morning or at dusk. Car ownership per road-mile is one quarter that of Britain, and traffic density is even less. There is almost no major road on a hill steep enough to require an indirect gear.

Direction signposting in the Republic is good on major roads; distances were formerly marked in miles, in black on white, but these are being converted to kilometres, in white on green; where there is room for doubt the sign writer is supposed to put 'mi' or 'km', but sometimes gets it wrong. However, direction signposting on minor roads is not good; many signposts are broken, and where not broken they merely point to an unsigned fork or crossroads. Beware of taking an unsigned turning that leads in the direction you feel you ought to be going – it may go for miles and miles with never a turning, to a dead end in the mountains.

Direction signposting is very good in N.I.; distances are currently all in miles; small country roads are usually marked with the name of the road, like a street in a town, and the name is that of the place the road eventually leads to.

The style of driving in the Republic is unagressive and relaxed – about equal to the undemanding road conditions – although drivers in Dublin may need great patience. Few Irish drivers use the dip-switch. Pedestrians tend to ignore road signals, as in London. The style of driving in N.I. towns is rather competitive, but otherwise is leisurely and shows an awareness of other road users.

'Major road works ahead' may mean a minor re-alignment or road widening, but is more likely to mean one man resting in traditional pose by a shovel. The continuous white line, which it is forbidden to cross and should be reserved for dangerous stretches, is liable to be used wherever the road is not dead straight.

The registration number of a car registered in the Republic consists of three numbers and three letters; in N.I., of letters followed by four numbers. Red rear number plates are legal in the Republic; yellow rear number plates are legal in the U.K.

WHERE TO STAY

The Northern Ireland Tourist Board and Bord Failte publish booklets which list all hotels and most other accommodation. Local tourist offices will recommend a place according to your taste and means, and make a booking on the spot for a telephone fee. At the cheap end, there is a wide choice in the Republic not listed in official booklets.

Hotels and Guesthouses

These are listed in *Hotels and Guesthouses* (50p) issued every year by Bord Failte and in *All the Places to Stay* (50p) put out by the Northern Ireland Tourist Board annually. An hotel provides restaurant, bedroom and public rooms, and is often an entertainment centre as well (dancing or cabaret) – in many small towns the hotel is the only focus of local life. A guesthouse is a private house given over entirely to accommodation for visitors, and the lounges are reserved for guests and not open to the general public. Hotels, from luxury establishments through to the modest equivalents of a coaching inn, are nearly all Irish-run for a mainly Irish clientele.

There are plenty of modern, high-standard hotels in the main towns, with the possible exception of Belfast, while in the country, especially near noted golf courses or fishing centres, old country houses or castles have been converted into hotels. Many hotels are agreeably old-fashioned, not impersonal.

In the Republic prices must be displayed in the hotel. The requirement to display in the North is in the pipeline but is not yet statutory.

Bed and Breakfast

Many farmhouses in the country and private houses in towns will receive guests, and some of them are listed in the booklets *Irish Homes* issued by Bord Failte, *Farm Holidays in Ireland* issued (with a photograph of each property) by Irish Farm Holidays Association, and *Northern Ireland – Farm and Country Holidays*. The Town and Country Homes Association, Gentian

Hill, Salthill, Galway, publishes an illustrated guide to those homes which are members of the association. 'Registered' accommodation means the good lady has put her name on the Tourist Board list, while 'approved' accommodation means it has also been inspected by the Tourist Board and found to be up to standard. In the Republic, in popular touring areas, there are many more houses that offer accommodation. (In Northern Ireland the law is that all guest rooms must be registered with the Tourist Board, but there are a few in seaside towns which are not registered.) All these properties, registered and unregistered, can be recognized by the sign 'B & B', and allow you to meet the Irish people at home. You can expect a friendly welcome – tea and a plate of biscuits on arrival, as to a friend rather than a paying customer.

The price of bed and breakfast runs from below the cheapest guesthouse rates up to considerable luxury, fabulous food and cost to match.

Self-catering Accommodation

In most of the well-touristed areas there are houses, chalets or cottages to rent – details from local or regional tourist offices. A full list for the Dublin area is given in the booklet *Holiday Homes to Let* from Dublin Tourism, 14 O'Connell Street. Commercial organizations with self-catering holiday packages include Aer Lingus, B + I, Sealink, Joe Walsh, Ashling of Waterford and Trafalgar Travel. 'Rent-an-Irish-Cottage' has a chain of purpose-built holiday bungalows, mainly in the Shannon area – details from Shannon Airport. In Northern Ireland the National Trust has a number of holiday cottages to let. These are listed in *All the Places to Stay*.

Romantic Accommodation

Horse-drawn caravans, a modern version of the tinker's caravan now nearly vanished, can be rented in certain areas. They are for seeing the countryside slowly, making friends and enjoying a break from routine. Average distance covered is 20km/12mi per day. A number of companies in the Republic have horse-drawn caravans (trailers) for hire. Get the Irish Tourist Board Information Sheet number 14 for details of organizations currently providing this service. Horse-drawn caravans are adequately equipped, and the horses are no trouble, but users are less than ecstatic about the comfort.

Many castles, including 19th-century castellated houses, have been converted to hotels – details from the Town and Country Houses Association. (Addresses p. 42.)

Tents and Trailers

You can park a caravan (trailer) or pitch a tent almost anywhere out in the wilds, or in a field with the permission of the farmer. As to fixed camp sites, in Northern Ireland there are over 100 privately owned caravan sites which can also be used for camping. Details in the booklet *Camping and Caravan Parks* published annually at 20p. Camp sites in Forest Parks can also be used. There are two types: Forest Caravan Sites are for an extended stay and Forest Touring Caravan Sites, with fewer facilities, are for a stay of not more than three nights. In the Republic there are about 800 'organized' camp sites of which just over 80 are of a standard to get Bord Failte approval – list of these from Bord Failte.

The bottled gas generally available to campers in the Republic is Kosangas (yellow bottles); fittings are not interchangeable with Calor gas. Blue Camping Gaz is also available, but not everywhere.

Cheap Accommodation

There are 53 hostels of the Irish Youth Hostels Association, *An Oige*, and 10 of the NIYHA. Addresses in the International Youth Hostels Association handbook. Student hostels in Dublin, Galway and Cork. Colleges of summer education, *eg* in Sligo, Wexford and several parts of the Gaeltacht, have access to accommodation but only for students attending holiday courses.

EATING AND DRINKING

The tradition of Irish food is plain local produce, simply cooked; it's the same style of food as you will find in Britain, and prepared with the same finesse. The land produces meat (beef, lamb and pork), dairy products and potatoes, and these are the staples of cooking. 'No appetizing sauces or elaborate presentation are necessary', or attempted. It is basically simple country food, considerably upgraded in response to rising prosperity, tourist demand and the example of a few up-market places. Fried food is widespread. For the gourmet, the Kinsale area is reckoned the safest bet, but the *Good Food Guide to Ireland* remains significantly slender.

Characteristic Irish dishes: crubeens (pigs' trotters); drisheens (blood sausage); corned-beef-and-carrots; soda bread, which is really good but don't fill up on it before you reach the main course; cabbage-and-bacon pie; colcannon (cabbage-and-potato pie, may be highly seasoned); Irish stew, which is just a stew, very popular in pubs serving bar snacks; a side plate of jacket potato, in addition to any potato in the meal; bracks (sweet bread with currants).

Irish dishes found in hotels: trout, usually brown trout caught locally (much tastier than rainbow); salmon (poached or boiled), always beautifully fresh and when there is a glut in summer it can cost less in Dublin than on the west coast where it was caught; lobster, when you can get it – expensive because too much good Irish lobster goes to France; oysters, by tradition washed down with Guinness – the Galway Oyster Festival in September is the great place for oysters. All the ham is good, but pale Limerick ham is reputedly the best.

Where to Eat

Hotel food is usually adequate but unadventurous – hotels are required by law to provide a cooked meal at reasonable hours.

In the larger towns, you can find a fair range of restaurants, from the expense account variety through genteel cafés in big stores, to little eating-places round the corner. Smaller towns may have no restaurant at all, or one newly opened place with a French name, Frenchified menu and Irish food. More often there's a café or snack bar serving fish, grills and chicken, with greater zest and less grease than its British counterpart.

Growing fast is the takeaway; not an attraction exactly, but having the great merit that you can find one nearly everywhere and that it stays open till very late at night. In main towns, American-style fast-food joints, hamburger houses, pizza palaces and Chinese restaurants are spreading fast, and are well patronized. For a midday meal, many pubs have noticed the dearth of restaurants and the surplus of customers for them, and offer decent 'Pub Grub'. Best value at the cheaper end is an ordinary-looking house in a side street with the door open. A typical very moderately priced menu would be soup, roast meat and veg. (no choice), jelly and ice cream or jam roll and custard, biscuit and cheese, tea or coffee.

Eating Habits

Breakfast is a substantial meal (unless you specifically ask for a continental breakfast): fried bacon and egg, sausage, and usually tomato, toast and marmalade, and plenty of good tea or indifferent coffee. Midday meal is called 'dinner' in traditional Ireland, but 'lunch' where the habit of a cooked evening meal is taking hold; service of lunch in restaurants starts before 1200, and may be finished by 1400. The same meal served in the evening costs twice as much as at lunch. Afternoon tea is a bit of a problem for British visitors – very often there is nowhere you can go for just a cup of tea; the lounge of a pub, which is usually quiet in the afternoon, is a good alternative – non-alcoholic drinks and sandwiches. Evening meal is by tradition 'high tea', served from about 1800 to 2000, a substantial meal of tea and cakes following a cooked meat or fish dish; 'dinner', served from about 1930 onwards, is taking over.

Drinking

Drinking, and the companionship that goes with it, is a major attraction of the Irish scene. Drinking and generally socializing are the most common Irish pastimes – an astonishing 13% of the national income is spent on drink. Notwithstanding this, the temperance movement is very strong still, and its founder, Father Matthew, is a revered figure in the Republic's 10,500 pubs.

In Northern Ireland, pub hours are 1130 to 2300 from Monday to Saturday, closed on Sunday; however, the troubles have taken some of the pleasure out of pubbing in the North and it is only when you have become known that you get to know the regulars. In the Republic, pubs are open from 1030 to 2330 in summer, to 2300 in winter, and in Dublin and Cork they close for the Holy Hour (1430 to 1530); Sunday times are 1230 to 1400 and 1600 to 2200. In main towns, licensing hours are adhered to; there may be a grill across the entrance an hour before closing time but you may still be admitted. In the country it is unsporting of the *Gardai* to prosecute if the pub stays open only an extra half-hour.

Persons under the age of 18 are not, according to the law admitted in pubs at all, and there are printed notices warning of this. Underneath, you may see a larger, handwritten notice saying, 'No children after 6pm'.

Most pubs are called by the name of the proprietor, *eg* Donovan's Bar, but there are a few with a pub name *eg* The Running Fox, and these tend to be more luxurious.

The old-style country pub was the grocery shop, offering tins of beans, beer and stamps for sale over the bar, petrol outside, gossip all the time and funerals by arrangement; a few of these are left. The old-style town pub was the front room of O'Hara's place, with a bare wooden floor, barer wooden benches, and a bar for Guinness and talk; plenty of these are left. Formerly women were not admitted in pubs by convention – or were segregated in the 'snug' (a small room off the main bar), but few now would make a lady visitor unwelcome; still use your discretion. Out of deference to the old taboo, some bars won't serve a woman a pint, but allow her two halves.

The range of pub styles almost parallels the English equivalents and they serve the same purpose — somewhere to drink alone or in company as the mood takes you, to meet and mingle, to collect information (true, false and irrelevant), and agree on the stupidity of politicians and horse-trainers. The rules are: one person pays for each round as it comes (fight for the privilege of getting the first round), and everybody buys a round. That's all there is to it, apart from deciding what to drink.

Irish Whiskey About half the whiskies drunk in Ireland are Irish, the rest are Scotch whisky. The brands to look out for are Jameson's, Towers, and Paddy, distilled in the Republic; and Old Bushmills, distilled in the North. In 1984, for the first time since it received its royal charter in 1608, Bushmills brought out a pure malt whiskey called Bush Malt. Irish whiskey tastes at least as different from Scotch as cognac does. For an opinion on each one's merits, consult the next man at the bar. Spirit measures are generous — 24 glasses from a standard bottle, compared to the British 32.

Most restaurants have a licence permitting the sale of **wine** only, not beer or spirits. There are three vineyards in Ireland not yet producing wine commercially.

Beer Irish ale is the same sort of drink as English bitter: Smithwick's is a good example, rather bland; Hunter's is sharp, almost fruity; McArdle's has some depth of flavour; Cherry is a bitter beer, not a fruit drink. Lager is the nearest to American-style beer; there are over 20 brands, none pre-eminent. The classic Irish beer is stout, a beer made black by the addition of a small amount of roasted barley. About 30% of the beer drunk in Ireland is ale, about 14% is lager, and the remaining 56% is stout. Beamish & Crawford and Murphy's are two lesser brands, but stout in Ireland overwhelmingly means Guinness. To come to Ireland without trying it is improper.

Guinness has to be drawn slowly from the barrel with a hand-pump called a 'beer-engine', to form the characteristic deep, creamy head. To an expert the depths of head have different names — Cardinal, Bishop and Prior — and every man is an artist at pulling his favourite head. To speed up the slow ritual of dispensing Guinness, the brewers invented a special pump which is used for other people's drinks, but devotees won't let it be used on the purple stout itself.

For the record, all the Guinness sold in Ireland is brewed in Dublin, using Irish barley but not the water from the Liffey. The Guinness sold in southern Britain is brewed at Park Royal, outside London, and in northern Britain it is a blend of Park Royal and Dublin-brewed Guinness. This is to match local preferences, but Dublin-brewed is better — tastes best of all when sampled at the brewery (see p. 48). The stout supplied to the brewery hospitality room is the same as that supplied to any pub in Ireland, so the moral is — try your Guinness at a pub with a big turnover, so you can be sure it is in good condition.

ENJOY YOURSELF

For all the main activity holidays in Ireland — fishing, boating, golfing, riding/pony trekking — there are package tours available which combine transport to Ireland, accommodation and the activity of your choice. Aer Lingus promotes its inclusive holidays, but there are dozens of other packages; details from the tourist boards.

Golf

The weather promotes the growth of soft green grass, and as a result there are 300 golf courses (250 in the Republic, nearly 90 of them 18-hole, and another 70 in N.I.). On many courses there is no green fee for the occasional visitor in local, registered accommodation. If you want to sample a number of courses, there are so many you hardly need to plan a route. (Few courses have clubs for rent.) Many hotels specialize in catering for golfers and are associated with a particular course; golfing long weekends are popular. The most famous course is probably the Royal Portrush; other well known ones are Waterville, Killarney Championship and Royal County Down. Many courses in the Dublin region.

Information from tourist offices. Full list of courses in the Republic in the leaflet *Visitor's Guide to Irish Golf Courses* from Bord Failte (including details of facilities, renting clubs, and professional golf). The information bulletin on golf produced by the NITB contains similar details and covers courses to which the public is admitted.

Cruising

The Shannon system and the Erne system are the two great waterways used by cabin cruisers and, in addition, there is some boating on the canals, and on Lough Neagh and Strangford Lough.

The River **Shannon** is about 240 miles long (385km) from its source in the Cuilcagh Mountains of north Leitrim, to the open sea, and about 140 miles (225km) of this is navigable by cabin cruiser. (Rapids beyond Killaloe.) There are over 500 cruisers for rent, ranging from two-berth to eight-berth vessels, for a quiet potter about catching a few fish, seeing a few sights, taking a few jars, in company or alone. Along the shores there are castles, abbeys, old fortifications, meadows, pubs, villages with grocery stores, and diesel supply stations. The major centre for boat rental is Carrick-on-Shannon, but also available at Athlone and Killaloe; regattas and boat rallies.

Lough Ree and Lough Derg, which are widenings of the main river, are small inland seas, and you should enquire about weather conditions before sailing across them. There are half a dozen smaller, more intimate lakes and one of the prettiest, Lough Key with its forest park, is just off the main stream.

To rent a cruiser there must be somebody over the age of 21 in the party to take charge, and at least one other person familiar with the controls. No licence is needed. You get instruction in handling the boat before taking it away. There are 13 companies renting self-drive cabin cruisers, including Carrick Craft at Carrick, Cormacruisers at Killaloe, Emerald Star at Carrick and Portumna, and Shannon Castle at Williamstown; other names from Bord Failte, also through Blakes of Norwich and Hoseasons of Lowestoft.

The **Erne** system, which sees its future as an alternative to the smaller and more crowded Norfolk Broads, consists of the River Erne, Lower Lough Erne, which is an open lake with a few islands, and Upper Lough Erne, which is a mass of small islands and interconnecting stretches of water, with Enniskillen in the middle, connecting the two lakes. The two loughs (770sq km/300 sq mi) lie wholly in Co. Fermanagh, but the River Erne starts at Belturbet in Co. Cavan and merges into the angling lakes of the Midland region.

The principal companies with cruisers to rent on the Erne system issue a booklet *Holidays Afloat*, with pictures and plans of the boats; obtainable from Northern Ireland Tourist Board. There are also smaller boats for rent by the day, and day cruises from Enniskillen.

The **Grand Canal** (not used by commercial traffic) is continuously navigable from Banagher on the River Shannon to Dublin, with a branch to the River Barrow at Athy. Boat rental from Celtic Canal Cruisers Ltd, Tullamore. The Royal Canal is not continuously navigable.

Lough **Neagh** is the largest single lake in the British Isles – over 400sq km/150sq mi, and in places over 300m/1000ft deep. It is a fairly featureless inland sea. For an agreeable day out on the water, cruisers can be rented at Oxford Island, Maghery (for Coney Island) and especially at Antrim (marina by the river mouth).

For **sea cruising** round the coast, you need your own boat. There are several races, regattas and festivals; details from the Irish Yachting Association, 87 Upper George Street, Dun Laoghaire. The association also has details of sailing tuition holidays which include accommodation, meals and oilskins.

Fishing

For the keen angler Ireland has a wide choice of game, coarse and sea fishing, while for the more casual fisherman who fancies an impromptu day with a rod when the sky is unpredictably overcast, there is brown trout nearly everywhere, in lake, quiet river or tumbling stream. 'Listen to the river and you'll catch a trout', may be a bit of an exaggeration, but it's the right idea. The best source of information is the pub or hotel you're staying in. They should be able to advise you where to go, and where to rent or borrow tackle. The more dedicated angler should take his own tackle. Irish coarse fish have a reputation for fighting hard and may need heavier tackle than normal in British waters. Irish waters are noticeably free of pollution.

Salmon in most rivers flowing to the west, north and east. Most prolific in Galway, where in summer you can watch them fighting to climb up the rivers, but Donegal, Dublin, Kerry and many other places are claimed by somebody to have the best salmon waters. From July onwards there can be a glut of salmon in the restaurants. A salmon licence (see below) also covers sea trout, called in Ireland white trout. Attempts to introduce rainbow trout have not been very successful.

Coarse fish, *ie* freshwater fish other than salmon and trout. Principal species are bream, roach and rudd, pike and perch. Found throughout Ireland but the best areas are probably the lakes of Cavan-Monaghan, Northern Ireland, around the Shannon south of Athlone, and the canals, *eg* at Prosperous and Athy. Most coarse fishing is by wading or from stands around the lake edge, but you can rent a boat around many lakeside fishing centres. For coarse fishing, there are two leaflets with details on where to go and what to use for bait. Bord Failte provides information sheet no. 43 while the NITB produces Colin Grahame's *Coarse Fishing in Northern Ireland*, Larry Nixon's 1984 publication *Northern Ireland Angling Handbook* (£2.50, Proctor Publishing Co.) covers game, sea and coarse fishing.

Sea fish. Haddock, whiting and rollack, and conger eels, all year; skate from May, especially in Strangford Lough; blue shark from June off Kerry and from July off Antrim – these are only some of the species which attract anglers. Portrush and the Causeway Coast have perhaps the best reputation for sea fishing (see Larry Nixon's *Sea Fishing off Northern Ireland*), but the west and south coasts also offer facilities and good sport – Kinsale is noted for deep sea fishing and the Dingle peninsula for shore angling. The many wrecks round the coast make rich feeding grounds.

No rod **licence** is needed for sea fishing. No rod licence is needed for coarse fishing in the Republic, nor in the area of N.I. covered by the Foyle Fisheries Commission (Co. Londonderry draining into the Rivers Foyle, Faughan and Roe). Elsewhere in N.I., covered by the Fisheries Conservancy Board, a rod licence is needed for coarse fishing. Licences from tackle shops or the Fisheries Conservancy Board, Portadown. A rod licence is needed for game fishing in both parts of Ireland, about £5.00 for two weeks. (Prices liable to change.)

In addition to the licence to use a rod, a permit may be needed to fish a particular stretch of water. Waters where no permit is needed are 'free' but even there you should get the landowner's verbal approval. All sea fishing is free. Most coarse fishing in the Republic is free and much in N.I. Elsewhere a fee must be paid for coarse fishing; in N.I. it is usually paid to the Fisheries Conservancy Board (£3 per year). Game fishing in the Republic and N.I. generally needs a permit – about £5 for two weeks – but is free in some of the western lakes (Conn, Corrib and Killarney.)

There is no close **season** for coarse fishing; close season for brown trout is roughly beginning of March to end of September (varies locally); close season for salmon is January 1 to end of August. Further information: Angling Section, Inland Fisheries Trust, Glasnevin, Dublin 9, or from Department of Agriculture, Fisheries Division, Stormont, Belfast. Bait, delivered to local stockist, from Irish Angling Services Ltd, Ardlogher, Ballyconnell, Co. Cavan.

Horses

If the description of the Protestant Ascendancy as 'horse Protestants' was ever accurate, then today's Irish are just as much 'horse Catholics'. A land of horses without being horsey. There are horses for hacking, hunting, racing and just watching.

Hacking In the Republic there are almost 120 riding schools and stables with horses or ponies for trekking and riding over farmlands, mountain and forest trails or along quiet sandy beaches. From the beginner to the top show jumper, Ireland is the place to ride. Most schools offer private tuition and a variety of courses is available. Some riding establishments offer inclusive holidays with a range of accommodation. An excellent publication, *Equestrian Guide* (50p) put out by the Tourist Board lists all the schools, the number of mounts, what tuition is available, costs, accommodation and so on. There are also chapters on hunting, polo, showjumping, riding for the disabled, stud farms and racing.

In Northern Ireland try Mount Pleasant Trekking Centre, Castlewellan, Co. Down, or Newcastle Riding Centre, Castlewellan, Co. Down; also at Ballycastle and Dungannon; ponies in Ballypatrick Forest.

Hunting There are 32 packs of foxhounds and over 40 harrier packs (another breed of hound originally used for hunting hares). Visitors used to hunting are welcome at most meets. If you are not a skilled huntsman don't try to learn in Ireland. The Galway Blazers and the Black-and-Tans are nearly as well-known as the Quorn and the Pytchley hunts, and less snooty; there are scores of others. By arrangement you can rent a mount for about £30 a day; 'cap' is about the same as in England, say £10. A good ride because the land is less built-up; not so good for followers by car because there is less road.

Racing The number of racecourses in the Republic (28) and in N.I. has meant that the 'sport of kings' has become the people's sport. Every man you meet at the racecourse is an expert and can tell you all the winners, then after the event can tell you why, by the sheerest fluke, they didn't quite win. Grandstands and other facilities are generally good – a betting levy, administered by the Irish Racing Board is used to keep the courses up to the standard of the bloodstock. On-course bookmakers are the 'books', not 'bookies'; turf accountants run off-course betting shops.

There is racing on 250 days of the year. On the flat in summer the courses of eastern Ireland are best known – the Curragh (Irish Derby, end of June), Leopardstown, Phoenix Park – with Killarney in August and Galway at the end of July. From Janu-

The hunt gathering at Dunsany Castle, Meath

ary to April there is steeplechasing; see Fairyhouse at Easter and Punchestown at the end of April.

Watching The Dublin Horse Show in August is a great time to see the horsey set — more fun than the horses! Also the RDS spring show (May) and indoor show (November); Belfast show in May; many local shows in July and August.

At the National Stud (Tully, Co. Kildare) there's a museum with the history of the Irish horse — recommended for pony-mad children and customers of the 'books'.

Dogs

A visit to greyhound racing is worthwhile; you'll see the Irish at their leisure even if you are no lover of dog racing. In addition to tracks where dogs chase an electric hare (two in Dublin, two in Belfast and about nine in the provinces), there is coursing after a live hare. This is mostly park coursing, where the hare is brought along and released, but there is still some open coursing, where the hare is flushed out by beaters. Clonmel is the 'greyhound capital of the world'.

Spectator Sports

The most popular winter sport is probably **soccer** though too many of the best players tend to find their way into British teams. **Rugby football** is also popular and is one of some half dozen international sports for which there is an All-Ireland team drawn from north and south. But summer is the great time for sport — Gaelic football and hurling. **Gaelic football** is a cross between soccer and rugby, faster than either with no stoppages for injury; it's close enough to Australian football for talk of merging the games to permit an international. **Hurling** is 'just not cricket' — it's a kind of handball-soccer, played with a near hockey stick called a *caman*, using a rugby goal. Any local will be delighted to give you a full explanation.

Gaelic football and hurling, both strictly amateur, are controlled by the Gaelic Athletic Association, which was founded towards the end of the last century to revive and promote purely Irish games as part of the nationalist movement. At first G.A.A. maintained the 'ban' — anybody who played a 'foreign' game like soccer was forbidden in a G.A.A. team. This was to make sure the clubs were not infiltrated by sporty detectives from Dublin Castle. Croke Park, Dublin, is the venue for the All-Ireland hurling final on the first Sunday in September, and the All-Ireland Gaelic final on the last Sunday in September. Re-run on television that night and in bars for the next week.

Swimming

The sea is rather cold for swimming unless you're hardy. Along the west coast and especially in the south west the Gulf Stream does bring warm water, as all the brochures say, just as the milder weather does encourage fuchsias and near tropical plant growth. But if you are told you can swim at Christmas, don't believe it. It's usually perfect for children who want to play on the beach and enjoy the occasional splash in the water. The best time for a swim is on a rising tide when there has been sun all day to warm the sand. The north east can be as warm as the south west. The Irish Sea is distinctly more chilly.

Other Sports

Tennis courts are mostly associated with hotels; there are few public courts.

The Adventure Sports Centre, 56 St Margaret's Avenue, Kilbarrack, Dublin 5, offers **active holidays** for teenagers and young adults, staying with families. You can specialize in riding, sailing, mixed adventuring, walking, seasports, canoeing. Bases at Creeslough, Co. Donegal; Tiglin, Co. Wicklow; Sherkin Island, Co. Cork; Saltee Islands, Co. Wexford; in Connemara and Co. Kerry.

Walking

For simple country walking, along footpaths, through forests and over mountains, meeting people and finding somewhere to stay as you go, Northern Ireland is very well organized. The Ulster Way is a 775km/481mi walk roughly around the borders of the province, along footpaths and country lanes, beaches and bogs, moorland and parkland. The Sports Council publishes a series of 11 leaflets, detailing different sections of the Ulster Way. These leaflets, plus an overall map sketch of the Way are available from the Sports Council or from the NITB.

The Republic is more free-and-easy, or less well organized. If you want help with plotting a walking tour, the Irish Hostels Association is helpful, but broadly speaking the country does not have a network of footpaths. Either you stick to the open mountains and uplands, or you're constantly negotiating fences and boundaries. Nobody minds where you walk so long as you do no damage. the highlands and cliffs of west Donegal, the Wicklow Mountains and the Killarney lakeland and Ring of Kerry are obvious places to choose to roam free on foot, but almost any of the 'mountains' should satisfy the walker. In the Slieve Bloom mountains (starting point, Birr, Co. Offaly) an effort is being made to open up tracks for ramblers.

There is a series of nine good walking guides available in bookshops, covering: 1) West, 2) South West, 3) North West, 4) South East, 5) East, 6) Dublin and Wicklow, 7) Mournes, 8) Killarney, 9) Connemara.

Climbing

The mountains of Ireland are generally for hill-walking and their summits can be reached without climbing gear, but both Muckish and Errigal in Co. Donegal attract rock climbers, and in the Mountains of Mourne there is fine climbing terrain. Other climbs are specialized — for information, contact the Federation of Mountaineering Clubs of Ireland (see p. 42).

Rock-climbing guide books to: 1) Mournes, 2) Dalkey, 3) Antrim Coast, 4) Donegal, 5) Malinbeg, 6) Bray Head, 7) Burren Cliffs, 8) Coum Gowlaun (Connemara) available from F.M.C.I.

Tracing Your Ancestors

There is now a Bord Failte information sheet no. 8 giving names and addresses of organizations who will, for a fee, help you trace your Irish ancestors back to at least 1830.

MUSIC AND DANCE

The harp is the symbol of Ireland — the only country in the world whose national emblem is a musical instrument. The harp itself has almost vanished from the popular music scene, but one of the styles of traditional music that you hear today is derived from classical harp playing — long, dreamy melodies, almost unstructured, with slow variation of content. Livelier melodies, for dancing more than for singing, are known as jigs and are best played on a flute. These 'classical' traditional styles, which you will hear at performances rather than impromptu playing, persist in the jollier up-to-date versions to be heard everywhere. All of them fit into the Irish tradition of making your own music and having your own fun.

Irish folk songs were assiduously collected in the 19th century by Bunting, Petrie and Pigot and are now published by the Department of Folklore at UCD. Strictly traditional songs are for solo voice, mostly in Irish but now often in English; this style is called *sean nos*. Accompanied singing is less demanding; traditionally by flute or fiddle or nowadays accordion or, most favoured, the guitar. The most popular type of song is the ballad, or song-with-story — mockingly about Finn MacCool, or fondly about the Tans. Many of the ballads which command greatest affection in Ireland are old and of some historical interest while others tell of more recent events.

You may still come across individuals playing the older music for their own pleasure but for the most part it is to be heard at performances organized by *Comhaltas Ceoltoiri Eireann*. Comhaltas was formed to 'strike a blow for the homeland's cultural identity'. Through its agency traditional music has been made available to thousands who would otherwise know Irish music only as after-hours singing in a pub.

The chief way to hear traditional music is at *Seisiun* – a group of musicians move round from hotel to hotel playing the local songs and dances; at the end of the evening there's a chance for everyone to join in. The time and place will be displayed in shop windows and hotel lobbies. Although they arose in response to demand from tourists to hear traditional music, *Seisiun* are patronized mainly by the Irish themselves. Village Airs, put on in the Shannon region, are rather more geared to the tourist market.

Festivals of music (*fleadh*, pronounced *flah*, plural *fleadhanna*) seem to take place at the drop of a hat. These are performances of traditional song and dance on a competitive basis – the competitors usually get together afterwards to play for their own pleasure and for anybody else who cares to listen. The big festival is the All-Ireland Fleadh, during the last week in August at a different venue each year – a bit like, the Welsh Eisteddfod but less serious. There are over 30 other *fleadhanna*, advertised in local press or details from tourist information offices. The *Fleadh Nua*, at Ennis, Co. Clare during May, is a more formal affair.

Siamsa, also organized through Comhaltas, is a theatrical performance, in music and mime, portraying the Irish way of life as it was 50 years ago. This is based at Tralee but the troupe goes out to Listowel and to the Dingle Peninsula.

In Dublin Comhaltas provides other opportunities to see and hear Irish music – *Fonntrai* (twice weekly in summer) which is nearer to a cabaret, and *Cois Teallaigh* which is more an instructive session where musicians demonstrate their art and explain what they are doing. Finally, the *Ceilithe* is a reconstruction of the traditional Irish party, or house dance (*Ceilidh*, pronounced *kayley*), with a small admission fee and the chance to learn the steps of the Kerry sets, a jig, a reel or formalized country dances like the 'Siege of Ennis' or the 'Walls of Limerick'.

In addition to the revivalist music and dance of Comhaltas, there is plenty of opportunity to join in the living tradition at hotels and pubs. The big hotels put on cabaret, sometimes with international names but mostly with local performers who play modern music in an Irish style. Pubs have 'Irish nights' which are cheerful, robust, rebellious, and accompanied by a firm rhythm that may not appeal to the more delicate ear. From the pub, if you get into a party, you may well move on to a *Ceilidh* for more of the same.

A singing pub is one where the customers are known to sing, as at the end of an Irish night, but without paid performers at the microphone to start them off.

Irish step-dancing – which is possibly the origin of tap-dancing – is rather similar to Scottish sword dancing in footwork, perhaps even more intricate, but the arms are held by the sides and it is danced on the stage with an unsmiling earnestness.

Galway Oyster Festival

Usually you will see step-dancing done by girls in 'traditional costume' (though you may wonder whether the country folk among whom step-dancing grew up could ever afford such fancy dress); if you are lucky, you may be around when an old boy, remembering the steps of his grandfather, gets up to answer the music and dance for himself.

North Kerry may be the only area where the old formalized dances are still danced because they know no other way. Dancing at a hop, a mixture of ballroom and disco laced with Comhaltas, is probably the most popular of all Irish entertainments (after telly).

WHAT YOU SEE

Landscapes

The **mountains** of Ireland, like the rim of a saucer round a central limestone plain, form the background to the Irish scene. For the most part they are bare hills, heather-blue or rock-grey or pine-black, an uncultivated framework seen across the patchwork of small green fields. Most of the ranges are small in extent, so that from the ridge you can look out over the spreading farmland on either side. Only the domed, granite Wicklow Mountains and the sandstone and lime peaks of Kerry (with Ireland's highest summit, Carrauntoohil, 1041m/3414ft) offer extensive tracts of wild mountain country where you get the feeling of being lost in the mountains.

The mountains of Donegal and Connemara are bleak upland, magnificent when seen from the distance, while the Mountains of Mourne and the Sperrins are open walking country, too high to be farmed. In the south there is a series of small patches of high ground made pretty by rivers and streams. The many other tracts of ground also called 'Slieve' (Irish for mountain) tend to be barren and boggy. At intervals along the west and north coasts the mountains come right to the sea in a range of cliffs, from Co. Cork right up to Fair Head; the Cliffs of Moher in Co. Clare, Slieve League in Co. Donegal and the Giant's Causeway must be the most visited, but there are other impressive cliffs along the Atlantic seaboard.

Drumlins are hillocks which create a switchback countryside that makes some of the mountains look flat in comparison. A belt of drumlins stretches across counties Down, Armagh, Leitrim, Cavan and Monaghan and extends right out into Strangford Lough. These are oval masses of boulder clay deposited during the Ice Age, and richly farmed now; the two cathedrals of Armagh are built on drumlins.

Bogs once covered nearly 14% of the surface of Ireland, though cutting and land restoration has reduced this in recent years to about 6%. A bog is a bed of peat, from one metre to ten metres deep (3–33ft), with a thin layer of soil that supports acid-loving plants like sphagnum, sedges and bog cotton; a bog can feel dry at the surface, and you can walk on it, but it is almost non-productive. In the wet, high ground of the west the bogs are 'blanket bog' – the peat spreads over the landscape, even on sloping ground; here the peat is cut by hand into blocks which, when dried out, are burnt instead of coal. The peat blocks, called turf, fill the cottages with the aromatic smell that still means home to exiled Irishmen. In the drier Midlands 'raised bog' has developed out of fen on overgrown lake basins; the acid conditions created mean that the bog feeds on itself. Here the peat is thicker and cut mechanically to provide fuel for power stations – although Ireland is heavily dependent on oil for its energy, about 20% of the Republic's electricity is generated by peat-firing. A ton of peat supplies about as much heat as half a ton of coal. The sight of a peat bog, cleared and levelled and raked out for mechanical harvesting, deep red under the white sky like a harrowed prairie, is a neglected beauty of the Midlands.

There are said to be 800 **lakes** in Ireland – but like the 650 pubs of Dublin, this must be an underestimation. Most of the small ones are the result of poor drainage, and lie hidden in fairly level country, reed-fringed, still, merging into the land – an angler's paradise, with a fishing stand somewhere along the edge, and a boat which you can rent or borrow. Some of the larger lakes in the north are set in wooded hills to create a composite lakeland picture; the lakes of Killarney are perhaps too famous for their views. The larger lakes on the Shannon – Lough Ree and Lough Derg – and the upper and lower reaches of Lough Erne, are for cabin cruising, while Lough Neagh, the largest lake in the British Isles, has a regular steamer service.

In the distant past nearly all Ireland was covered in **forest** but by the start of this century hunger for fuel and land had made this the most treeless land in Europe. Almost the only trees were on the estates of the great landowners. Since then, there has been a great revival of forestry and just over 5% of the total land area is covered by trees. Most of the forests have been opened to the public as forest parks, with car parking, toilets, adequate but unobtrusive signposting, and sometimes a café. There are forest parks in: Co. Antrim (Glenariff); Co. Armagh (Gosford and Slieve Gullion); Co. Cavan (Dun a Ri and Killykeen); Co. Cork (Guagan Barra); Co. Donegal (Ards); Co. Down (Castlewellan and Tollymore); Co. Fermanagh (Florence Court); Co. Galway (Portumna); Co. Monaghan (Rossmore); Co. Roscommon (Lough Key); Co. Tyrone (Davagh, Drum Manor, Gortin Glen and Parkanaur); Co. Wexford (John F. Kennedy at New Ross); Co. Wicklow (Avondale). In addition, there is much other woodland — Northern Ireland is especially well-endowed, with over 50 large and small forests, while for the Republic the Forest and Wildlife Service supplies nature trail leaflets describing another 13 stretches of woodland. All these scenic attractions are signposted in the vicinity as a 'scenic drive', and are provided with picnic sites — a couple of tables and benches, sited with care to blend into the scene — to make daily woodland visits an appealing part of any tour of Ireland.

The Irish coast, all 3000 miles (4800km) of it, seems to be one long chain of superb **beaches** (sometimes called strands). North Donegal must have the finest beaches of all, great curving arcs of sand with cliffs or rocks at the end to mark the start of yet another expanse beyond. If the sea were warmer, these would surely be the premier playground of Europe. Many of them are double-layered — a smooth, tidal stretch of land rising slowly to a rim of sand dunes, and then another flat stretch above the dunes; this is the result of a drop in sea level (3m/10ft) a few thousand years ago.

The sea is warmed by the Gulf Stream, but it is not warm. You can go into the sea for a bracing dip, and on many beaches never see another soul. The shapes of the rocks, the wildlife, the magic of a sunset over the chill water seen through the haze over the warm sand, these are another haunting, essential part of the Irish scene.

In the more accessible places, seaside resorts have sprung up where the Irish take their holidays. They have the simplicity and, for some, the charm of a minor English resort 50 years ago; a couple of amusement arcades, Victorian houses offering bed-and-breakfast (but with a welcoming landlady), pubs where mum and dad retire for the evening leaving the children with the landlady, boats and pony rides and ice cream.

Mountains and lakes, forest and bog create the setting for the Irish countryside, but the foreground is its **fields**. The farmed countryside is an endless patchwork of small fields, divided by thick hedges over most of the country but often by stone walls in the west, or by fences in Northern Ireland. The history of Ireland is written in its fields. Most farms are small even today — over half the farmed land is in units of less than 30 acres (12 hectares) — and even these have been formed by the consolidation of still smaller holdings. At the worst time of the pressure for land, little 'farms' as tiny as a quarter acre were sublet to starving tenants and over a century of state-assisted purchase by the countryman has not obliterated the pattern of a million little units. Any one field might be in Britain, but the combined effect of these little plots going on and on is what makes each one look uniquely Irish.

The working of the field size is seen most clearly at hay-making — throughout the summer and into the autumn. Most of the hay is mown by tractor now, and perhaps half of it is baled, but the turning is nearly all done by hand — the fields are too small to be worth bringing in a machine. Haying starts late in the morning, for it is the wind not the sun that dries it off; the hay is collected with forks into little haycocks which are shaken out daily until collected. All over Ireland you will see these little fields of haycocks with a plastic handkerchief on top to keep the rain off.

The large number of subdivided fields encourages mixed farming — a few sheep, a couple of pigs, a 'herd' of three cows. This strengthens the deeply rural feel of the country, especially in the west. The principal farm product of Ireland is cattle, both dairy and beef, but even in the solid dairying country of the Golden Vale of Limerick and Tipperary where the rich ground encourages ranching, the small field pattern persists. The grain and sugar beet districts of Kilkenny and Carlow, and Northern Ireland are the chief areas where you see more open farming. Only the sheep, on hillsides from Cork to Donegal, have wide open spaces to graze on. The picture of the Irishman and his pig is very out-of-date now — in the Republic there are few more pigs than are required for domestic consumption, and pig production, like chickens, is concentrated in Northern Ireland. Altogether, about two thirds of the land area of Ireland is farmland, and 90% of this is grass.

Buildings

The building which has become the symbol of Ireland is the low, whitewashed cottage looking out from its single window to the bleak beauty of the bog. From here the

Killaloe on Lough Derg, Clare

Sligo farmhouse

Cooley Peninsula, Louth

Dooagh, Achill Island, Mayo

Upper Lake, Killarney, Kerry

Kilbaha Bay, Clare (Background: Navar Forest, Fermanagh)

visitor's ancestors fled, and the modern version is where the visitor now stays in Rent-a-Cottage. But this is a very restricted view of Ireland — there is so much more to see.

Dolmens are scattered all over Ireland — a sloping capstone supported on three pillars, a former Neolithic tomb from which the earth covering has been removed. In legend each dolmen is the resting place of the fugitives from Finn MacCool (p. 14) and it is said there are 366 of them — one for each day of the year that Dermot and Grania were pursued. 'Diarmaid and Grianna's Bed' is the usual name for a dolmen. Rather later than the dolmens are the **passage graves** of the Boyne Valley (p. 54); their chief interest for the casual visitor is the decorations.

The pre-Christian nomads have left very little on stone — their most interesting remains are the stone forts: the Grianan of Aileach (p. 103), Staigue Fort in Kerry (p. 76) and Dun Aengus on Inishmore (p. 88).

There are plenty of early Christian remains — **beehive huts,** and the **round towers** which are nearly as prominent as castles. The stone huts, or clochans, were hermits' hideouts and their remains are concentrated in the Dingle Peninsula and on Skellig Michael (p. 71 and 70). There are over 70 round towers scattered throughout Ireland; they are up to 30m/100ft high, and a dozen of them still have the original conical cap. These towers served as watchtowers, bell towers, and as a temporary refuge to which the monks could retire from a passing band of Danish or Irish raiders. The entrance, about 5m/16ft above ground level, had to be reached by ladder.

The round towers are usually associated with **monastic ruins** but these have for the most part been rebuilt at a later date. The most visited remains of Celtic monasticism are probably those at Glendalough (p. 57) and Clonmacnoise (p. 121); peaceful by the flat river or overshadowed by the hills, both become magical in the evening when the crowds have gone.

Celtic crosses mostly date from the 9th to the 12th centuries; also called high crosses. They are stone crosses carved with figures assumed to be a simple representation of biblical stories; Irish nationalists have left study of the deeper meaning of the high crosses to German anthroposophists. The best-known examples are at Monasterboice (p. 56), Kells (p. 58) and Durrow (p. 120).

The ancient buildings whose remains you see by the hundred are **castles.** The Normans started the fashion for castle building and the two best-preserved examples are Carrickfergus Castle and King John's Castle, Limerick; the ruins of Trim Castle are probably the most romantic. Norman castles are generally rounded while native Irish castles, like Cahir, are squarer. Most of the square based buildings called castles are in fact **tower houses**; there are nearly a thousand in the Shannon area and hundreds elsewhere. These are not really castles, built to rule the surrounding countryside, but the domestic buildings of unsettled times, homes that could be defended when trouble rolled by. They were built as late as the 16th century. The best known are Bunratty Castle (p. 82) and its fellow castles on the banquet circuit, and Blarney Castle (p. 67).

When the destruction of the Elizabethan wars died down, a new nobility appeared bringing a new style of house with it. At first people opened up the tower house with larger and larger windows, but these have succumbed to the weather. Then as a landed gentry of English origin began to settle into Ireland in the 18th century there sprang up the **grand houses** which are open to visitors today. They set out to build copies of the contemporary English style, but just as this gentry was absorbed to become the Anglo-Irish, their houses soon assumed an Irish look. There are about 20 major houses open to the public which are members of the Historic Irish Tourist Houses Association (Castle Street, Dalkey, Co. Dublin) and another eight in the care of the National Trust for Northern Ireland (Rowallane, Saintfield, Co. Down). One of the interesting things to notice if you tour historic houses, built to English models, is how characteristically Irish they look if you compare them with their parallels back east, and yet how alien they appear in the Irish landscape. Westport, Co. Mayo; Riverstone, Co. Cork; and Lissadell, Co. Sligo are three examples still preserved as houses; there are scores of others converted now to schools or colleges, and scores more decayed to nostalgic ruins. As ruins, they merge completely into the landscape like the tumbled cottages.

At the same time as the landlords were building their homes-from-home, the dispossessed natives were managing with the humble **cottage**. There are two basic types. In the west and north of Ireland, the roof is gabled, which gives a stronger though less watertight structure than a hipped roof. The roof is usually of thatch, and in Donegal roped down against the wind; sometimes stone slabs are used, supported on ancient timbers dug out from beneath the bog. This type of cottage which you see all along the western seaboard has a central door, tiny windows or

Grey Abbey, Down

Muireadach's Cross, Monasterboice, Louth

Ancient carvings, White Island, Fermanagh

One of the preserved cottages at Glencolumbkille, Donegal

no window at all, and a fireplace at one end away from the door. The narrow cabin is often widened at the fireplace to form an alcove for the bed. In the south and east a different type of cottage is seen with a hipped roof and a central door facing a central fireplace; with these cottages there soon appears a wall between the door and fireplace to stop the draught, and the little cottage is divided into rooms, becoming a more conventional farmhouse.

In the barren open country of the west the cottages stand naked on the moors, empty now and reverting to piles of stone; where they are grouped together, they cluster in straight lines, an extension of the stone walls. In the softer east the cottages, nearly always alone and perversely angled to the road, hide shyly behind a hedge or low wall.

These traditional cottages, long and low, whitewashed or stone-black, are the image of 'Oul Ireland'. They are vanishing now, but examples are preserved in outdoor museums. At Glencolumbkille (p. 103) there are Donegal cottages of different dates; at Bunratty Folk Park (p. 82) you can follow the development from simple cottage to more elaborate farmhouse; the Ulster Folk and Transport Museum, Belfast (p. 114) exhibits rural buildings in the different tradition that evolved in the North. A different style again is preserved in the Ulster-American Folk Park, Omagh (p. 107); these are the original and traditional Ulster houses, some belonging to prominent Americans alongside which are straightforward replicas of American log farmhouses and cabins.

There are still plenty of the traditional cottages left, though most have been downgraded to cattle stores or picturesque emptiness. On many the thatch has rotted to form rootage for bright green grass, and on many more it has made way for corrugated iron. But generally the cottage has been replaced by more modern buildings – square, slate-roofed bungalows provided by local councils, or comfortable two-storied houses for the more prosperous small farmer – both these styles would not look out of place anywhere in Britain. Strangely, it is not in the country but on the edges of the towns that you find a direct echo of the long, low cottage.

Around the country towns there are terraces of red-brick, black-slated single-storied houses – an urbanized version of the traditional cottage, put up in the last century when towns began to grow. This style is repeated in the new estates going up today on the other side of the town. Today's preference is for detached bungalows, still long and low, with a Romanesque arch to the front door and stonework around the picture window. These modern developments look as though the Irish are trying to get back to their roots and reproduce the old cottage in more comfortable form.

The **Georgian period** (18th century) was the time when the elegant town houses of the well-to-do were built. Dublin of course is famous for its streets and squares of handsome charm, more generously proportioned than their English counterparts. Outside Dublin there are many towns with a little Georgian housing – Fermoy, Westport, Armagh get away from the standard pattern of an Irish small town because of this. But the Georgian style in Ireland is expressed with a marked Irish accent – more spacious in places, or frequently more severe as in the country houses. Today, revived Georgian is the most popular style for modern private houses but without a trace of an Irish accent.

SHOPPING

Unless you're in the market for an oil-tanker or fleet of aircraft, the characteristically Irish products that you'll want to take home are clothing and crafts.

Woollen goods Aran handknit garments such as sweaters are traditionally made in undyed wool, and the pattern in the garment is created by different types of stitch; a really good Aran sweater is made of wool still heavy with natural oil, but the wool for most garments is scoured to an oil-free whiteness. 'Aran' now refers to the pattern and does not mean the product is from the Aran Isles.

Tweed can come as a heavy and very tough, but smooth, fabric made up into a top-coat or cloak, or can be more delicately woven to a lightweight fabric suitable for an evening dress.

Carpets, as from the factory at Killybegs, are superbly made, last it seems for ever, but may take forever to pay for.

Linen was the foundation of the prosperity of industrial Ireland. Although the industry has declined now, linen is still made (from imported flax) and is available as sheets, tablecloths, shirts and blouses – high quality; probably a better buy in Ireland than abroad.

Ireland is noted for its lead crystal **glass**. The principal glass factory is at Waterford (the factory can be visited but the products are not sold on the premises); a more recent one is in Dungannon, Co. Tyrone (sub-standard products available from the factory). There is also Cavan crystal and Galway crystal, which are products cut from glass made elsewhere.

Lace-making is a traditional Irish craft, but it has largely died out; most of the attractive **lace** products in the shops are factory-made; three places still hand-produce lace which may be bought on site – Limerick, Carrickmacross and Youghal. 'Clones lace' is a style of lace, but it is no longer made in Clones, Co. Monaghan.

The most famous **pottery** is from Belleek; an extremely hard porcelain, the designs are mostly Victorian in spirit. More modern designs from individual studios are available over much of Ireland, and there are new factories in Cork, Galway and Wicklow.

The green **marble** of Connemara is used for statuary, ornaments, chess pieces and the like. **Pewter** from Mullingar is sold in the form of drinking vessels, candlesticks, trays. Irish **silver** work dates back to before the Celts; the tradition has been revived and there is much jewellery for sale nowadays – the Claddagh ring (see Galway, p. 90) has enjoyed a great revival in popularity among the Irish.

Basketry, from willow and more typically from rushes, is widely available and good value but rather bulky.

Where to buy: most of these goods are sold in gift shops, Irish craft shops, and large stores all over Ireland; prices are much the same everywhere. There is possibly a wider choice if you shop in the district of production, *eg* at Letterfrack or Maam Cross for Connemara products, Galway for Claddagh rings.

The products of individual craftsmen can often be found only in local shops – sweaters, pottery, pictures in tweed, oil or enamel. For Northern Ireland there is a very useful index of craftsmen listed by name and product, which can be had from the Local Enterprise Development Unit, 17 Linenhall Street, Belfast BT2 8BS with sub-offices in Londonderry, Omagh and Newry. There seems to be no similar list for arts-and-crafts workers in the Republic, but Kilkenny Design Centre is a national organization promoting individual craft workers – main office opposite the castle in Kilkenny.

If you have missed getting your souve-

elleek craftsman, Fermanagh

nirs while travelling around Ireland, there is a comprehensive collection of the standard commercial lines at Shannon Airport in the duty-free shop; prices, free of sales tax but with the higher mark-up of an airport, are about the same as in an Irish shop. In Dublin, there is a fairly complete display at the Irish Life Arcade on Eden Quay; the Kilkenny Design Centre in Nassau Street; Giftcraft in Upper O'Connell Street; Gifts from Ireland in Duke Street. And if you're really desperate, Shannon Free Airport runs a mail order catalogue and will despatch to anywhere at prices calculated to just undercut US retail prices after payment of import duty.

As to more basic shopping, you will find small local shops with a limited range of goods, relatively high prices but willing personal service; chain stores for food and household products in Dublin and other main towns — Woolworths and its Irish sound-alike Wellworths, Marks and Spencer and its Irish look-alike Dunnes, Quinnsworth which is the most comprehensive of the food-and-goods stores, even Tesco and British Home Stores; individually owned department stores in the larger towns, which look and feel as though they have remained unchanged since the 1930s and are just being modernized. If you are looking for elegance, try Grafton Street, Dublin. Normal hours are 0900 to 1730. Some of the smart shops in Dublin (south of the river) still close at 1300 on Saturday. Outside the centre there are food shops open from 0700 to 2400 six days a week, and until midday on Sunday. New shops have opened in Belfast city centre alongside old favourites such as Littlewoods, C & A, British Home Stores and Marks and Spencer.

WHAT YOU NEED TO KNOW

Churches

In the Republic, about three million people or 94% of the population are Catholic, and just over 100,000 are Protestants. In Northern Ireland, there are nearly half a million Catholics, just under one third of the population, and a million 'Protestants and others' — the 'others' being mainly people of no religious belief but with a Protestant background. The majority of Northern Ireland Protestants are Presbyterians, a substantial minority are Episcopalians, and there are smaller numbers of Methodists and others. The churches on the most prominent sites throughout Ireland belong to the Church of Ireland, and can be recognized by a plain black notice board outside with the times of services, and by the absence of religious statuary. The Church of Ireland is the Protestant (Episcopalian) church, which was established by law as the sole legal church of Ireland during the Reformation, and disestablished only in 1869. For much of that time Catholics were not allowed to build churches.

Electricity

The standard supply is a nominal 240 volts AC, usually delivered at 220 volts AC; frequency is 50 Hz. Most hotels have sockets for an electric razor adapted to 110 volts.

Holidays

Public holidays throughout Ireland are: January 1; March 17 (St Patrick's Day); Good Friday (not an official holiday in the Republic); Easter Monday; December 25 (Christmas Day); December 26 (Boxing Day in the North, St Stephen's Day in the Republic).

Additional public holidays in Northern Ireland are: July 12 (Orange Day), or following Monday; last Monday in August; 1st Monday in May (May Day); last Monday in May (spring bank holiday); December 27 (bank holiday).

Additional public holidays in the Republic are: 1st Monday in June; 1st Monday in August; last Monday in October.

Ascension Day is not an official holiday, but the occasion of many absences in the Republic.

Festivals

(other than public holidays)

Festivals linked to certain towns are mentioned in the gazeteer but get the *Major Festivals and Events* sheet published annually by Bord Failte. This gives precise dates as well as telephone numbers for further information on individual festivals.

There are a great many festivals in Northern Ireland. Details from the TIC in Belfast or any Northern Ireland Tourist Board. Here is a list of some of the more important ones. **March** Belfast Music Festival, speech, drama and music competitions for the young, held annually. St Patrick's Day celebrations, processions and pilgrimages in Downpatrick, Horse Ploughing, Ballycastle, International Motor Cycle Trials, Bangor. **May** Belfast City Marathon, North West 200, motorcycle road race, Royal Ulster Agricultural Society Show. **June** Irish Festival of Good Beer, Ulster Games, Northern Ireland Games and Country Fair, the premier field sports event. **July** City of Belfast

Rose Trials – international competition for catalogued roses, Fiddle Stone Festival, part of the 10-day Belleek Festival, John Donnelly International Moto Cross, Battle of Boyne celebrations, Lady of the Lake Festival, Irvinestown, Lughnasa Medieaval Fair & Crafts Market, Carrickfergus Castle. **August** Ulster Grand Prix, Belfast, Oul' Lammas Fair, Ballycastle, oldest of Ireland's big traditional fairs. **September** Belfast Folk Festival, Dromore Horse Fair, Harvest Fair, Newtonards. **October** Royal Ulster Academy of Arts Exhibition, Belfast, Ulster Antiques & Fine Art Fair. **November** Belfast Festival at Queens's – after Edinburgh the UK's biggest arts festival.

Leprechauns

The 'little people' of folklore, fairies dressed as elves. (The word comes from the Old Irish *luchorpan*, from 'lu', small and 'corp', body). The Irish affect not to believe in leprechauns and joke about people who do, but awareness of the devilment and wilfulness of nature is still strong. Any sighting of a leprechaun should be reported to the Bord.

Lost Property

The main lost property office of CIE is at Transport House, 12 Bachelor's Walk, Dublin; the main lost property office of UTA, covering Ulsterbus, is in Oxford Street, Belfast, tel 220011. The main office for general lost property in Belfast is at Musgrove police station in Ann Street, tel 237212, ext 50. In Dublin phone 741851 for CIE; 751107 for taxi lost property. In Belfast phone 58345.

Maps

Maps of the whole of Ireland are available from Bord Failte £1.50 each – 12 miles to the inch (tourist sites shown, and with handy town plans) – or can be bought cheaply at filling stations on a somewhat larger scale than the Bord map. Bartholomew's at 9 miles to the inch is clearer but less detailed; identifies scenic areas; Bartholomew also produces a 4 miles to the inch map. For the extra detail needed when touring, both the Ordnance Survey of Northern Ireland and the Ordnance Survey Office, Dublin, issue a set of maps covering the whole island at 1:126,720 (½ in to 1 mi) and 1:575,000 (1 in to 9 mi); both series available from booksellers. In addition, there is a new series of 1:50,000 maps covering the whole of Northern Ireland on 18 sheets.

Police

The police force in Northern Ireland is the Royal Ulster Constabulary, who wear green uniforms, are always armed, and are more often engaged in security duties than in ordinary police work. There is, strictly speaking, no police force in the Republic. The *Garda Siochana*, the social guard, who act as the police force wear navy blue uniforms and are normally unarmed. The Garda are not in principle a general law-enforcement agency but concerned only with criminal activity and breaches of public order. In practice, their duties are much the same as the police in any developed country. For an emergency telephone call to the police, dial 999 in both parts of Ireland.

Some of the former Irish police forces are preserved in legend. The Royal Irish Constabulary was the police force of all Ireland under the Union, engaged on police work but also a paramilitary force for suppression of nationalist resistance. The Dublin Metropolitan Police was an unarmed force in Dublin under the Union, very similar to the old-time London bobby. The Auxies (Auxiliary Constabulary) were a small, elite force, nominally part of the R.I.C., engaged mainly in intelligence work during the Anglo-Irish War (1921). The Black-and-Tans were ex-soldiers (they wore police tunics and army trousers) originally called in to supplement the police during the Anglo-Irish war. (The Black-and-Tans are also a well-known hunt in Tipperary, and in an English but not an Irish pub, black-and-tan is a mixture of Guinness and bitter.)

Post

British stamps must be used on letters posted in Northern Ireland (red post boxes) and Irish stamps on letters posted in the Republic (green post boxes). Post offices are open 0900 to 1800 Monday to Friday, 0900 to 1230 on Saturday in Northern Ireland; 0900 to 1730 Monday to Saturday (some close 1300 to 1415) in the Republic. The General Post Office, O'Connell Street, Dublin, is open from 0800 (0900 Sundays) to 2300. There is a 24-hr post office at Shannon Airport.

Telephones

Telephone booths in Northern Ireland are red, in the Republic they're green. All call boxes in the North are on S.T.D. (subscriber trunk dialling) so you can make direct calls to almost anywhere in the world; they take coins of 5p and 10p, and a few boxes *eg* at the airport take 50p coins. Otherwise you can make international calls from a private phone (ask for an A.D.C. call – advice of duration and charge) or on a metered hotel phone. Phone boxes contain full instructions for use.

METRIC CONVERSIONS

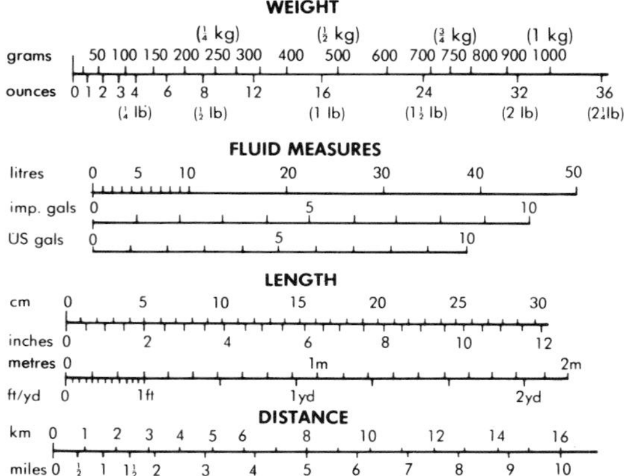

In the Republic the telephone system is being converted to S.T.D. and in a few years should be operating as in N.I. At present there are many intermediate stages of conversion. On the whole, for anything but local calls, it is much easier to find an hotel or private phone. International calls usually require that you get the operator, and this can involve a very long wait. Coin boxes have slots for coins of 5p and 10p but some may work on 10p pieces only. If there are buttons A and B, put the money in first to dial your number, and press button A when the call is answered. Button B gives your money back if there is no answer, or ends a call – it's always worth pressing button B when you've finished, you may get your money back anyway. If there is a handle, you have to crank this to get the operator before making a call. In Northern Ireland the minimum charge from a public call box is 10p, the same as in the UK.

Dial 100 for the operator in N.I.; in the Republic dial 199 for the operator, or 0 in a press-button box.

There is one telephone directory for N.I. and two for the Republic, one covering Dublin and one covering everywhere else. Both the Republic and Northern Ireland have Yellow Page directories.

Television and Radio

There are at least five television channels in Ireland: BBC 1 and BBC2, transmitted from Northern Ireland and from Britain and picked up over all N.I. and by about four fifths of the receivers in the Republic; Ulster Television (commercial) transmitted from N.I. and picked up over most of the northern part of Ireland; and RTE 1 and RTE 2, transmitted from Dublin or substations in the Republic and received over nearly all the Republic and most of N.I. RTE 1 is generally similar to BBC 1; RTE 2 is nearer to British commercial television, except for an hour a night of Irish culture.

There are two radio stations with programmes in English from the Irish radio service; these are the most frequently heard although British stations can be received over most of Ireland. There are special radio programmes in Irish for the Gaeltacht areas, and various local radio programmes, mostly transmitted from mobile, low-power studios.

Time

In winter, all of Ireland is on Greenwich Mean Time, *ie* 1200 in Dublin, Belfast and London is 0700 in New York. In summer, all of Ireland is on British Summer Time, which is one hour ahead of G.M.T. (end March to end October).

The sun rises and sets 23 mins later in Dublin than in London, and in the extreme west 40 mins later than in London.

Tipping

The standard rate of tipping to paid staff as in an hotel or restaurant is 12%, simply add this to the bill; where the money is handed over personally, *eg* to taxi drivers, 10%. When service charge has already been added, there is no need to add anything further. It is not customary to tip in pubs, shops, cinemas or ticket offices.

If somebody does you a service over and above what would normally be expected in their job, show your appreciation with thanks and a smile, not with money which may offend; but if that someone is a public employee whose job frequently exposes him to such duties, the offence is less if the tip is accompanied by the words 'Get yourself a drink'.

Toilets

Toilets are adequate at stations and the like, but other public conveniences are fairly rare. This is no hardship because you can nearly always go into a pub. In the Republic, gents' are labelled FIR and ladies' MNA.

Weights and Measures

The traditional measures in Ireland are the imperial measures (pound, pint, gallon and mile), but these are gradually being replaced by metric measures except in pubs. The pint in Ireland is 20 fluid ounces, and the gallon is 160 fluid ounces ($4\frac{1}{2}$ litres).

The old Irish mile was longer than the Imperial mile (47 Irish = 60 English) and the old Irish acre larger than the statute acre (1 Irish acre = 7840 square yards); these old measures are never used today, but take care if you read old statistics.

USEFUL ADDRESSES

(Tel. nos in brackets)

The tourist board for the 26 counties is the Irish Tourist Board, called in this book by its Irish name *Bord Failte* (board of welcomes), and for the six counties is the Northern Ireland Tourist Board; they are the first and best sources of further information on places to stay and things to do. **Bord Failte** head office: Baggot Street Bridge, Dublin 2 (765871). Other addresses: **UK** Ireland House, 150 New Bond Street, London W1 (01-493 3201), Glasgow (041-221 2311), Birmingham (021-236 9724), Manchester (061-832 5981). **North America** 590 Fifth Avenue, New York, N.Y. 10036 (212 246 7400), also in Chicago, San Francisco, Los Angeles, Toronto. **Australia and New Zealand** MLC Centre, 37th Level, Martin Place, Sydney 2000 (232 7460), also Auckland. Within the Republic there are regional tourist offices which co-operate with but are not part of *Bord Failte* and often have local information that you do not get from the national board, their offices are: **Dublin City** 14 O'Connell Street (747733); the **East** 1 Clarinda Park North, Dun Laoghaire (808571); **Midlands** Mullingar (8671); the **Mid West** Limerick (47522); **Donegal–Leitrim–Sligo** Sligo (5336); the **South West** Cork (23251); the **South East** Waterford (75823); the **West** Galway (63081). Apart from Donegal–Leitrim–Sligo, the regions are the same as adopted in this book. **NITB** head office: River House, 48 High Street, Belfast (231221). Other addresses: **UK** The Ulster Office, 11 Berkeley Street, London W1 (01-493 0601) – also in Glasgow (041-221 5115) and Sutton Coldfield (021-354 1431). **USA** 3rd floor, 40 West 57th Street, New York, NY 10019 (212 581 4700).

There are local offices of the NITB at Larne and at Belfast International Airport as well as most major towns in NI. There is also a NITB information desk in Clery's department store in O'Connell Street, Dublin. Apart from the above, you can contact the British Tourist Authority.

Travel

Air Aer Lingus, Dublin (for head office 370011, reservations 377777; transatlantic 377747; also a direct Freephone at the central bus station, Dublin); Belfast (245151); Cork (24331); Shannon (Limerick 45556); London, 52 Poland Street, W1 (01-734 1212); for transatlantic flights 01-437 8000) and in seven other cities in the UK; New York (590 5th Avenue, NY (212 557 1110), offices also in Boston (Dunfay Parker House Hotel, 60 School Street – 1 800 223 6537). This number also locally serves Chicago, Philadelphia, San Francisco and Washington. British Airways, London, Cromwell Road Terminal, London SW7 (01-370 5411); Glasgow (041-332 9666); Belfast (40522); Dublin (686666); Cork (961411); Shannon (61477); New York, 530 5th Avenue (212 687 1600), and 36 other cities in the USA; Toronto, 60 Bloor Street West (595 2500), and 11 other cities in Canada. Air Florida, Miami (305 592 8550). Air UK, Norwich (0603 44288); British Midlands Airways, East Midlands Airport, Derby (0332 810552); Brymon Airways, City Airport, Plymouth (0752 707023); DanAir, Newman House, 45 Victoria Road, Horley, Sussex RH6 7Q9.

Central reservations 02934 5622. Loganair, Glasgow Airport (041-889 3181). Delta Airlines, Atlanta (404 765 2600). Eastern Airlines, Miami (305 873 2211). North West Orient, St Paul, Minnesota (612 726 2611).

Sea Sealink, Victoria Station, London (01-834 2345 or 834 2122), and at Stranraer (0776 3531), Holyhead (0407 2304), Dun Laoghaire (Dublin 742931) and Rosslare (Wexford 33115). There is also a teledata number for general Sealink enquiries and bookings (01-200 0200). For latest information on what is happening at the ports ring Holyhead on (0407 3031) or Fishguard (0348 873523). B+I, Reliance House, Water Street, Liverpool (051-227 3131), 155 Regent Street, London (01-734 4681), and at Cork (021 23024), Dublin (724711), Pembroke and Rosslare (053 33311); Brittany Ferries, 42 Grand Parade, Cork (021 507666) and at Plymouth (0752 21321); Irish Continental, Aston Quay, Dublin (01 774331); Townsend-Thoresen, 1 Camden Crescent, Dover (0304 203388), Cairnryan (058 12 276) and Larne (0574 4321).

Trains British Rail, Euston Travel Centre (01-387 9400) or Paddington, Travel Centre (01-262 6767); CIE City Booking Office, 59 Upper O'Connell Street, Dublin (787777) and stations throughout the Republic; Northern Ireland Railways telephone enquires to Belfast 230310 or 235282 and at stations throughout the Province, also British Rail at 24 Donegal Place, Belfast (0232 27525).

Buses CIE City Booking Office as above; Busaras (bus station), Store Street, Dublin (742941), 35 Abbey Street Lower, Dublin, in office hours; Ulsterbus, 10 Glengall Street, Belfast (220011; 220574 after 1800).

Consulates

Australia Fitzwilton House, Wilton Terrace, Dublin (761517); **Canada** 65 St Stephen's Green, Dublin (781988); **UK** 33 Merrion Road, Dublin (695211); **USA** 42 Elgin Road, Dublin (688777) and Queen's House, Queen Street, Belfast (28239).

Accommodation and Activities

An Oige (Irish Youth Hostels Assn.), 39 Mountjoy Square, Dublin: Y.H.A. of N.I., 56 Bradbury Place, Belfast; An Taisce (National Trust for the Republic), 41 Percy Place, Dublin; National Trust for N.I., Rowallane, Saintfield, Co. Down (510721); Irish Farm Holidays Assn., Ashton Grove, Knockraha, Co. Cork (Cork 821 537); Town and Country Homes Assn., Shangri-la, Newtown, Bantry. Co. Cork (Bantry 244); Farm and Country Holidays Assn., 76 Kilbroney Road, Rostrevor, Newry, Co. Down; Assn. for Adventure Sports, Tiglin Adventure Centre, Ashford, Co. Wicklow; Union of Students in Ireland Travel, 7 Anglesea Street, Dublin; Erne Charter Boat Assn., 37 Townhall Street, Enniskillen; Inland Fisheries Trust (Angling Section for the Republic), Glasnevin, Dublin; Fisheries Conservancy Board for N.I., 21 Church Street, Portadown, Co. Armagh (for rod licence); Fisheries Divn. of N.I. Dept. of Agriculture, Stormont Castle Grounds, Belfast (for controlled fishing permit); Sports Council for N.I., House of Sport, Upper Malone Road, Belfast; Federation of Mountaineering Clubs of Ireland, 20 Leopardstown Gardens, Blackrock, Dublin; Inland Waterways Assn. of Ireland, Kingston House, Ballinteer, Dublin; Forest Park and Wildlife Service, 22 Upper Merrion Street, Dublin (for information on forest parks and shooting); Ordnance Survey of the Republic, Phoenix Park, Dublin; Ordnance Survey of N.I., Ladas Drive, Belfast; O'Mara Travel Ltd, 4 St Stephen's Green, Dublin and Travel Ireland, Dripsey, Co. Cork for walking, canoeing, cycling, riding holidays; Irish Caravan Council, 164 Sutton Park, Sutton, Co. Dublin.

Cultural

Irish Arts Council, 70 Merrion Square, Dublin; Northern Ireland Arts Council, 181a Stranmills Road, Belfast 9; Royal Dublin Society, Ballsbridge, Dublin; Gaeltarra Eireann, Na Forbacha, Galway; Irish Georgian Society, Castletown House, Celbridge, Co. Kildare; Comhaltas Ceoltoiri Eireann (Irish music and dance) Culturlann na Eireann, Belgrave Square, Monkstown, Co. Dublin; Ulster-Scott Historical Foundation, Balmoral Avenue, Belfast; Historic Irish Tourist Houses and Gardens Assn., c/o Fred's Travel, Castle Street, Dalkey.

Miscellaneous

Automobile Association, 23 Suffolk Street, Dublin and 108/110 Great Victoria Street, Belfast; Royal Automobile Club, 65 Chichester Street, Belfast; American Express, 116 Grafton Street, Dublin and 9 North Street, Belfast; TI-Irish Raleigh Ltd (rent-a-bike), Broomhill Road, Tallaght, Co. Dublin; Irish Workcamp Movement, 23 Essex Quay, Dublin; Rent-a-Cottage, Shannon Free Airport, Co. Clare; Public Record Office, 66 Balmoral Avenue, Belfast (ancestor tracing in N.I).

DUBLIN CITY
AND THE EAST

Over a million people, one third of the Republic's population, live in Dublin's Fair City, yet the conurbation does not appear to be collapsing under the strain of its own gravitational pull. Instead the impression is of a stately, rather frayed but smiling centre of life for a large handful of urbanites. The most obvious sign of the modern disease is the volume of traffic, and even then it moves slowly.

Superficially it is Georgian Dublin, with elegant 18th-century houses and people still moving and talking with a Georgian politeness and leisure. Just underneath, or round the back, is 19th-century Dublin – it could fairly be called the last Victorian city in the British Isles – with its street markets, derelict warehouses, plain front rooms opening onto the sidewalk, old-fashioned nameplates of redundant but still active clubs and unions, corner shops with simple stock and bigger glossy shops, begging mothers, brawling men; gutsy, tolerant and liveable.

These aspects of Dublin are bound together by modern developments and the Liffey. As a real capital and centre of government, with a role to play in international affairs, it is enlivened with administrators and bureaucrats, academics and communicators, whose numbers ensure that Dublin moves with the times, if a little bit behind. The River Liffey rules the city almost unnoticed. With its steep, low-walled banks and traffic along the quays, it could almost be the Seine but for the absence of bookstalls; at its best at night – a long winding gap through the low sky-line, with few bright lights and very little advertising.

Dublin is one of the more human cities in Europe, certainly the most human capital, and is, above all, a happy city. Dubliners themselves have the reputation among out-of-towners as smart alecks, inclined to look down on their country cousins. But with the continued growth of the population, most Dubliners now have their roots in the country, and it's a city of countrymen at home in the town – slow-moving, slow-talking but with an eye to a fast buck.

A number of places open to the public have set opening times which may be changed from time to time. Dublin Castle, used for visits of foreign dignitaries and other important occasions has to be closed to the public from time to time. Many places, such as the National Museum and the Municipal Art Gallery are closed on Mondays. It is best to check up-to-date opening times either with the tourist information office in O'Connell Street or in the current Dublin official guide which is published annually.

History

Dublin, or in Irish *Baile atha Cliath,* was known to the classical geographer Ptolemy as *Eblana* (AD 140). However, the story of the city does not really begin until seven hundred years later when a wooden town was built here by the Vikings, to be used as a base for raiding further up the Liffey.

At Clontarf, now a seaside suburb of north Dublin facing the B + I ferry terminal, the Vikings were defeated by Brian Boru on Easter Day 1014. Dublin remained in Irish hands until in 1170 it was taken by the Anglo-Normans. It was held by the English until Easter Monday 1916, when it became Irish for the third time at the opening of the War of Independence.

In late mediaeval times Dublin and its immediate surroundings were almost the only part of Ireland obedient to the English king. The native Irish were squeezed outside the city walls to today's suburb of Irishtown, which lies south of the Liffey. Dubliners backed the losing side every time in the wars in Britain that spilled over into Ireland, but their luck improved with the landing of Cromwell in 1649. From the end of the 17th century Dublin began to flourish as a wealthy Protestant city.

At first the town grew up on the north side of the river, and parts which are now struggling against decay, like Mountjoy Square and Parnell Square, were home to rich aristocrats. But from the middle 1700s fashion moved south, and the squares of Georgian houses which remain the pride of Dublin began to appear –

Trinity College

The Four Courts

Custom House and Liberty Hall

Merrion Square in 1752, St Stephen's Green in 1780, and Fitzwilliam Square as late as 1820. The Wide Streets Commission was established in 1757, to enforce the generosity in the proportions of the streets and houses which makes Dublin so pleasant to walk in today.

When the Irish parliament became independent in 1783, the flowering of Dublin society reached its height. The Four Courts were completed, the parliament building (now the Bank of Ireland) was built in 1785, and the Custom House was built in 1790. Dublin was the second city of the British Isles in size, and the first in glittering elegance.

This metropolitan development was cut off by the enforced union with Britain in 1800, after which the Irish parliament was dissolved and the aristocrats retired to England or to their country estates. The growth of modern Dublin began in the Victorian era. Drains were laid which are only now beginning to deteriorate, the railway arrived (Heuston Station, 1845, preserves a splendid Victorian ironwork roof), industry developed, and Dublin Corporation was created in the form in which it still tries to manage the city's problems. The poor were poorer than the London poor, with no Dickens to immortalize them, and the characteristic Dublin humour emerged, strikingly like Cockney humour. Terrace after terrace of little houses were built to house the growing working class — houses which are now becoming desirable residences round the edge of the inner city. Most of the pubs also date from this time.

An appreciation of the theatrical and literary movement from the end of the Victorian era — Yeats and Synge, the expatriates Oscar Wilde and George Bernard Shaw, and later Sean O'Casey and James Joyce — set the tone for a witty, conversational society which persists in Dublin today. The wealthy enjoyed receptions at the Lord Lieutenant's little court.

But while London was the heart of an Empire, Dublin was a colonial outpost. From the steps of the General Post Office in O'Connell Street the Republic was declared in 1916. The events of the following years are Irish history, not just Dublin history, but they led to the emergence of Dublin as the capital of a small, poor and uncertain but independent state. The damage of the Anglo-Irish war and the Civil War was repaired, cars replaced horses and buses replaced trams, and Dublin changed very little for another 30 years.

From the 1950s, as the novelty of independence wore off and post-war wealth seeped in, Dubliners began to take a new view of their town, and to try to make it a fair city again. The Georgian squares, which had decayed to gloomy tenements, were restored; speculative development was checked, so that today there is only one tower block in the centre, but at the cost of leaving considerable derelict property awaiting redevelopment; and some of the picturesque but dingy warehousing and tenements were torn down. This has left Dublin the happy mixture of cities you see today.

Prominent Features

(Nos. relate to map, p. 46/7.)

Trinity College (13), generally known as TCD, has a main entrance right at the heart of Dublin, and if you stand by the railings for a while you're bound to see someone you know walking past, if you know anybody at all in the fair city. In case you don't know anybody, the portico has notices of lectures, talks, film shows, debates, plays, recitals — activities for nearly all tastes.

TCD was founded in 1591 as a Protestant university, to further the Reformation, but most of the buildings are 18th century. They are grouped to create a wonderful cloistered calm, enlivened by the students on their way to lectures or to the tearoom in the new Arts Block.

For the visitor, the chief interest of TCD is the **Old Library**, high and dark and still used for study, housing hundreds of thousands of centuries-old books in buff leather bindings. Pride of the library is the *Book of Kells* (from the monastery of Kells about 64km/40mi from Dublin p. 58), an illuminated manuscript of the gospels compiled in the eighth century. One page is turned each day. Other treasures in the library are the *Book of Armagh*, a ninth-century New Testament with the Confession of St Patrick; the *Book of Durrow*, a seventh-century gospel; and an ancient harp which is the official symbol of the Irish President (called the harp of Brian Boru, it is probably 15th-century).

The **King's Inns (3)**, at the end of Henrietta Street (off North Bolton St,), functions as a training ground and club for those lawyers who intend to practise at the bar (barristers).

About ten minutes' walk from the King's Inns, the **Four Courts (2)** is a late 18th-century building overlooking the Liffey, housing the superior courts of the Republic. During the Civil War the Four Courts was occupied by anti-treaty forces who were shelled out by Michael Collins' artillery, destroying the original building, but it has been completely restored in its original form. The chambers that open off the central circular hall were originally the Courts of Chancery, King's Bench, Com-

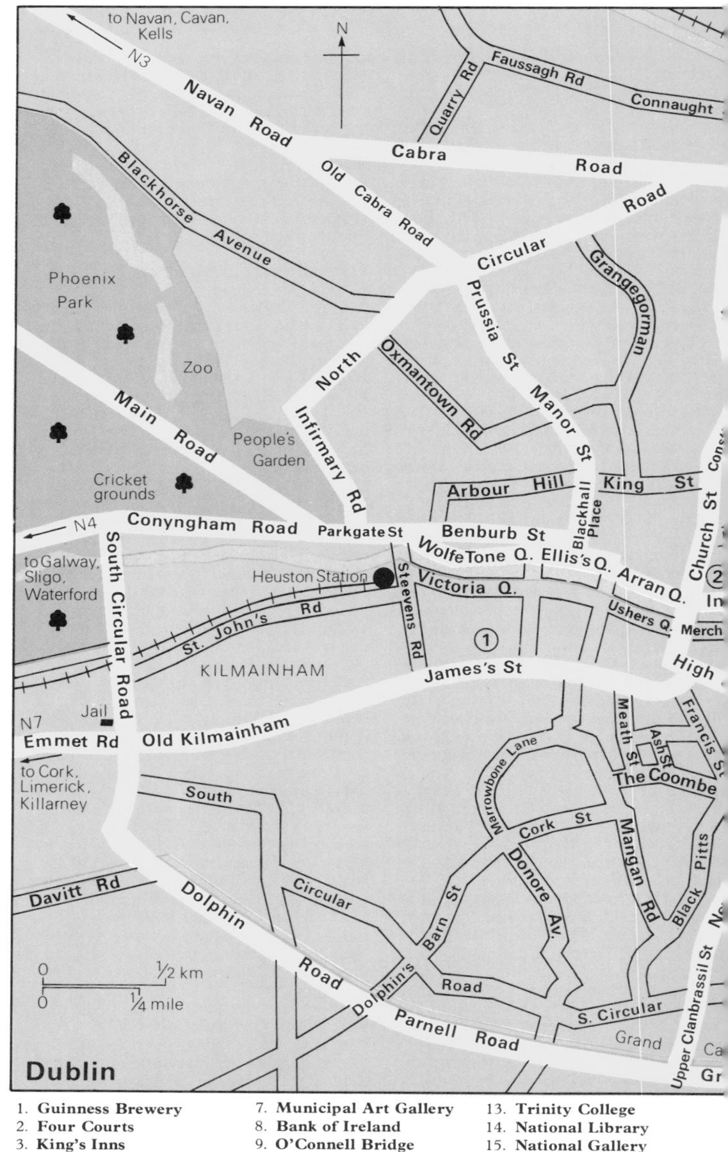

1. **Guinness Brewery**
2. **Four Courts**
3. **King's Inns**
4. **Christchurch Cathedral**
5. **St Patrick's Cathedral**
6. **Dublin Castle**
7. **Municipal Art Gallery**
8. **Bank of Ireland**
9. **O'Connell Bridge**
10. **Catholic Pro-Cathedral**
11. **Liberty Hall**
12. **Custom House**
13. **Trinity College**
14. **National Library**
15. **National Gallery**
16. **National Museum**
17. **Leinster House**

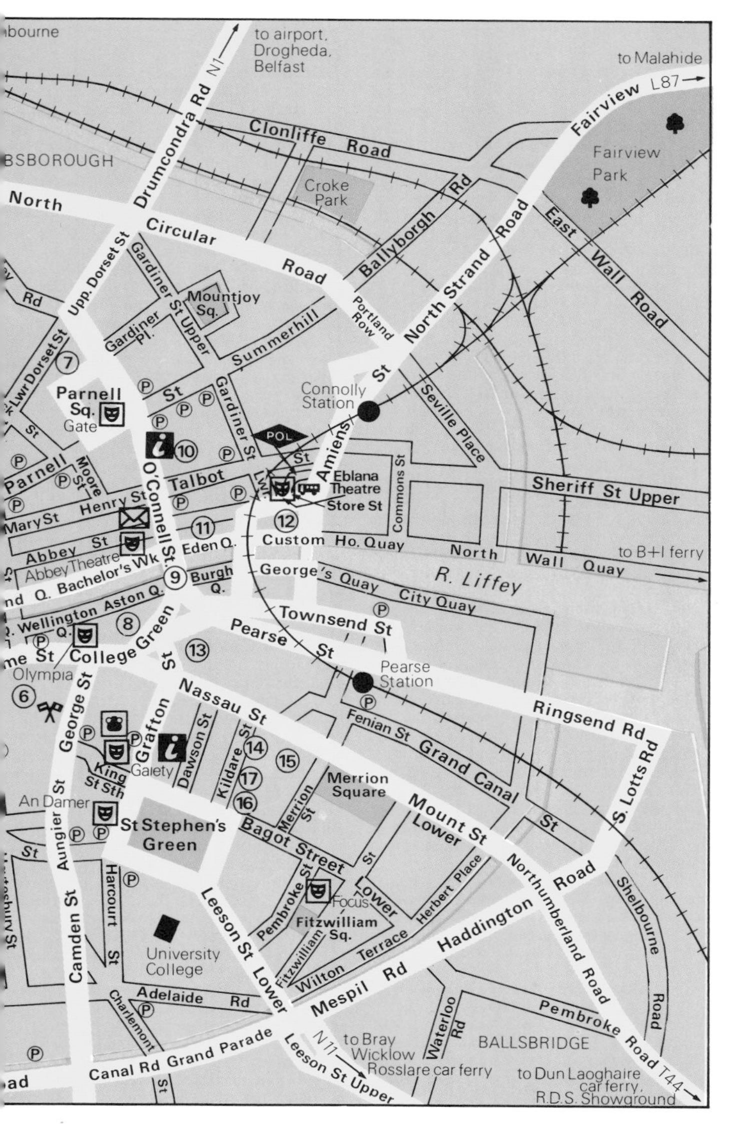

depository of records until it was burnt down in 1921, it has been completely restored and today houses government offices. Some genealogical records are still stored here if you're ancestor hunting.

Liberty Hall (11), a tower of greenish glass (11 stories), is the only high block that has been allowed near the city centre, so the Dublin skyline is on the whole graceful, peaceful, 19th-century and mon Pleas and Exchequer. That outmoded legal system has been superseded in Ireland, but the barristers and judges still wear wigs and robes in court and haunt the nearby bars in mufti.

The **Custom House (12)**, with a splendid front to the river which you can see best from George's Quay on the south bank, is probably the finest public building in Dublin. It was designed by James Gandon and completed in 1791. Liberty Hall is headquarters of the Irish Transport and General Workers' Union.

Leinster House (17), the former town residence of the Duke of Leinster (the only Irish duke), was built in 1745 and acquired by the Irish government in 1922 to be the seat of the Irish Parliament (*Oireachtas*). There is an 18th-century suite of rooms for the Senate (60 members), and a more modern oval chamber for the *Dail* (lower house, of 148 members). The public are admitted when the house is not sitting, entry from Kildare Street.

The **National Library (14)** is on the left of Leinster House, the National Museum on the right. Both date from about 1890. There is a closed access system as in the British Museum but visitors may be allowed to consult books without a reader's ticket. Splendid collection of photographs and Irish newspapers. Gaps in the collection of books. For the less studious, there are interesting exhibitions in the downstairs entrance hall.

The **National Museum (16)** has an excellent collection of Irish antiquities, especially pre-historic; representative collection of Irish silver, glass, swords and costume; informative special exhibitions. A visit to the upstairs hall of military history (mainly mementoes of the War of Independence) may help you understand what the Irish feel about themselves. Natural history is an annexe round the back, in Merrion Street.

The **National Gallery (15)** also has its entrance in Merrion Street. Spacious, handy restaurant; a major gallery for a small country. Houses part of the country's portrait collection; the remainder has been moved to Malahide Castle.

The **Municipal Art Gallery (7)**, at the top of Parnell Square is devoted to modern art, mostly a bequest from Sir Hugh Lane. Even if you're not partial to 20th-century painting, the interior of the gallery is worth sitting in – the 1762 town house of the Earl of Charlemont.

The cathedrals are **Christchurch (4)** and **St Patrick's (5)**, both Church of Ireland and nearly next door to each other, and the Catholic **Pro-Cathedral (10)** at the back of O'Connell Street. Christchurch was founded in 1173 by Strongbow, on the site of a church built by the Danish king, Sitric. The original crypt remains. It is the diocesan church for the bishoprics of Dublin and Glendalough. St Patrick's, founded in 1190 because the authorities did not trust the Dano-Irish alliance at the church across the road, is the national cathedral of (Protestant) Ireland. Jonathan Swift (*Gulliver's Travels*) was Dean of St Patrick's from 1713–45. Both Christchurch and St Patrick's were heavily restored in the 1870s.

St Mary's Pro-Cathedral was built around 1825; from outside it looks like the Temple of Hephaestus snatched from its hill in Athens, to stand in a flat side street – the Protestant Ascendancy would not allow the cathedral to be built on a commanding site – but the calm interior is worth seeing.

For church interiors, the newish Dominican church at the back of Merchant's Quay is to be recommended. A short distance beyond the Protestant cathedrals is the **Guinness' Brewery (1)**, home of the deep purple stout. It is no longer possible to tour the brewery, but in Crane Street there is a public room (open 1000 to 1500) where you can see a filmed explanation of the company's history and the brewing process, and afterwards you can sample the brew at its very best in the hospitality room.

Dublin Castle (6) is a must if you're sightseeing; guided tour every half hour. Dublin Castle was started as a Norman castle, added to over the years, and reconstructed finally in the 18th century. For seven hundred years it was the base of Norman, then English, then British rule in Ireland and 'the Castle' in Irish history sounds nearly as ominous as in Kafka's book of that name. The sumptuous State Apartments are where the Lord Lieutenant entertained and gave balls or banquets for the upper crust of Irish society, like a king – indeed, he was generally called the Viceroy. The rest of the castle, not now open to the public, housed the administrative offices of the Chief Secretary, the effective head of government in Ireland in place of a prime minister.

With independence, the state apartments fell into neglect for a time. But as Ireland came to appreciate her Georgian heritage, they were richly and colourfully refurbished, but tastefully, without the ostentation of viceregal days. Now they are used for state functions such as the inauguration of a president or a reception for the heads of government of the EEC. They are worth visiting for the Killybegs carpets alone, or for the truly sumptuous toilets.

Kilmainham Jail, just outside the

The Throne Room, Dublin Castle

centre of Dublin on the road to Naas, was the temporary home of a succession of Irish nationalists – Fenians, Land Leaguers, Parnell, the Invincibles – and it was here that the leaders of the Easter Rising were shot, ensuring the final success of the Rising. The jail has been partly restored as a museum of Irish martyrdom, and is open to the public on Sunday afternoons.

Phoenix Park is huge (708 hectares/1750 acres); mostly flat grassland with well-spaced trees. The American ambassador's residence is in the grounds, and the former viceregal lodge is the official residence of the President of the Irish Republic. Busy at weekends with sports being played, and at any time with strollers and riders. Cattle roam free and deer can be seen at night. The People's Garden is a colourful flower garden by the south-east entrance nearest to the city centre, and then past the lakes near the entrance is Dublin Zoo.

At Glasnevin, the **Botanic Gardens** house a great variety of plants and trees, with rock gardens, hothouses and a mill-race. Open 0900 to 1800, or to sunset.

City Layout

This section should be read in conjunction with the map on p. 46/7.

The Inner City is the area between the Grand Canal in the south, and the North Circular Road, with the River Liffey running through the middle from west to east. It is easy to walk from one side to the other in 30 mins, and the best way to see and enjoy Dublin is on foot.

Buses coming to the very centre are marked *An Lar* (Irish for 'The Centre'), and a standing joke among Dubliners is to ask where this mythical place is – nobody seems to know. Who are the Anlarians, skulking there unseen? *An Lar* buses may stop anywhere from Parnell Square to College Green – a good 10 mins apart.

The centre may be taken as **O'Connell Bridge (9)**, broader than it is long. North from the bridge runs **O'Connell Street**, a wide avenue with chromium-plated cafés, restaurants, Clery's store, The Gresham and Royal Dublin hotels, a Tourist Information Office, and the famous **General Post Office**. The GPO on a Saturday afternoon is the place for political speeches, while processions and demonstrations usually take place in O'Connell Street. The grid of small streets either side of O'Connell Street is where you find the chain stores and less expensive eating-places; beyond Capel Street to the west, there is an interesting bit of older Dublin. At the top of O'Connell Street is **Parnell Square**, which marks the start of an area of old houses which can be recognized as Georgian but look more like Victorian tenements. This continues to Mountjoy Square, formerly very fashionable but now struggling to recover from a sad decline. Gardiner Street, both at its upper end around Mountjoy Square and at its lower end, intersecting with Talbot Street, is good for cheapish lodgings.

The streets on each side of the river are called the **Quays**; pubs, warehouses (many deserted), bright in places with an antique shop or book shop, dingy in other places. The north quays are one-way from east to west and the only streets in Dublin where traffic rushes; the south quays are one-way from west to east, and full of buses.

South from O'Connell Bridge, Westmoreland Street curves up an incline past the **Bank of Ireland (8)**, with buskers and jewellery sellers under its arches, to **College Green**, the short stretch of road in front of Trinity College. Here is the focal point of Dublin and the start of its elegant quarter. **Dame Street**, the extension of College Green, is the nearest there is to a commercial street in Dublin, and its continuation past the castle meanders into a dark-and-bright area; several good eating-places, some buildings awaiting development.

Grafton Street, a low hill down which the traffic slowly oozes trying to get to the front of Trinity College, is a street of fashionable shops and the widening triangle south east of the junction of Grafton Street with Nassau Street is the most select part of Dublin. Here the expensive shops and good, old-fashioned, hotels give way to the residences of the well-to-do — almost all Georgian houses which have been kept in, or restored to, 18th-century comfortable elegance. The three famous Georgian squares are **Merrion Square, St Stephen's Green** where office redevelopment has started, and the little jewel **Fitzwilliam Square**, but all the easy broad streets are Georgian in appearance and proportion. The general feel of affluence continues beyond the canal to Ballsbridge, which is the first suburb of Dublin and shelters the more modern of the up-market hotels.

Eastwards of Trinity College — City Quay, Townsend Street and **Pearse Street** — there is no pretence to elegance; a land of motor repair shops, car rental offices, defunct institutions, leading to factories and the docks.

Merrion Square

West of **St Stephen's Green** the main roads are Georgian terraces, still broad and comfortable, but less self-conscious, hiding backstreets of early Victorian artisans' dwellings, small corner shops, pork butchers, 'Wood, Turf, Coals Supplied' shops, Chinese restaurants, a violin shop selling apples, a second-hand books-and-tyres shop, Iveagh House, old warehouses and modern offices.

For a tour round Dublin to see the historic landmarks you can't do better than follow the route suggested by Dublin Tourism in their booklet 'Tourist Trail – Signposted Walking Tour of Dublin'. The walk takes about three hours, not counting stops. The booklet gives an illustrated explanation of what you see. Available from the Tourist Information Offices in O'Connell Street.

The Tourist Trail concentrates on historic, decorative Georgian Dublin. A little departure from it will show you a completely different city – Victorian Dublin. For example: Gardiner Street, Frenchman's Lane, across the river to Tara Street Station, on to Pearse Station and take a train for a few stops, to, say, Sydney Parade or Booterstown – from the train window look out onto the backs of the houses. Having returned, amble back past the south side of St Stephen's Green, Kevin Street, find Ash Street – good modern housing which retains an Irish style – and next to Ash Street is Park Terrace – old houses in a distinctively Irish style. Just beyond is the Liberty Market in Meath Street where you will see the Dublin of Molly Malone, and then down Steevens' Lane past Dr Steevens' Hospital. Cross the river beyond the station and find North King Street – the area is rundown now because it is threatened with clearance to make way for the Inner Tangent relief road, but while it lasts you can see old Dublin, in a spirit that underlies much of the more touristed bits. Up Capel Street, which was James Joyce's favourite, and along the rise to the edge of Phibsborough perhaps, and then through the backstreets, partly cleared, to Parnell Square and across to Mountjoy Square where you started.

A third walk would be the literary trail. Start at the Joyce Museum in the Martello Tower, Sandycove (see below).

Taxi ranks in O'Connell Street, College Green, St Stephen's Green, and at bus and train stations. In phone book under 'Taxicab ranks'; or radio cabs on 772222/776528. Horse-drawn cabs on 755 995.

Outer Suburbs

On the buses you will see the names of destinations in outer Dublin, all meaning something in particular to Dubliners. Here are some of them, to tempt you to just hop on a bus and go there. An interesting feature of Dublin is that there is no feeling of segregation despite social differences between areas.

Ballsbridge is the poshest residential suburb, just beyond the South Ring. Here are embassies, the showgrounds of the Royal Dublin Society, and sophisticated hotels offering entertainment. There are a few pockets of working-class cottages, while **Herbert Park** is a sub-suburb, without quite the same cachet – more the home of fairly successful intellectuals.

Ballymun was on the northern edge of the city when built a few years ago, but expansion has crept past it. Dublin's only experiment with high-rise flats it has experienced the troubles common to tower blocks. However, the kids of Ballymun have found a salvation unique in urban alienation – they've learned enthusiastically to speak Irish (with a strong working-class Dublin accent).

Castleknock (beyond Phoenix Park) is modern, neo-Georgian, and not too hard up.

Crumlin is a mixture of corporation housing and struggling private estates. Don't confuse the Crumlin Road, leading to it, with the better-known Crumlin Road in Belfast.

Dalkey is a settled, old-established, middle-class suburb by the sea.

Donnybrook New home of University College, Dublin. The centre of the college is at Bellfield, and a student flavour spreads throughout the surroundings. Whereas TCD is the single college of the University of Dublin, UCD is one of the constituent colleges of the National University of Ireland. The whole range of academic subjects is studied at UCD, and since the main campus moved here from its cramped premises at the back of St Stephen's Green, Donnybrook has become quite lively. Also the home of Irish television.

Drumcondra Pink-brick terraces and pebble-dash, semidetached houses.

Dun Laoghaire is known to many visitors as the terminal for the ferry from north Wales, but it is also a busy, prosperous little town in its own right, independent of Dublin city, with good entertainments and shopping. Just outside Dun Laoghaire is a small block of low, Irish-cottage-style terraces to remind you how very English all the rest looks.

To the south east at Sandycove is the Martello Tower, now the Joyce Museum. James Joyce stayed here with his friend Oliver St John Gogarty in 1904. Get a copy of *Dubliners* and see how many of the characters portrayed there survive in spirit today.

Greystones A residential area, hardly a resort although by the sea; genteel. Fills up in the evening when commuters tumble off the Dublin train.

Howth Visit the Howth Peninsula for the view across Dublin Bay from the summit; bus to the top follows the worn-out markings of the 'Viking Route'. Follow this with a meal in the fishing harbour overlooking the small island called Ireland's Eye, or a walk through the rhododendron-filled demesne of Howth Castle. Villas mingled with neo-Georgian bungalows are springing up anywhere on the peninsula in sight of the sea. Elsewhere are streets of semidetached houses and grey concrete flats. All very quiet.

Famous in nationalist history for the jetty where arms were landed in 1914 for the Republican cause.

Irishtown Formerly a very down area but now improving, an extension of Ringsend. (Dog track.)

Killiney One stop on the train beyond Dalkey and very similar – more aware of the sea. Killiney Hill Park is very pleasant with great views over Killiney Bay.

Malahide A seaside resort distinct from Dublin, but getting caught up as an outer suburb; castle.

Monkstown Takes its name from the enforced movement of the monks from Dublin. Now comfortably prosperous like Dun Laoghaire, strong in entertainment.

Phibsborough Just north of the centre, formerly a dense concentration of artisan houses, now office blocks are appearing, and the whole area is coming up.

Portobello Strongly working-class, older housing.

Ranelagh, Rathmines, Rathgar, Rathfarnham. A line of suburbs stretching south west, all fairly prosperous. James Joyce was born at 41 Brighton Square West, Rathgar.

Ringsend Dockland; working-class, old Dublin.

Sallynoggin A working-class pocket between Dalkey and Killiney, out of sight of the sea.

Sandymount An older area, spacious not smart.

Terenure A continuation of the Rathmines line, with the memory that this was once open country.

What to do in Dublin

Theatre There are probably more new plays of quality and interest on the Dublin stage than in London, creating excitement, an acceptance of short runs, and an interest in theatre that goes beyond a theatre-going crowd. The Abbey Theatre in Lower Abbey Street does the Irish classics and some modern works; the Peacock underneath the Abbey is for new plays with something to say; the Gate at the top of O'Connell Street puts on international classics; the Gaiety in South King Street presents popular modern plays, grand opera twice a year, musicals and pantomime; the Olympic in Dame Street also has musicals; the little Eblana, Store Street, specializes in modern plays and revues; Focus in Pembroke Street; Victor Theatre, Dun Laoghaire, is all-purpose. More avant-garde are the Project Theatre, East Essex Street, and the Players in TCD. Lambert Mews in Monkstown is a puppet theatre.

Cinema Cinema-going is still prominent in Dublin life, and there are nearly 30 cinemas in the city centre.

Music There's no proper concert hall but the Francis Xavier Hall, just north of Mountjoy Square, is used by the Radio Symphony Orchestra for concerts. Classical music is put on from time to time in St Anne's, Dawson Street, the Hugh Lane Museum (lunchtime), the National Gallery (teatime) and at the Royal Dublin Society – opera. There's Irish music, pop, jazz and traditional, and folk, at pubs and hotels all over Dublin. The city centre and older inner suburbs are full of music of one sort or another, maybe less in the newer suburbs. Open-air bands in Phoenix Park, Dun Laoghaire, Killiney. Details from tourist offices, *In Dublin* magazine and evening papers. *Culturlann na Eireann* is the headquarters of CCE at Belgrave Square, Monkstown, and provides a summer programme of Irish music.

Pubs Dublin pubs are similar to London pubs (contrary to the conviction of good Dubliners), but are even more a feature of Dublin life. Many more have remained in the pure Victorian style, and there's a greater sense of escape into the Irishman's castle. Most guide books, the *In Dublin* free map, and the Tourist Board's free *Inside Guide to Dublin,* have their own list of recommended pubs, and all the lists are different. The official figure is 650 pubs in Dublin; on our count, there's that many in the inner city alone. It's best to find your own type of pub. Quiet in the afternoon; too full on a Saturday night.

Nightlife Several establishments are advertised as nightclubs (mainly around Leeson Street), but a Dublin nightclub is not what you'd expect in New York or Paris – it's more of an expensive disco.

Cabaret at some of the big hotels – see evening papers.

Sport Croke Park, just beyond Mountjoy Square, is the venue for Gaelic games

Hurling, Croke Park

(football and hurling) and soccer while Lansdowne Road, between Irishtown and Ballsbridge, is the home of rugby football. On a Sunday morning you can watch the above games played in Phoenix Park. Dog-racing at Shelbourne Park Stadium, Ballsbridge (Mon., Wed., Sat. evenings) and at Harold Cross Stadium (Tue., Thur. and Fri. evenings). Golf at fourteen 18-hole golf courses and at about as many 9-hole courses within easy reach of the city centre; there are public courses at Donabate and Howth. Horseracing at Phoenix Park (very friendly and local) and Leopardstown, and more important meetings further out at the Curragh and Naas, Co. Kildare; in April at Punchestown; and at Easter at Fairyhouse, Co. Meath. Off-shore sea fishing from nearly all the little resorts up and down the coast. Public tennis courts at: Herbert Park, Ballsbridge; Bushy Park, Terenure; Ellenfield Park, Whitehall; St Anne's, Dollymount; Johnstown Park, Finglas. Yachting clubs at Dun Laoghaire and many resorts north of Dublin. Rowing on the Liffey at Islandbridge. And there is ten-pin bowling at Stillorgan.

Shopping Go north of the river, in the side streets off O'Connell Street, for basic shopping; less pricey. Clery's in O'Connell Street is a big department store, a Dublin institution, straight out of the 1930s; Arnott's in Henry Street is another. Mary Street market for real cut prices and quality to match.

South of the river the shops are more select. When the goods are the same as north of the river they are not necessarily more expensive. The principal shopping street is Grafton Street, with the two main stores, Switzers and Brown, Thomas, to remind you that the original market for better Dublin wares was the Anglo-Irish, a tweedy, conservative but eccentric lot. The fashion boutiques, couturiers and Irish craft shops in the streets between Grafton Street and Kildare Street, and thereabouts, are still not short of tweeds. Antique shops are spread along the quays by the Liffey, with more in the Grafton Street area – furniture and silver. Bookshops, there are ten general booksellers; Green's (Clare Street) and Webbs (Crampton Quay) are second-hand bookshops and Fred Hanna (Nassau Street) has a second-hand department; Books Upstairs (South King Street) for the alternative society; Starry Plough Bookshop (Gardiner Place), socialist and Sinn Fein Workers' Party; New Books (Essex Street) communist; An Phoblacht (Parnell Street) provo Sinn Fein.

Street markets remain an important part of the Dublin scene, to see and hear the old Dublin humour and ill-humour in action, and get the occasional bargain. Moore Street market near Parnell Square, and the Liberty market, Meath Street (the 'Liber-ties' were those parts of Dublin outside the jurisdiction of the Lord Mayor) offer foodstuffs, plastics and some second-hand goodies; Iveagh market, Francis Street, for old clothes, furniture and books; Cumberland Street market, second-hand things, especially shoes; Gaiety Green is an arcade with separate shops rather than stalls.

THE EAST

Any part of the eastern region can be visited on a day's outing from the city centre. The hills and vales of the Wicklow Mountains – the Garden of Ireland – can be a holiday centre in themselves, with never a need to visit the city. The Cooley Peninsula is another holiday centre for lovers of countryside, ideal for a tour of St Patrick's country and the Mountains of Mourne further north. The Boyne Valley is rich in antiquities if that's your interest, otherwise there are stately homes, racecourses, grand estates and seaside resorts.

Arklow P9

Co. Wicklow A shop-lined street winding down the hill to the bridge; during the summer full of holidaymakers from the beaches and holiday camps to north and south, tourists making for the lakes of southern Wicklow, and locals out for a few errands and to meet friends. Plenty of bars, cafés and traditional Irish music; pottery.

Athy N3

Co. Kildare A market town on the River Barrow. An attractive small square is flanked by old, arched buildings and the open banks of the river – the scene of notorious floggings by the British in suppressing the rising of 1798. White's Castle (1507) on the bridge is still a private residence. The Grand Canal joins the Barrow at Athy.

Avoca O8

Co. Wicklow The village, starting point for a tour of the **Vale of Avoca**, is a pretty place tucked into one side of a hill, overlooking the river – a couple of pubs with carpets and a couple of cafés. The vale is a scenic route; steep wooded valleys overlook rock-strewn streams, many picnic places have been set up on the hillsides and there are horse-drawn caravans. The Meeting of the Waters, confluence of three streams and a renowned beauty spot, has its river banks paved and gardened, and is no longer the romantic wilderness of Thomas Moore's poem. Alongside this there is an unaffected local life, as at the cattle market in **Aughrim** where every man has his stick to prod his chosen beast.

Avondale, 7km/4mi north of Avoca, is the former home of Charles Stewart Parnell and is now the training centre of the Irish Forestry Service. (Open to the public 1400 to 1800 from Friday to Monday, May to September.) The house sits in a large forest park (214 hectares/530 acres); nature trail open all year round.

Blessington L6

Co. Wicklow A centre for touring western Wicklow, this 17th-century village has one long, wide street. Visit **Russborough** a grand Georgian house 5km/3mi further south, and see the Beit Art Collection, items of Irish silver and the miniature railway exhibition. Open 1430 to 1830 on Sundays, Bank Holidays, Wednesdays (June to September) and Saturdays (July and August).

Bray L9

Co. Wicklow A rather barren seaside town – long esplanade of Victorian houses, cafés closed in July. Bray Head (241m/791ft) is an extension of the Wicklow dome and sticks out into the sea; it is very striking viewed from a distance, especially in the early morning light. **Glen Dargle** (4km/2½mi inland) is thickly wooded, with a favourite path along the river.

Carlingford B8

Co. Louth Chief village of the **Cooley Peninsula** – wooded hills looking across Carlingford Lough to the Mountains of Mourne, winding lanes, cattle fields, well-to-do farms and the swimming pools of extremely well-to-do expatriate Americans. Ravensdale Forest Park. Carlingford village is rather unremarkable, but the massive castle overlooking the harbour (narrow gateway to allow just one horseman at a time) and the tower house by the square, remind you of its long history. To the south, **Giles Quay** has an attractive little harbour.

Drogheda F7

Co. Louth (pop. 22,000) A major industrial centre, also a port, and formerly one of the chief towns of Ireland. Entertainment centre for people staying in the area to visit the Boyne Valley (archaeology, monastic ruins and the Battle of the Boyne).

The passage graves of the Boyne Valley at **Dowth, Knowth** and the most famous at **Newgrange**, are roughly 7km/4mi west of Drogheda, and about a mile from each other. Built around 2500 BC by the Neolithic predecessors of the Celts, the tumuli contain burial vaults with corbelled roofs, entered through a 20m/66ft-long passage. Each entrance is marked by decorated stones carved with flint chisels, celebrated examples of New Stone Age art. Absorb these designs and see if you can connect them with Celtic patterns. In legend, the builders were the *Tuatha De Danann*, the Celtic Gods, who still live there underground and emerge as the fairy

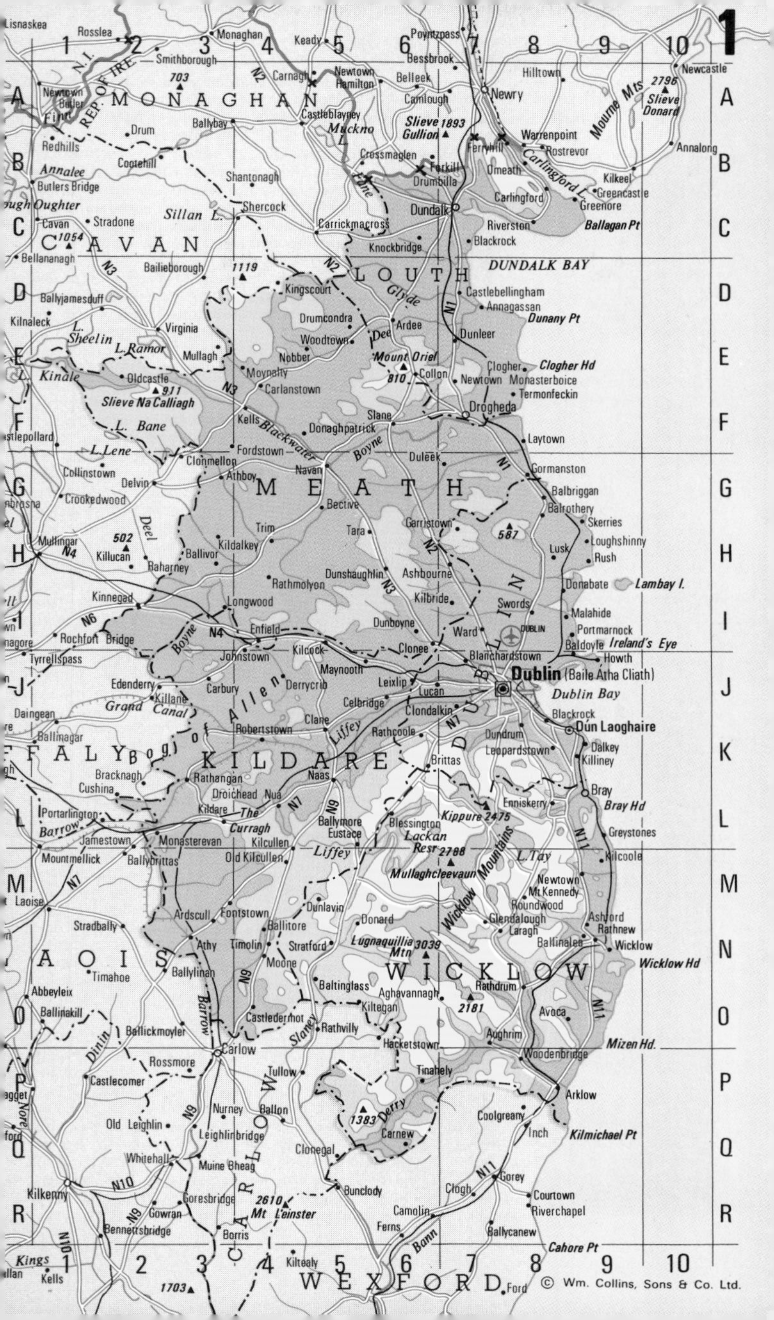
1
1 2 3 4 5 6 7 8 9 10
A B C D E F G H I J K L M N O P Q R
Lisnaskea
Rosslea
Monaghan
Keady
Poyntzpass
Bessbrook
Hilltown
Newcastle
Smithborough
N.I.
REP. OF IRE.
703
Carnagh
Newtown Hamilton
Belleek
Newry
Mourne Mts
2796
Slieve Donard
Newtown Butler
MONAGHAN
Camlough
Castleblayney
Slieve Gullion 1893
Muckno L.
Drum
Ballybay
Warrenpoint
Rostrevor
Ferryhill
Annalong
Redhills
Crossmaglen
Forkill
Cootehill
Omeath
Carlingford L.
Kilkeel
Annalee
Shantonagh
Drumbilla
Greencastle
Butlers Bridge
Fane
Carlingford
Greenore
Lough Oughter
Shercock
Dundalk
Sillan L.
Cavan
Stradone
Carrickmacross
Riverston
Ballagan Pt
1054
CAVAN
Knockbridge
Blackrock
Bellananagh
N3
Bailieborough
1119
N2
LOUTH
DUNDALK BAY
Kingscourt
Glyde
Castlebellingham
Ballyjamesduff
Annagassan
Drumcondra
N1
Dunany Pt
Kilnaleck
L. Sheelin
Virginia
Ardee
Dee
Dunleer
L. Ramor
Woodtown
Mullagh
Nobber
Mount Oriel
Clogher
Clogher Hd
L. Kinale
Oldcastle
Moynalty
810
Collon
Newtown
Monasterboice
911
Carlanstown
Termonfeckin
Slieve Na Calliagh
Drogheda
L. Bane
Kells
Blackwater
Slane
Castlepollard
Donaghpatrick
Laytown
L. Lene
Fordstown
Boyne
Clonmellon
Duleek
Gormanston
Collinstown
Navan
Athboy
Delvin
MEATH
Balbriggan
Crookedwood
Bective
Balrothery
Garristown
Skerries
Deel
Trim
Tara
587
Loughshinny
Mullingar
502
Kildalkey
N4
Killucan
Ballivor
Lusk
Rush
Raharney
Dunshaughlin
Ashbourne
Rathmolyon
N3
Donabate
Lambay I.
DUBLIN
Kinnegad
Longwood
Kilbride
Swords
Malahide
N6
Dunboyne
Portmarnock
Enfield
Ward
Rochfort Bridge
Boyne
Baldoyle
Ireland's Eye
Kilcock
Clonee
Howth
Johnstown
Blanchardstown
Tyrrellspass
Maynooth
Dublin (Baile Atha Cliath)
Edenderry
Carbury
Derrycrib
Leixlip
Lucan
Dublin Bay
Killane
Allen
Celbridge
Grand Canal
Clondalkin
Daingean
Clane
N7
Blackrock
Bog of Allen
Robertstown
Rathcoole
Dundrum
Dún Laoghaire
Ballinagar
Liffey
OFFALY
KILDARE
Leopardstown
Dalkey
Brittas
Killiney
Bracknagh
Rathangan
Naas
Cushina
Bray
Droichead Nua
N9
Enniskerry
Bray Hd
Portarlington
Kildare
The Curragh
Ballymore Eustace
Blessington
Kippure 2475
Barrow
Lackan Resr
Greystones
Jamestown
Monasterevan
Kilcullen
2788
Mountmellick
Ballybrittas
Old Kilcullen
Liffey
L. Tay
Kilcoole
Mullaghcleevaun
Wicklow Mountains
Newtown Mt Kennedy
Laoise
Roundwood
Dunlavin
Ardscull
Fontstown
Donard
Glendalough
Ashford
Stradbally
Ballitore
Laragh
Rathnew
Lugnaquillia Mtn 3039
Athy
Timolin
Stratford
Ballinalee
Wicklow
Moone
Wicklow Hd
LAOIS
Ballylinan
WICKLOW
Timahoe
Baltinglass
Rathdrum
Aghavannagh
Abbeyleix
2181
Kiltegan
Ballinakill
Castledermot
Avoca
Ballickmoyler
Rathvilly
Slaney
Dinin
Aughrim
Mizen Hd.
Hacketstown
Carlow
Woodenbridge
Rossmore
Tullow
Tinahely
Castlecomer
Arklow
Nurney
Ballon
Derry
1383
Old Leighlin
Coolgreany
N9
Leighlinbridge
Carnew
Inch
Kilmichael Pt
Clonegal
Whitehall
Muine Bheag
Gorey
N11
Kilkenny
N10
Bunclody
Clogh
Goresbridge
2610
Courtown
Gowran
Mt Leinster
Riverchapel
Camolin
Ferns
Bennettsbridge
Borris
Bann
Ballycanew
Cahore Pt
Kings
Kiltealy
Kells
1703
WEXFORD
Ford
CARLOW
© Wm. Collins, Sons & Co. Ltd.

folk. Exhibition on site. Tumuli closed Monday.

Monasterboice, 8km/5mi north of Drogheda, has the remains of a monastic settlement of the fifth century. Here are the ninth-century round tower, still standing 30m/100ft high, and three Celtic high crosses. The famous Muireadach's Cross (South Cross) is the one you will often see on picture postcards. It dates from AD 1000 and is covered in sculptured panels depicting scenes from the Gospels. The others are the larger West Cross and the simpler North Cross.

The coming of the Normans was heralded by the building of Mellifont Abbey in 1142 – the first Cistercian house in Ireland. The ruins stand 8km/5mi north west of Drogheda.

Parliaments were held in Drogheda in pre-Tudor times but in 1494 Poyning's Law was enacted here, decreeing that Irish laws had to be ratified in England.

The notorious siege of Drogheda was in 1649, when the town held out against the English parliament in support of the executed king. When Cromwell finally took the town, he had the garrison and leaders of the townspeople massacred and many others transported to Barbados. The massacre – whether the total slain was 500, 2000 or 30,000 as different interested parties claim – has left as deep a mark on Irish Catholics as the next event in the Boyne Valley has made on northern Protestants.

Passage grave entrance, Newgrange

The Battle of the Boyne is recalled every year by Orange parades in Northern Ireland, and every day in the conflict there. It took place in 1690 on July 1st by the old calendar, now July 12th – the date when the drums beat and King Billy rides his white charger to remind the Catholics who lost on that day.

The battleground is about 6km/4mi south west of Drogheda (near Duleek), and signposted. James II, King of Great Britain, had been deposed because he was a Catholic (or because he made no secret of it), but he remained king in Ireland for that same reason.

James's army consisted of 7000 French troops, lent by Louis XIV ensuring that British involvement with Ireland could never cease; some Swiss troops who provided the papal guard; about 10,000 half-trained infantry (including some Protestants) who were part of the British army – these men fought for land and not on religious grounds; and about 10,000 untrained but wildly enthusiastic Catholic-Irish cavalry.

James's opponent, William, was Prince of Orange (hence the orange colour of the Protestant sash) and husband of James's daughter Mary; William had been invited to replace James in England. William (King Billy) had no invitation to Ireland, no rights in Ireland, and no wish to go to Ireland, but he had to prevent a comeback by James. His army consisted of the Dutch Blue Guards (he was ruler of the Netherlands), the Danish Red Guards (James's other son-in-law was king of Denmark), some regiments of German mercenaries and some Finnish troops lent by the Czar. Starting the Protestant tradition of drumming, his army was led by a drum band lent by Pope Alexander VIII. The newly raised English army had left their horses back home, ploughing in East Anglia, and was kept out of the way. A force of Protestant volunteers from Enniskillen and Londonderry (the first Inniskillen Fusiliers) provided William's personal guard.

William was no soldier and did not want to fight: James was an experienced general – he had commanded both the French and the Spanish armies and the English navy at various times – but was tired, disillusioned and determined not to fight. When James ran off, the Protestant cause was secured for three hundred years. In Drogheda, or Belfast, you will no doubt read differing accounts of the Battle of the Boyne.

Landscaped gardens, Powerscourt

Dundalk C6

Co. Louth (pop. 25,000) A busy manufacturing town – tours of the brewery and cigarette factory. In front of the Courthouse in Market Square, a well-illustrated map guides you through the Cuchulain country of the Cooley Peninsula. Cuchulain was a legendary hero, a leader of the Red Branch Knights, who defended the peninsula against the cattle-raiders from the west. A large mound at **Dun Dealgan** (20m/66ft), 3km/2mi west of Dundalk, is his birthplace; **Knockbridge**, 8km/5mi south west of Dundalk, is where he died, having tied himself to a rock that he might die facing his enemies.

Theatre, traditional and modern entertainments; Dundalk Maytime festival around May 20th.

Enniskerry L8

Co. Wicklow (pop. 1000) A pretty, grey hamlet at a crossroads by the foot of a hill; noted as the nearest point to **Powerscourt**, greatest of the demesnes of the Anglo-Irish. The house, a stately home on the grandest scale, was destroyed by fire in 1974, but the armoury and magnificently landscaped gardens are open to the public. The demesne, 5666 hectares/14,000 acres of choicest scenery set aside as a private park, is open for visits to the waterfall, a silver trickle over rocks 60m/200ft high.

Glendalough N7

Co. Wicklow The glen of the two lakes. A beautiful valley shut in by mountains; wooded, good walking and hill climbing. The lower lake has the more important remains of many monastic settlements – the gateway which was the entrance to a monastic city, the round tower, the ancient Church of Our Lady, the Priest's House (12th-century Romanesque) and the ruins of the cathedral and 7th-century St Kevin's Church. The upper lake, more romantically pretty, has the ruins of the Reefert Church and a Bronze Age fort; the church on the rock, on the south shore, has to be reached by boat. Both lakes are very crowded in summer.

The village for Glendalough is **Laragh**, a few houses facing a triangular green from which the roads climb up over the mountains. The north-west road, above Glendalough, leads high over bare rock-strewn hills to the Wicklow Gap and on to the man-made lake of Blessington reservoir. The road due north is the Military Road, opened up after the 1798 rebellion to bring artillery to Irish freedom fighters/brigands. This leads across bleak moorland to the Sally Gap, a crossroads near the source of the River Liffey, with bogs on either side made impassable by peat cuttings. Dubliners like to buy themselves a bit of bog and come out here at weekends to cut turf. The road north east leads through the wooded valley of a little stream called the Annamoe, and through the pretty village of **Annamoe** to the even prettier village of **Roundwood**.

Glenmalure is another ravine south of Glendalough; less visited, more rugged, popular with climbers.

Kells
Ceanannus Mor F4

Co. Meath (pop. 2400) The *Book of Kells* was produced here in the monastery around AD 800. It was preserved until taken by Cromwell's troops to Trinity College Dublin, where it is now on view in the library. The monastery was dissolved during the Reformation, and the most prominent remains are the five Celtic crosses. The most elaborate, though the top of the cross and wheel has been knocked off, is in the marketplace; the others including the oldest, by the round tower, are in the graveyard of St Columba's (C. of I. church) – see facsimile of the Book of Kells. St Columba's House (Columcille's House) is similar to the chapel at Cashel, p. 61.

Kildare L3

Co. Kildare (pop. 3000) This little town, spread along the main south-west road from Dublin, is rather nice – a small parking lot round a stone memorial, and a larger one in the market square overlooked by a winding, high-walled road that leads to the cathedral. Lovely St Brigid's Cathedral, with a round tower in the grounds, is well maintained and the little notice there asking visitors for funds 'because there are only twenty families in the area for upkeep and cleaning of the cathedral' tells you all you need to know about the status of the Church of Ireland in the area.

Kildare is the centre of the Irish horse breeding and training industry. Just to the south of the town is the National Stud at Tully; in the grounds the Japanese gardens, portraying the several stages in the life of man, and the Irish Horse Museum are open Easter to October 1030 to 1230 and 1400 to 1700, Sundays 1400 to 1730. East of Kildare is the Curragh, a vast plain of grass and gorse, surrounded by riding

The paddock, Curragh racecourse

stables. The plain is used for riding and racing (the Irish Derby is held here), and for sheep grazing. At its eastern end is the chief military training camp of the Irish Defence Forces. The Curragh Mutiny took place here in 1914 when British cavalry officers declared they would take no action to enforce Home Rule on northern Protestants, and so made partition the only option for the British government.

Maynooth J5

Co. Kildare (pop. 500) Pronounced *M,nooth.* All you see of the village initially is a few houses, pubs and takeaways, spread along the main road. A side street leads to the cloistered calm of St Patrick's College in Main Street, training centre for the Catholic priesthood and now part of the University of Ireland. Carton House (open Sunday afternoons) is an imposing Georgian mansion at the east end of Maynooth but far more magnificent is nearby **Castletown** (open daily in summer except Tuesdays), a grand Palladian mansion at Celbridge, now the headquarters of the Irish Georgian Society.

Celbridge is on the Liffey; Leixlip (Danish for salmon-leap) is downstream, where the river is crossed by the main road from Dublin to the west. There you can watch the salmon climb the fish ladder at the hydroelectric dam.

Naas K5

Co. Kildare (pop. 4000) Pronounced *Nace.* A comfortable town on a rise in the Dublin-Cork road. Naas racecourse is for flat racing, while **Punchestown**, 5km/3mi south east is for steeplechasing. **Robertstown**, 8km/5mi north west of Naas, has a restored hotel beside the Grand Canal; in summer banquets are given in the style of Georgian Ireland.

Navan and Tara An Uaimh G5

Co. Meath (pop. 5000) As it curves down the hill from the marketplace to where the Blackwater meets the Boyne, Navan has the layout of an English country town and buildings direct from the Irish Midlands. There are several castles within easy reach of Navan — Liscartan, Rathaldron, Dunmoe and Dunsany — but of greater interest are the ancient Irish centres on two nearby hills. The **Hill of Tailte** (outside Donaghpatrick, 8km/5mi north west of Navan) was the ancient site of the all-Irish games, a form of Olympics founded in prehistoric times and continuing intermittently until the Norman invasion. Another such festival was held on the **Hill of Ward** (near Athboy, 20km/12mi from Navan).

The **Hill of Tara** was the 'capital' of Celtic Ireland. Every three years a *feis* (assembly) was held at which the tribes tried to settle their differences without war. At the *feis*, unlike the games held on the Hill of Tailte, there was a truce and all who came vowed to do no violence to each other. The last *feis* was in AD 554.

Tara was also the seat of the Kings of Meath, and around AD 76 King Tuathal the Lawful made himself High King; there were about 40 High Kings in the pre-Christian era, and six more after King Laoghaire allowed St Patrick to preach the faith from here. The footings of the Banqueting Hall (House of Meadcircling) of the Kings of Meath are still here on this green, wind-blown hill 8km/5mi south west of Navan. One of the kings was Niall of the Nine Hostages, but the alleged dungeon on Tara's hill where Niall kept his hostages has proved to be a Neolithic grave. The legend of Tara as remembered, in Thomas Moore's song ('The harp that once through Tara's halls the soul of music shed') is just legend, but the symbolism of Tara is powerful. Brian Boru saw its propaganda value when he made himself High King and received here the homage of the King of Meath, and Daniel O'Connell held here the greatest of his monster meetings in pursuit of Irish independence. The hill can be visited at all times.

Rush H9

Co. Dublin A pleasant little backwater by the sea (more agreeable than the adjacent and better known **Skerries**), with a patch of sand and a jetty from which you can get a boat to the bird sanctuary at Lambay Island (with prior permission from the steward).

Trim H4

Co. Meath (pop. 1700) The remains of the Norman castle, two acres of ruins along the southern bank of the Boyne, are a most impressive sight. There is a keep (28m/90ft high), and five of the original ten towers of the outer wall remain. These should prepare you for a village in which you can still see the mediaeval town. In 1399 Henry IV was imprisoned in Trim Castle by his cousin Richard II.

Wicklow N9

Co. Wicklow (pop. 4000) Lying parallel to a narrow creek, Wicklow has a small harbour. A long, narrow main road rises towards the marketplace. Holiday atmosphere, many sailing regattas. Nearby beauty spots include the **Mount Usher** Garden Demesne near Ashford, and the **Devil's Glen** (8km/5mi north) on the Vartry River.

THE SOUTH EAST

The South East is where the Norman invaders first arrived from across the channel and where their mediaeval followers settled most densely. The results of the settlement can be seen in the countryside today. Although the South East lay outside the Pale – the area which remained under royal authority – it has retained a more English appearance than the Pale, and the visitor who lands here from across the channel may wonder if he has left home. Within living memory the dialect of Wexford retained constructions and an accent that came straight from Early English, unmodified by the language of Shakespeare.

But the region holds an honourable place in the history of Irish nationalism. Kilkenny – to Irish eyes an English-looking town – was the base of the Catholic Confederation of native Irish and Old English who came together against the Protestant English, and Wexford is famous as the last fight of Wolfe Tone's rebellion. The Kennedy family originated from here, and are remembered in the John F. Kennedy Memorial Park, near New Ross.

Statistics show that the South East has more hours of sunshine per year than any other part of Ireland, and indeed in May to July the 'sunny South East' is noticeably warmer, but the region still gets its full share of rain.

The eastern part of the region is a land of broad, slow-moving rivers and rich farmland. Mainly limestone, it has been broken up into small patches of tillage – fields have high hedges so you can't see much from the road. Rivers Slaney, Nore and Barrow attract anglers and boaters. This is a very prosperous part of Ireland with new houses appearing everywhere. The Blackstairs Mountains are a ridge of bare or heather-covered hills but the higher Comeragh and Knockmealdown Mountains have been more strikingly sculpted by the ice, which left steep corries popular with rock climbers.

Further west the fields are larger, coming towards the Golden Vale (the great area of dairy-farming pasture which begins around Tipperary). The River Suir (pronounced *Shure*) flows gracefully past the Galty and Comeragh Mountains and is graced by a string of attractive old towns – Cahir, Clonmel, Carrick. The best stretch of the River Blackwater is south of the Knockmealdown Mountains. In the mountains themselves, the Vee is a noted viewing road (Clogheen to Lismore) through the Knockmealdown Gap.

The east coast, on the Irish Sea, is flat, but the south coast has several sandy seaside resorts and further west low cliffs, coves and headlands (Saltee Islands bird sanctuary). Lobster fishing at many ports enlivens the diet. Apples grown around Kilkenny and Clonmel.

Festivals End of June, Tipperary festival (Irish and modern music, dancing, exhibitions); July (earlier or later) Cashel Week of traditional Irish music, song and dance; September, Waterford light opera festival; late October, Wexford festival of opera, a major international event.

Cahir L3

Co. Tipperary (pop. 1800) A picturesque old town on the Suir. Battlemented castle in good state of preservation (or restoration), overlooking old market square. New market square at top of town.

Carlow G10

Co. Carlow (pop. 10,000) Basically one long, rather narrow street, centre of a plain of large fields growing barley which is malted in the town, and sugar beet processed in a factory just outside. Carlow Castle is what the locals will recommend you to see, but the county museum is the real delight – two rooms of assorted junk, old farm implements, an 'old' bar similar to the ones you can still see in out of the way pubs, and old newspapers. Several tumuli and dolmens in the area, the largest at Browne's Hill (3km/2mi east of Carlow).

Carrick-on-Suir M6

Co. Tipperary (pop. 5000) Encircled by hills, this was a favourite town of Anne Boleyn (Henry VIII of England's second wife). See the manor house and beside it the old keep overlooking the river. Riverside pavement used for fishing. Twisting, old streets on the hills south of the modern town. Broad main street with many eating-places, coffee shop used by young people, and good bookshop. But the town still has a simple economy – a truck stops in the street to sell its wares, and signs say, 'Sugar bought, any quantity' or 'Home-made jams bought'.

Cashel K3

Co. Tipperary (pop. 2500) Essentially one short, wide street with a cross at each end, visitors come to the town of Cashel to see the Rock which stands over 60m/200ft above the town. This rock was the seat of the early Kings of Munster. It was here that St Patrick first used the shamrock to illustrate the Trinity, and from the time Brian Boru was crowned here as King of Munster (around AD 1000, before going on to make himself High King of Ireland), Cashel was the base of a development that could have spared Ireland many of the troubles of its history if it had not been cut off by the Normans. Feudal structures in an Irish style, blending church and state, were beginning to replace the chaotic tribal organization. There is some reflection of these structures in the ruins now open to the public on the Rock of Cashel. Cormac's Chapel, built around 1130, is a blend of European and Irish buildings. This is incorporated in the Cathedral (13th-century), now ruined, which replaced an earlier cathedral founded at the time the Normans landed. The building that looks like a castle is the Choristers' Hall. The Rock is open 1000 to 2030 in summer, 1000 to 1930 in winter.

Castlecomer H8

Co. Kilkenny (pop. 2000) Former centre of a small coalfield; pleasantly laid out with a tree-lined avenue and broad streets creating a sense of space. Wooded valleys to the immediate north; further north, the uplands between Carlow and Castlecomer are part field, part bog , with an anthracite mine at **Rossmore** where a handful of miners still work.

Dunmore Cave immediately south of Castlecomer on the road to Kilkenny is well-lit; the bones of some of the hundreds of people who sought refuge from the Danes were found here.

Clonmel M4

Co. Tipperary (pop. 12,000) A strong sense of civic past in this town on the River Suir, entered from the east through its ancient gate. Unusually well gardened. Centre of Ireland's greyhound racing. Forest park nearby on road towards **Clogheen** (climbing); further south the valley of the River Nire is an especially pretty route.

Dungarvan P5

Co. Waterford (pop. 6000) Administrative centre of County Waterford, market town for its region; some industry (leather), yet the impression you are left with of Dungarvan is a fishing village based on the stone harbour, south of Dungarvan town. Helvick Head is a promontory to the south, beyond the Irish-speaking fishing villages of **Ringville** and **Ballynagaul**.

Enniscorthy K12

Co. Wexford (pop. 7000) Runs sharply

Cashel

down to the Slaney River; attractive little market square at the top of the town, dairy co-operative and lumber yard by the river. The Norman castle is now a museum (open 1000 to 2000 in summer). View to Vinegar Hill, with a memorial to the last stand of the rising of 1798. Good base for climbing in the **Blackstairs Mountains**.

Kilkenny · I8

Co. Kilkenny (pop. 14,000) A long main street running up and down a low hill; interesting little back streets. You can sense the town's long history in the old buildings – notably the Tholsel (old town hall – 1761) and the House of Bishop Rothe (1594) – but also its modern vigour.

Kilkenny Castle (18th-century), looking as though it had never seen a day's fighting, is by the river – gardens, parkland, children's playground. Directly opposite the gates of the castle are Kilkenny College and the Design Workshops (open every day). Several interesting 13th-century churches to visit, and Smithwick's Brewery.

During Kilkenny Arts Week in August there are many exhibitions, concerts and fringe events. The Kilkenny Hunt meets regularly at **Thomastown**.

Make an outing to the ruins of **Jerpoint Abbey**, 19km/12mi south of Kilkenny. This is probably the finest monastic (Cistercian) ruin in Ireland.

Inistioge on the road between Kilkenny and New Ross is a strikingly attractive village on a bend in the river – trees in the square and woods surrounding.

New Ross L10

Co. Wexford (pop. 5000) Mediaeval town, with narrow streets winding up and down the hills, some passable only on foot. The main road leads down to a long bridge over the River Barrow. A farmhouse in Dunganstown (8km/5mi south) was once the home of the Kennedy family, and is now overlooked by the **John F. Kennedy Memorial Park** (open 1000 to 2000), with arboretum and exhibition centre.

Rosslare Harbour N14

Co. Wexford Where the boats arrive from Fishguard and from Le Havre. (Plenty of Bed and Breakfast in surrounding countryside.) **Rosslare** town is some miles from Rosslare Harbour; described as a 'well-known seaside resort', it has a bare curving beach of shingle alternating with sand, and looks depressed and depressing. Beyond Rosslare, the extreme south-east tip of Ireland is **Carnsore Point**, proposed site for Ireland's first nuclear power station which may be ready when the peat runs out.

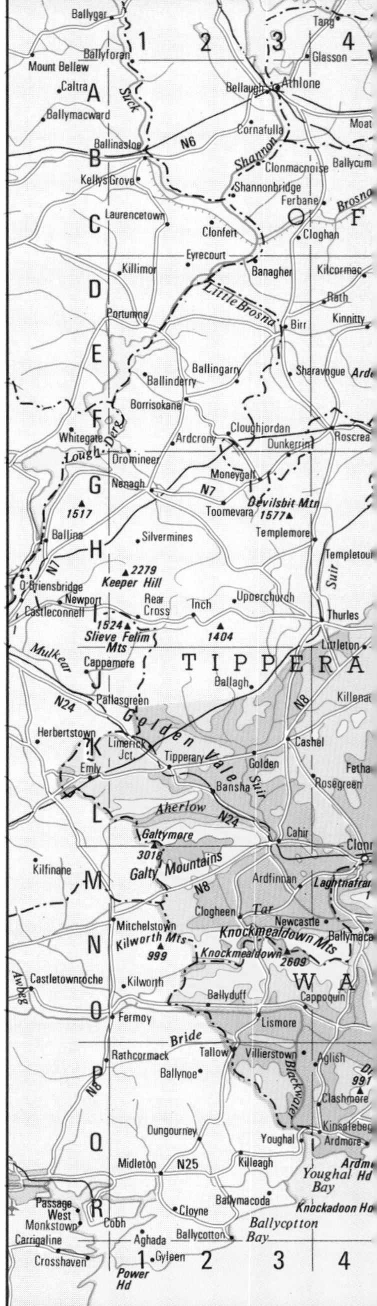

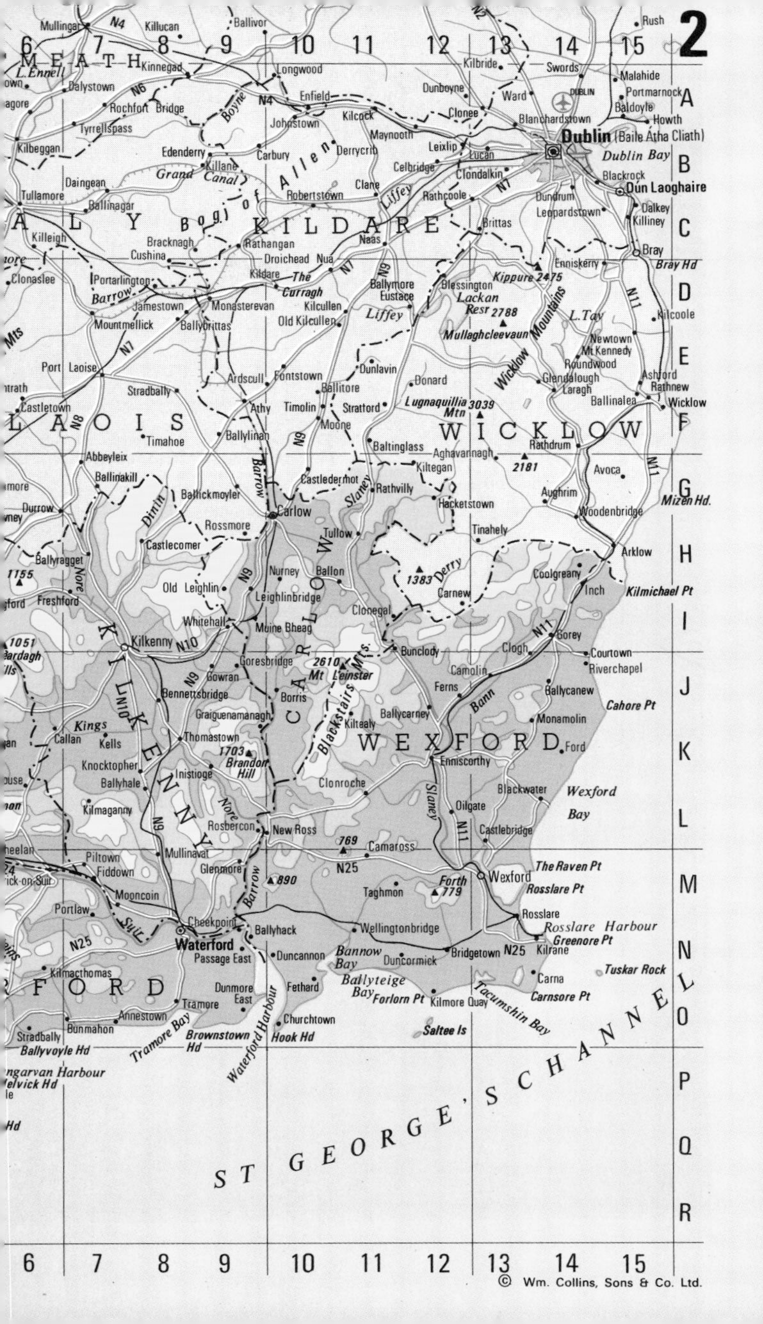
2
6
7
8
9
10
11
12
13
14
15
A
B
C
D
E
F
G
H
I
J
K
L
M
N
O
P
Q
R
MEATH
KILDARE
LAOIS
WICKLOW
KILKENNY
CARLOW
WEXFORD
FORD
ST GEORGE'S CHANNEL
Mullingar
Killucan
Ballivor
Rush
L. Ennell
Kinnegad
Longwood
Kilbride
Swords
Malahide
Dalystown
Dunboyne
Portmarnock
Enfield
Ward
Baldoyle
Rochfort Bridge
Boyne
Johnstown
Kilcock
Clonee
Howth
Tyrrellspass
Maynooth
Blanchardstown
Dublin (Baile Átha Cliath)
Kilbeggan
Edenderry
Carbury
Derrycrib
Leixlip
Lucan
Dublin Bay
Killane
Grand Canal
Bog of Allen
Celbridge
Clondalkin
Blackrock
Daingean
Clane
Dún Laoghaire
Tullamore
Robertstown
Liffey
Rathcoole
Dundrum
Ballinagar
Leopardstown
Dalkey
Killiney
Brittas
Killeigh
Naas
Bracknagh
Rathangan
Bray
Cushina
Droichead Nua
Enniskerry
Bray Hd
Clonaslee
Kildare
The Curragh
Kippure 2475
Portarlington
Ballymore Eustace
Blessington
Barrow
Lackan Resr 2788
Jamestown
Monasterevan
Kilcullen
Old Kilcullen
L. Tay
Kilcoole
Mountmellick
Ballybrittas
Mullaghcleevaun
Mountains
Newtown Mt Kennedy
Roundwood
Port Laoise
Dunlavin
Wicklow
Glendalough
Ashford
Donard
Laragh
Rathnew
Stradbally
Ardscull
Fontstown
Ballitore
Ballinalea
Wicklow
Castletown
Athy
Timolin
Stratford
Lugnaquillia Mtn 3039
Moone
Timahoe
Ballylinan
Rathdrum
Baltinglass
Aghavannagh
Abbeyleix
Kiltegan
2181
Avoca
Ballinakill
Castledermot
Rathvilly
Aughrim
Mizen Hd.
Ballickmoyler
Slaney
Hacketstown
Woodenbridge
Durrow
Carlow
Rossmore
Tinahely
Dinin
Tullow
Castlecomer
Arklow
Ballyragget
Nore
Nurney
Ballon
1383
Derry
Coolgreany
1155
Old Leighlin
Inch
Freshford
Leighlinbridge
Carnew
Kilmichael Pt
Clonegal
Whitehall
Muine Bheag
Gorey
Kilkenny
N10
1051
Bunclody
Clogh
Courtown
Goresbridge
2610 Mt Leinster
Camolin
Riverchapel
Gowran
Bennettsbridge
Borris
Ferns
Ballycanew
Bann
Cahore Pt
Blackstairs Mts.
Graiguenamanagh
Kiltealy
Ballycarney
Monamolin
Kings
Callan
Thomastown
Kells
1703
Brandon Hill
Ford
Knocktopher
Enniscorthy
Inistioge
Ballyhale
Clonroche
Blackwater
Wexford Bay
Kilmaganny
Oilgate
Rosbercon
New Ross
Castlebridge
769
Camaross
Mullinavat
Piltown
Glenmore
N25
The Raven Pt
Fiddown
890
Wexford
Carrick-on-Suir
Forth 779
Taghmon
Rosslare Pt
Mooncoin
Portlaw
Rosslare
Cheekpoint
Suir
Ballyhack
Wellingtonbridge
Rosslare Harbour
Greenore Pt
Waterford
Bridgetown
Kilrane
Passage East
Duncannon
Bannow Bay
Duncormick
Kilmacthomas
Carna
Tuskar Rock
Ballyteige Bay
Dunmore East
Fethard
Forlorn Pt
Kilmore Quay
Carnsore Pt
Tramore
Tacumshin Bay
Annestown
Churchtown
Bunmahon
Tramore Bay
Waterford Harbour
Saltee Is
Stradbally
Brownstown Hd
Hook Hd
Ballyvoyle Hd
N4
N6
N7
N9
N11

A glass cutter at work in the Waterford Crystal factory

1798 Memorial in Market Sq., Enniscorthy

Waterford fruit bowl

Cahir Castle

Tipperary K2

Co. Tipperary (pop. 5000) Market town of the Golden Vale, Tipperary is surrounded by co-operative creameries. Very lively. Excursion point into the rather over-rated **Glen of Aherlow**. The song *It's a long way to Tipperary* was written in 1914 by an Englishman, Jack Judge, who had never been here.

Tramore O8

Co. Waterford (pop. 4000) A seaside resort; good sand, beach cleaned and guarded, calm sea generally (no breakers), amusement arcades, fish and chips. Bed and Breakfast on approach to the town, and plenty of boarding houses. Nearly all the holiday-makers are Irish, and then there are the locals. Tramore is ideal for a simple, undemanding, relaxed holiday. The young may complain that it is behind the times, but it will remain so partly because there is not the pressure of population to change it.

The coast road west from Tramore is a succession of open cliff tops and small coves. Inland there is a riot of wild growth

Waterford N8

Co. Waterford (pop. 35,000) On the slopes above the River Suir; a fairly busy town, part harbour, part industrial centre. Quiet in the evenings. The single bridge over the Suir may be something of a traffic block; from the bridge runs the South Quay to Reginald's Tower, a massive circular stone fortress built as part of the Danish defences in AD 1003 and now a municipal exhibition centre. The Theatre Royal is used for professional and amateur productions, and in September there is the Waterford International Festival of Light Opera (two weeks).

The Waterford Glass Factory is two miles south (3km), on the Cork road. (Closed last week in July, first two weeks in August.) Tours should be booked in advance with the Tourist Office on Waterford Quay.

Wexford M13

Co. Wexford (pop. 15,000) A considerable industrial town but visitors to the festivals see none of this; instead, the quays along the winding harbour front remind you that this was once a major port, while the main street behind the quay, which dates back to before the 17th century, is so narrow you can almost reach across from one pub to take a glass from the pub opposite. The Bull Ring was the scene of bull-baiting in Norman times; the statue of a pikeman here recalls that Wexford was held for a week by pike-armed insurgents against the English in 1798. Current pastimes are more peaceful – light opera at the Wexford Festival at the end of October; theatre plus dinner during the summer season; classical and Irish music; occasional mumming with Father Murphy and his pikemen in place of the traditional English characters; bird-watching from observation points on the Wildfowl Reserve (Greenland Geese) on the mud flats facing Wexford harbour.

Wexford harbour

THE SOUTH WEST

Foreigners adopt the soft accent of Cork when trying to put on an Irish brogue, and the Kerryman is the butt of hundreds of jokes circulating in Ireland, as popular (and unjustified) as the Irish jokes so common in Britain. Why the South West should be singled out in this way is hard to understand, for it is the softest part of Ireland – in climate and landscape, if not in history.

The weather is warm thanks to the celebrated Gulf Stream. However it does not, as you may be told, make the sea so warm you can swim at Christmas – indeed, you need to be hardy to stay in the sea even in summer – but it does prevent frost, so that sub-tropical plants can flower in favoured spots and overall there is a richer vegetation.

Geology is a contributory factor in the profusion of plant life in the area. It is a region of sandstone ridges with limestone in between, a deeply indented coast and great mountains. The South West is part of a great tract of sandstone formed early in the earth's history, represented by the Pembroke Peninsula in Wales, the Cornish Peninsula in England, and the Brittany Peninsula in France. Similarities can be seen in the 'bones' of these regions, though recent history has made them very different.

Because of its position, the South West has looked across the sea to the rest of the continent, and not across the narrow channel to Britain like the east, or into itself like the north. The earliest invaders, the Tuatha De Danann, and after them the Milesians (probably successive waves of Celts from France or Spain), landed here and their queen (daughter of the Pharaoh of Egypt) is buried here. To the Romans the people of the South West were known as Ivernii, and have given their name to the whole island as Hibernia. The King of the World (all but Ireland) landed at Ventry, where he was defeated by the legendary Finn MacCool. The mediaeval lords of the region, the Desmonds, led rebellions against the English monarchy and started the tradition that has survived in the name Rebel Cork; an attempt to colonize the area with English settlers under Sir Walter Raleigh was a total failure (16th century), and it was to the South West – to Kinsale,

Allihies, Beara Peninsula

Bantry House

Bantry, and Bantry again – that aid for Irish rebellion came from France and Spain. In the Anglo-Irish war of 1920, Rebel Cork was again the leader of the fight, and it is here that you will still be told tales of the battles and burnings in the true tradition of Irish storytellers.

Scenically the four peninsulas stretching south west into the sea are most impressive. The Dingle Peninsula, though small, is famed for its fishing and total lack of development, and is the most strongly Irish-speaking part of the South West. Around the Iveragh Peninsula runs the Ring of Kerry, a 100-mile-long scenic road (160km) beginning and ending at Killarney. Its name is almost synonymous with the lush beauty of lakes and mountains, and gentle ferns. The Beara Peninsula, which extends from the Gouganebarra Forest Park, is centred on Glengarriff, home of Mediterranean warmth. The Bantry Peninsula is the least spectacular of the four; gentler country merging into the south coast. Inland, the Blackwater River wanders through a fertile limestone country of fields and cows, becoming more barren towards the south west as the mountains begin to pile up.

Local produce includes pottery (Youghal), woollens (Dripsey), knitwear (Ross Carbery), lobsters (all round the coast, but mostly sold abroad).

Festivals The whole region is very strong in Irish 'traditional' entertainment, details from local tourist offices; the 'set' dancing of North Kerry is danced unselfconsciously; May, Cork Choral Festival; May, Killarney Pan-Celtic Week; June, Cork Film Festival; early August, Puck Fair at Killorglin; September, Rose of Tralee Festival.

Ballybunion F8

Co. Kerry (pop. 1300) A family resort, centre for outings, one of the world's best golf links. At the north end of the flat beach (3km/2mi long) start the cliffs which stretch along the coast almost to the Shannon – many caves, 5km/3mi walk to Leck Castle. Amusement 'casinos', seaside entertainment, Bed and Breakfast in glass-porched houses facing the sea. Ruined Ballybunion Castle. **Knockanore Hill**, 5km/3mi east, offers splendid views to Galway Bay and the mountains of Tralee and Killarney. Immediate countryside is flat, even marshy.

Bantry O9

Co. Cork (pop. 3000) A quiet little town with a large market square; sheltered by the hill overlooking Bantry Bay. Here came the French in 1689 to aid James II, and then in 1796 to try to support Wolfe Tone's rebellion. The bay now receives oil tankers heading for the terminal on Whiddy Island. Bantry House and grounds open 1000 to 1800, summer to 2000. **Sheep's Head Peninsula** west of Bantry has scenic coastal drives.

Blarney L15

Co. Cork (pop. 1100) Five miles north of Cork (8km), with a triangular green enclosed on two sides by shops and hotels for visitors, and Blarney Castle on the third side. Legend has it that here in the castle

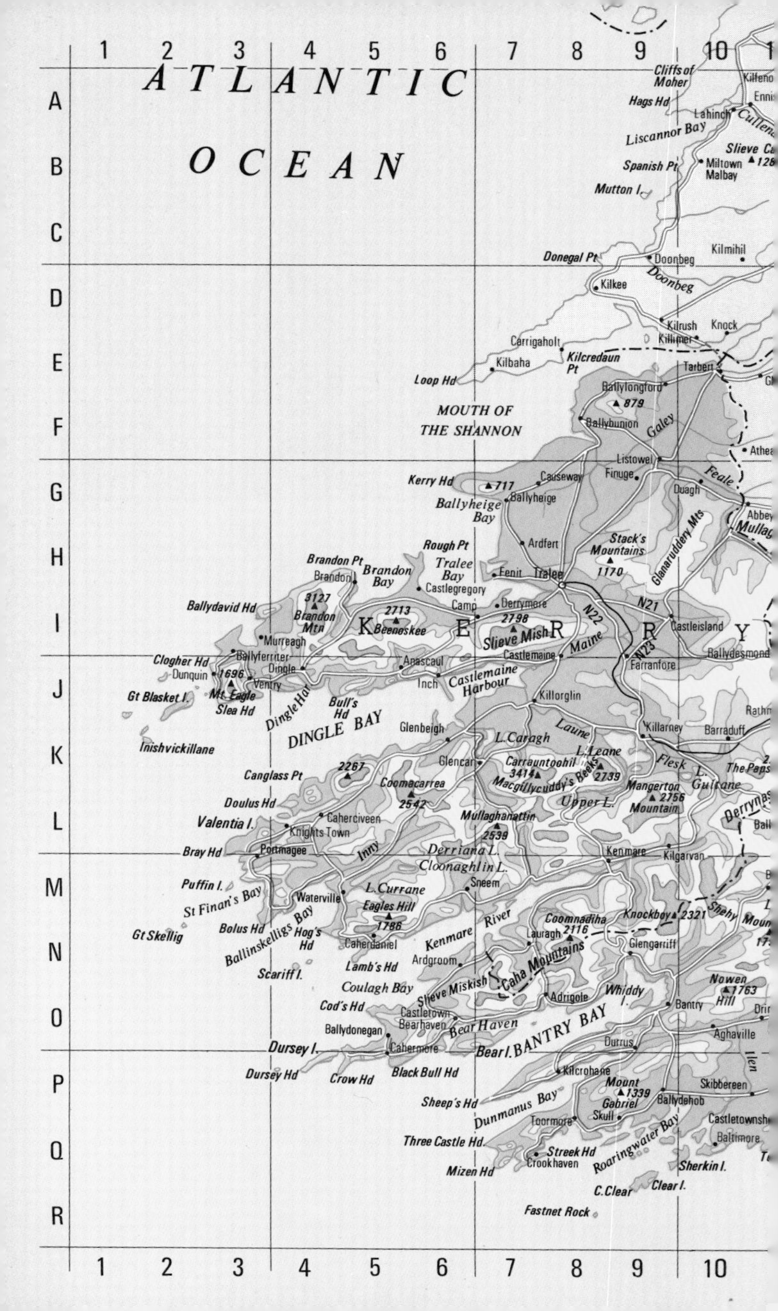

1 2 3 4 5 6 7 8 9 10
A B C D E F G H I J K L M N O P Q R
ATLANTIC
OCEAN
Cliffs of Moher
Hags Hd
Lahinch
Liscannor Bay
Spanish Pt
Miltown Malbay
Mutton I.
Kilmihil
Donegal Pt
Doonbeg
Doonbeg
Kilkee
Kilrush
Knock
Killimer
Carrigaholt
Kilbaha
Kilcredaun Pt
Tarbert
Loop Hd
Ballylongford
879
MOUTH OF THE SHANNON
Ballybunion
Galey
Listowel
Finuge
Feale
Kerry Hd
717
Causeway
Ballyheige
Ballyheige Bay
Duagh
Glanaruddery Mts
Ardfert
Stack's Mountains
1170
Rough Pt
Tralee Bay
Fenit
Tralee
Brandon Pt
Brandon Bay
Brandon
Castlegregory
3127
Brandon Mtn
2713
Beenoskee
Camp
Derrymore
2798
Slieve Mish
N22
N21
N23
Castleisland
Ballydavid Hd
K E R R Y
Murreagh
Maine
Clogher Hd
Ballyferriter
Dingle
Anascaul
Castlemaine
Ballydesmond
Dunquin
1696
Ventry
Inch
Castlemaine Harbour
Farranfore
Gt Blasket I.
Mt Eagle
Slea Hd
Dingle Har
Bull's Hd
Killorglin
DINGLE BAY
Glenbeigh
Laune
Killarney
Barraduff
Inishvickillane
L.Caragh
L.Leane
Glencar
Carrauntoohil 3414
2739
Flesk
The Paps
Canglass Pt
2267
Coomacarrea
Macgillycuddy's Reeks
Mangerton Mountain
2756
L. Guitane
Doulus Hd
2542
Upper L.
Mullaghanattin
Valentia I.
Cahersiveen
Knights Town
2539
Bray Hd
Portmagee
Inny
Derriana L.
Cloonaghlin L.
Kenmare
Kilgarvan
Puffin I.
L.Currane
Sneem
St Finan's Bay
Waterville
Eagles Hill
1786
Knockboy
2321
Shehy
Coomnadiha
2116
Gt Skellig
Bolus Hd
Ballinskelligs Bay
Hog's Hd
Caherdaniel
Kenmare River
Lauragh
Glengarriff
Caha Mountains
Ardgroom
Scariff I.
Lamb's Hd
Coulagh Bay
Slieve Miskish
Nowen Hill
1763
Whiddy I.
Adrigole
Cod's Hd
Castletown Bearhaven
Bear Haven
Bantry
BANTRY BAY
Ballydonegan
Aghaville
Dursey I.
Bear I.
Durrus
Cahermore
Ilen
Dursey Hd
Crow Hd
Black Bull Hd
Kilcrohane
Mount Gabriel
1339
Skibbereen
Sheep's Hd
Ballydehob
Dunmanus Bay
Skull
Toormore
Castletownshend
Baltimore
Three Castle Hd.
Streek Hd
Crookhaven
Roaringwater Bay
Mizen Hd
Sherkin I.
C.Clear
Clear I.
Fastnet Rock
1 2 3 4 5 6 7 8 9 10

3
13
14
15
16
17
18
19
20
21
22
A
B
C
D
E
F
G
H
I
J
K
L
M
N
O
P
Q
R
L. Cutra
1314
Knockannis
L. Graney
1243
Sharavogue
Arderin
1734
Borrisokane
Borris-in-Ossory
N8
Crusheen
Feakle
Whitegate
Lough Derg
Cloughjordan
Roscrea
N7
Inchicronan L.
Scarriff
Ardcrony
Dunkerrin
Dromineer
N18
CLARE
Tuamgreney
Moneygall
Donaghmore
Tulla
Nenagh
Quin
Arra Mts
1517
N7
Toomevara
Devilsbit Mtn
1577
Rathdowney
1748
Glennagalliagh
Slieve Bernagh
Templemore
Clarecastle
Ballina
Silvermines
Killaloe
Silvermines Mts
Templetouhy
Newmarket-on-Fergus
2279
Keeper Hill
Johnstown
1155
Fergus
Sixmilebridge
Suir
Shannon
Hurlers Cross
O'Briensbridge
Urlingford
N19
Bunratty
Ardnacrush
Newport
Rear Cross
Inch
Upperchurch
N18
Castleconnell
Thurles
Shannon
Shannon Airport
1524
Slieve Felim Mts
1404
Limerick
Pallaskenry
Mungret
Mulkear
Littleton
1051
Slieveardagh Hills
Kildimo
N20
Cappamore
TIPPERARY
Caherconlish
Ballingarry
Askeaton
Patrickswell
Ballagh
Killenaule
Pallasgreen
N24
Deel
Maigue
N21
Golden Vale
Adare
Croom
L. Gur
Herbertstown
Limerick Jct.
Cashel
Drangan
Rathkeale
LIMERICK
Bruff
Hospital
Emly
Tipperary
Golden
Fethard
Ninemilehouse
Ballingarry
N20
Bansha
Suir
Rosegreen
Newcastle West
Bruree
Aherlow
N24
Slievenamon
2368
Rockhill
Mahoonagh
Galtymore
Cahir
Kilmallock
3018
Clonmel
Kilsheelan
Rath Luirc
Galty Mountains
Suir
N24
Carrick-on-Suir
Kilfinane
Comeragh Mountains
Milford
Newtown
N8
Ardfinnan
Laghtnafrankee
1703
1710
Ballyhoura Mts
Clogheen
Tar
Nire
Freemount
Mitchelstown
Newcastle
Knockmealdown Mts
Kilworth Mts
Ballymacarbry
Buttevant
Kildorrery
999
Knockmealdown
2609
Monavullagh Mts
2597
Doneraile
WATERFORD
Awbeg
Castletownroche
Kilworth
Kanturk
N20
Ballyduff
Cappoquin
Mallow
Fermoy
Lismore
Banteer
Blackwater
1406
Knocknaskagh
Bride
Nagles Mountains
Tallow
Villierstown
Dungarvan
Rathcormack
Aglish
Blackwater
Drum Hills
Boggeragh Mountains
Ballynoe
991
Ringville
Musheramore
N20
Watergrasshill
N8
Clashmore
N25
Mine Hd
Kinsalebeg
CORK
Dungourney
Youghal
Ardmore
Ardmore Bay
Sallybrook
Ardmore Hd
Blarney
Midleton
N25
Killeagh
Youghal Bay
Macroom
Dripsey
Coachford
Cork
Lee
Ballincollig
Knockadoon Hd
N22
Passage West
Great I.
Ballymacoda
Cloyne
Ballycotton Bay
Crookstown
682
Monkstown
Cobh
Aghada
Ballycotton
Ballinhassig
Carrigaline
Crosshaven
Gyleen
Cork Harbour
Power Hd
Inishannon
Enniskean
Bandon
Bandon
Kinsale
Summer Cove
Ballinascarty
Frower Pt
Old Head
Kinsale Harbour
Timoleague
Clonakilty
Courtmacsherry
Old Head of Kinsale
Courtmacsherry Bay
Seven Heads
Clonakilty Bay
Galley Hd

Blarney Castle

visitors gain the power of eloquent speech from the rush of blood to the head as they hang upside down to kiss the Blarney Stone in its perilous position beneath the battlements. (Open 0900 to sundown, June/July to 2030; Sundays 0930 to 1730.) The origin of 'Blarney', meaning fair words to deceive without offending, lies in the 16th century when Queen Elizabeth's deputy pressed the Lord of Blarney Castle to hold his lands not as a chief, but as though they were a grant from the queen. The loquacious lord strung the deputy along for years with soft answers. The legend of the Blarney Stone is itself Blarney, created about a century ago.

Caherciveen L4

Co. Kerry (pop. 1500) The largest town on the Ring of Kerry, the scenic circuit of the Iveragh Peninsula, with some spectacular stages on the road to **Glenbeigh** (walk the Glenbeigh Horseshoe) and to **Glencar**. Two miles north west (3km) of Caherciveen is Leacanabuaile stone fort (ninth-century, pre-Christian site). From nearby Kingstown there is a ferry to **Valentia Island** (also reached by road bridge from Portmagee) with its cliffs, tropical vegetation and seascapes. Boats from Valentia Island to the **Skelligs** – jagged rocks nine miles (14km) out to sea. Skellig Michael (the Great Rock) rises massively to over 200m/700ft; stone steps lead up to a deserted monastery with a lighthouse below.

Cobh M17

Co. Cork (pop. 6000) A modern town, formerly an important port of call for transatlantic steamships, now an occasional port of call for liners. The last view of Ireland for many departing emigrants. A German freighter with arms for the Easter Rising was scuttled here in 1916. Irish Steel smelter at Haulbowline Island.

Cork L16

Co. Cork (pop. 150,000) A commercial and industrial city (the third largest in Ireland), centred on an island between two channels of the River Lee. The docks and car ferry terminal begin about 4km/2½mi downstream, with the smell of mills, shipbuilding, brewing and tanning. Smelling more strongly of money, the commercial area around the South Mall and the entertainment and shopping districts of MacCurtain and St Patrick's Streets.

It's a city of broad thoroughfares and narrow alleys, and very steep hills (some of them with steps). 'God's own city and the devil's own people' is one accusation hurled at Corkonians – unjustly, for though they've a strong-minded sense of independence, they're proudly friendly.

During the war of independence, one Lord Mayor was assassinated, allegedly by British auxiliaries, the next starved himself to death in protest, and much of the centre was burnt down, undoubtedly by British troops. There's not too much of interest left: Shandon Church (St Anne's) with its famous bells dominates the north side of the city; St Mary's Catholic Cathedral has a presbytery with records going back to 1748 for ancestor hunters; St Finbarr's C. of I. Cathedral is built on the site of the original church founded by Cork's patron saint, and is near the Marsh (Washington Street), the oldest part of the city.

The statue to Father Matthew, founder of the Irish temperance movement, stands at the bridge end of St Patrick's Street; called simply 'The Statue', it is the principal reference point for finding your way in Cork.

Irish plays and revues in summer at the Opera House, and modern and classical plays at the Everyman Playhouse. Open-air market at the Coal Quay (Cornmarket Street). University College Cork is set in pleasant grounds by the south channel of the Lee, just beyond St Finbarr's; noted collection of Irish music and dance.

Dingle J4

Co. Kerry (pop. 1500) The **Dingle Peninsula** is the most northerly of the four peninsulas of south-west Ireland, and a scenic and holiday alternative to over-touristed Killarney. Much smaller than the Iveragh Peninsula, it retains a more strongly traditional character. The north-west coastal plain remains Irish-speaking, with secluded hamlets and picturesque groupings of people in the rain.

Dingle village is the largest on the peninsula, a blend of fishing port and holiday base. A good harbour, pubs, a few streets twisting up the hills. **Ventry Bay**, 6km/4mi west of Dingle, is a splendid yachting harbour and leads to the rugged rocks of Slea Head, overlooked by Mount Eagle. Dunquin, on the far side of Mount Eagle is the starting point for a trip by boat or currach to the **Blasket Islands**; uninhabited since 1953, these were the home of a great tradition of story-telling which has been preserved in books such as *The Islander* and *Twenty Years A-Growing*.

A splendid outing from Dingle is to drive over the **O'Connor Pass** (Dingle/Camp road); an almost soft outlook south of the summit but forlorn and romantically sad on the north side, looking across an empty lake-strewn valley to the heights of Brandon Mountain. West of the pass, a succession of sleepy hamlets lead to windy **Brandon Point** and then you can walk over the grass-covered cliffs to the top of Brandon Head. Eastwards towards Tralee is a flat plain sprouting modern bungalows, backed by the bare Slieve Mish.

The south coast road east from Dingle overlooks the sea from low cliffs (Red Cliffs), with a quiet pub and slipway at **Inch** beach and peninsula.

Every fisherman will be delighted with Dingle's coast. For others, the region is rich in antiquities. **Gallarus Oratory**, an early Christian church in the shape of an upturned boat, is of unmortared stone but still watertight (6km/4mi north west of Dingle, off road to Ballyferriter). The **Fahans**, on the southern slopes of Mt Eagle are a group of over 400 beehive huts, again unmortared, together with standing stones, sculptured crosses and ring forts. **Dunbeg Fort**, a stone wall defending a seaward promontory, is worth visiting. Twelfth-century Hiberno-Romanesque church at Kilmalkedar (north of Ballyferriter) – ogham stone.

St Finbarr's Cathedral overlooking the River Lee, Cork

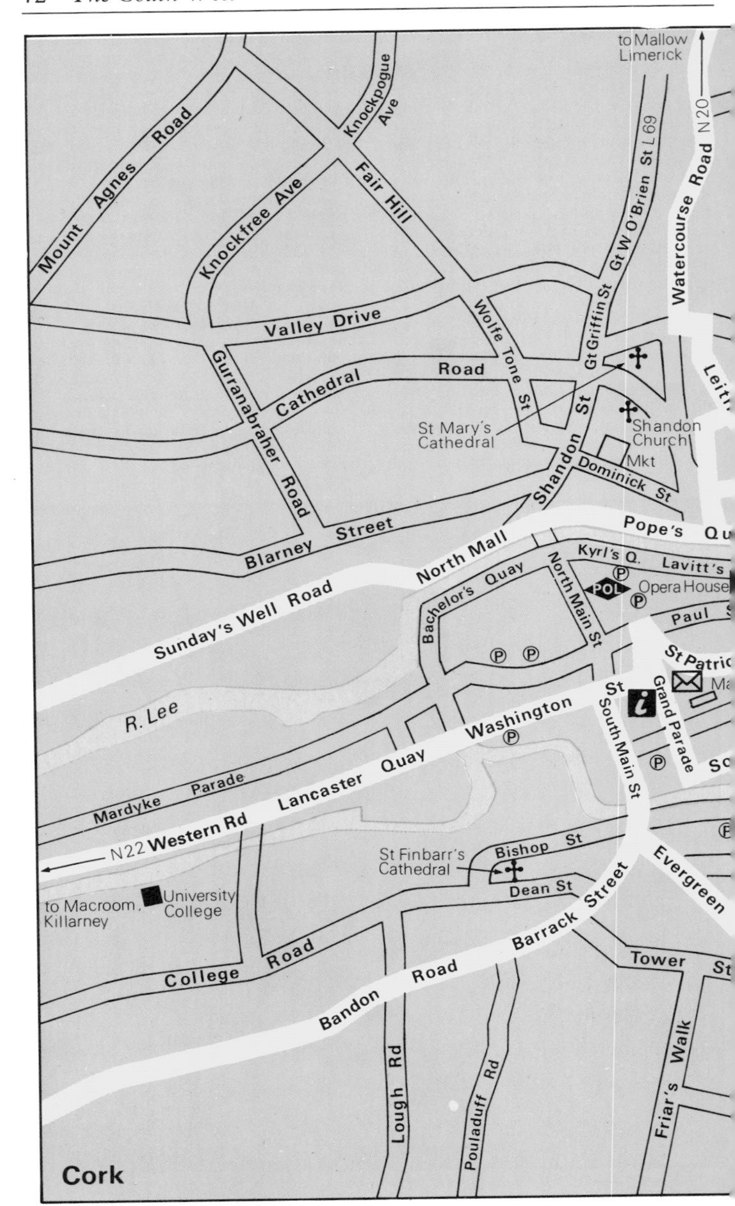
to Mallow
Limerick
N20
Watercourse Road
Gt W O'Brien St L69
Mount Agnes Road
Knockpogue Ave
Fair Hill
Knockfree Ave
Valley Drive
Wolfe Tone St
Gt Griffin St
Gurranabraher Road
Cathedral Road
St Mary's Cathedral
Shandon Church
Mkt
Shandon St
Dominick St
Blarney Street
North Mall
Pope's Qu
Sunday's Well Road
Kyrl's Q.
Lavitt's
Bachelor's Quay
North Main St
POL
Opera House
Paul
St Patric
R. Lee
Washington St
Grand Parade
South Main St
Mardyke Parade
Lancaster Quay
N22 Western Rd
St Finbarr's Cathedral
Bishop St
Dean St
Evergreen
to Macroom, Killarney
University College
Barrack Street
Tower St
College Road
Bandon Road
Lough Rd
Pouladuff Rd
Friar's Walk
Cork

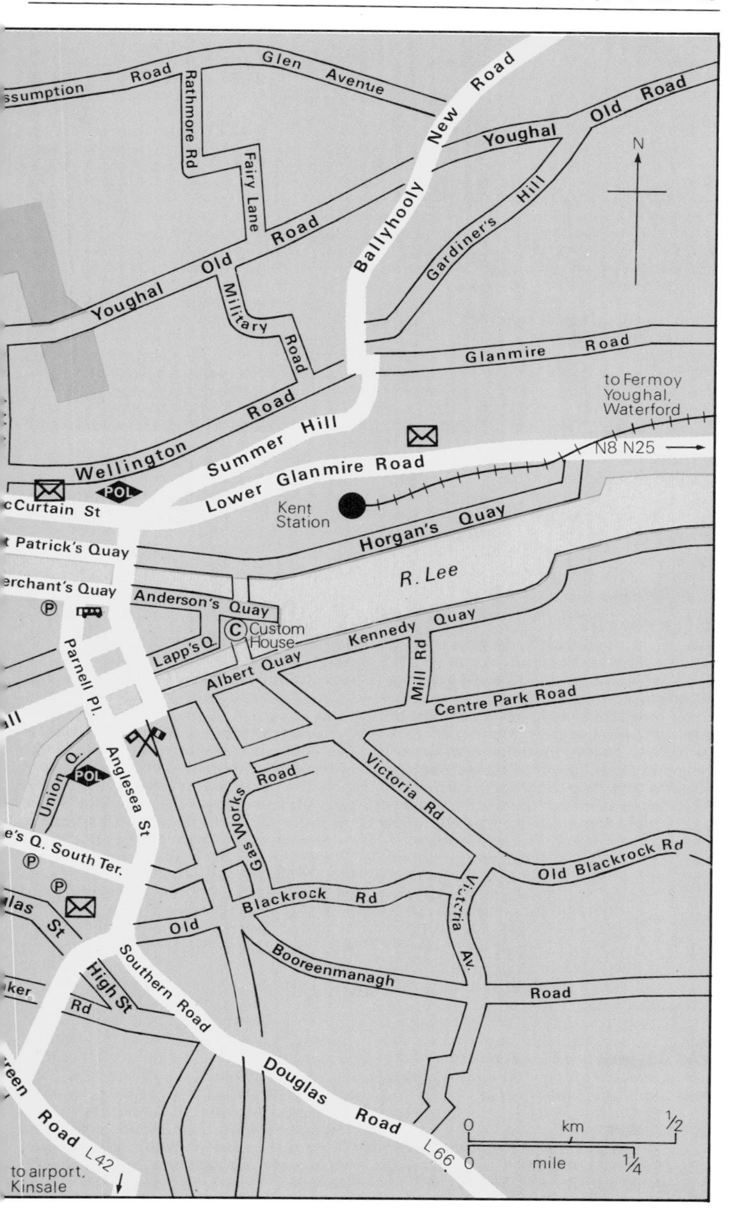
ssumption Road
Glen Avenue
Rathmore Rd
Fairy Lane
Ballyhooly New Road
Youghal Old Road
Gardiner's Hill
N
Youghal Old Road
Military Road
Glanmire Road
to Fermoy Youghal, Waterford
Wellington Road
Summer Hill
Lower Glanmire Road
N8 N25
POL
cCurtain St
Kent Station
Horgan's Quay
t Patrick's Quay
R. Lee
erchant's Quay
Anderson's Quay
Custom House
Kennedy Quay
Lapp's Q.
Albert Quay
Mill Rd
Parnell Pl.
Centre Park Road
Victoria Rd
Union Q.
POL
Anglesea St
Gas Works Road
e's Q. South Ter.
Old Blackrock Rd
las St
Old Blackrock Rd
Victoria Av.
Booreenmanagh Road
ker Rd
High St
Southern Road
een Road L42
Douglas Road
L66
0 km 1/2
0 mile 1/4
to airport, Kinsale

River Blackwater, Fermoy

Fermoy J17

Co. Cork (pop. 3400) The rapids in the River Blackwater, overlooked by Georgian houses, may make you pause in Fermoy and discover its delightful tree-shaded walks. Salmon- and trout-fishing centre.

Glengarriff N9

Co. Cork (pop. 250) A small village squashed between mountain and sea, but the chief holiday resort of the **Beara Peninsula.** About 30 miles long (48km), and at its broadest 10 miles wide (16km), the peninsula is a ridge of mountain, the Miskish and Caha Mountains – wild, with boulders and rocky outcrops; cut by streams and sheep pastures; surrounded by a narrow coastal strip which provides a celebrated scenic drive. **Healy Pass** crosses the mountains from Adrigole. On the southern shore of the peninsula (notably mild and scattered with fuchsia) is a corniche road, and the warmest point on it is Glengarriff. This village is a scattering of south-facing hotels on the rise overlooking Bantry Bay, centred on a rocky, wooded glen. Boat every ten minutes to Garinish Island, for subtropical plants in Italian gardens.

The western end of the peninsula is noted for sea angling – nightly fish auction at **Castletown Bearhaven** which is also a centre for forest walking and mountain climbing (Hungry Hill).

Kenmare L9

Co. Kerry (pop. 1000) A simple little town on the tourist's Ring of Kerry; just large enough to lead its own life. Local point lace and homespun woollens on display in the convent. Visit Sheen Falls 3km/2mi south. North of Kenmare, Windy Gap is a steep climb over the lakes and mountains, and then a descent to the green warmth of Killarney.

Killarney K9

Co. Kerry (pop. 7500) The Killarney region is rightly the most famous area of Ireland for scenic beauty, based as it is on three island-studded lakes set in mountains, surrounded by glens and wooded shores.

Killarney town has industry (engineering – container cranes, hosiery), but looks essentially a tourist town. It can be so crowded in summer that you will find it difficult to walk past the cafes and souvenir shops. The crowds become part of the town's charm – lively all the time; your fellow visitors are anxious to be friendly and spend their money while the locals are anxious to be friendly and help them spend it. Many pubs and varied nightlife.

Salmon and trout fishing are free in the Killarney lakes, trout fishing is free in some of the rivers; there are two 18-hole golf courses in the region and a racecourse; canoeing on the lakes.

The Killarney region is suitable for touring by car, with the odd expedition on foot, or by bicycle; or wholly on foot with the occasional help from a bus or lift-giver; or by pony rented in the town. You can rent a jaunting car (horse drawn, two rows of outward facing seats) conducted by a guide or jarvey, who will advise you where to go and regale you with stories on the way.

Below, a selection of the many sights:

Aghadoe Hill, overlooking the north side of the lower lake about 3km/2mi off the Killarney/Tralee road, provides a splendid panorama of the Killarney lakes although only 130m/400ft high. The 'cathedral' is a ruined church.

Black Valley (Cummeenduff Glen) A river valley opening into the mountains below Carrauntoohil; can be seen or walked to from the south end of the Gap of Dunloe.

Bourn Vincent Memorial Park (The Killarney National Park) Covers most of the Killarney lake district (4450 hectares/11,000 acres) and is full of walks and scenic drives. It was given to the Irish nation in 1932 by the Bourn and Vincent families.

Carrauntoohil, the highest peak in Ireland (1041m/3414ft). Can be walked – the easiest approach is probably from Gortbue School.

Devil's Punch Bowl A deep pool in the Mangerton Mountains, from which the water flows underground to feed the Torc Waterfall.

Gap of Dunloe A 7-mile-long track (11km) winding between Tomies Mountain and Macgillycuddy's Reeks; splendid mountain views. It is usual to traverse the gap from north to south. During the season cars must be left at Kate Kearney's Cottage, and then you continue on foot, by pony or in a jaunting car to finally take a boat from the head of the upper lake back to Killarney. Out of season (and at night) you can drive through the gap but a vehicle over 5m/15ft in length may not negotiate the bends.

Innisfallen Most picturesque of the islands in the lower lake, with much holly. Reached by boat from Ross Castle.

Kate Kearney's Cottage Once a coaching inn, now the starting point for rides through the Gap of Dunloe; refreshment centre.

Ladies' View A high point on the Killarney/Kenmare road, overlooking the upper lake with a splendid view over all three lakes and through the Gap of Dunloe.

Lough Guitane More bleak and sombre than Killarney's other three lakes; good trout fishing.

Lower Lake (Lough Leane) Largest of the lakes, with 30 islands and 30 legends for each island.

Mangerton A peak south of the middle lake (840m/2756ft) reached in about 3hrs walking from Muckross, with superb views from the summit.

Middle Lake (Muckross Lake) just below the Torc Waterfall, surrounded by colourful shrubbery.

Moll's Gap An opening into the Reeks, along the valley of a small stream (just before the metalled road to Kenmare); impressive views.

Muckross House A 19th-century

Killarney

manor house, now a living museum of Kerry life, with an active craft centre. The gardens are a mass of azaleas and rhododendrons, rock gardens, and lawns; free guided tours.

Old Weir Bridge At the Meeting of the Waters, where the upper lake flows into the middle and lower lakes. Luxurious shrubbery all round. Here boats returning from the upper lake to Killarney shoot the rapids.

Ross Castle A ruined castle on a peninsula in the lower lake, where you can hire boats. No entry to the castle.

Torc Waterfall (18m/60ft high) is reached by a footpath from the Kenmare road 6km/4mi outside Killarney. Rocks covered in ferns and mosses and soft greenery; best appreciated if you come down to its warmth on foot from Mangerton, or by car from the Windy Gap. (Tea, toilets, information centre.)

Upper Lake Connected to the other two lakes by the Long Range. From the head of the upper lake, near Lord Brandon's Cottage, you can take the boat back to Killarney.

Killorglin J7

Co. Kerry (pop. 1100) A grey stone village of open streets sloping down to a pretty bridge over the River Laune. Killorglin becomes alive in August when the Puck Fair is held and shops and pubs are open day and night. A goat is crowned King Puck and presides over a cattle and horse fair; a survival of pagan ceremonies.

Kinsale N15

Co. Cork (pop. 1600) A lovely old town of narrow, winding streets, steep footpaths and Georgian houses. A former naval port, now a fishing village with a fine natural harbour, it is primarily a tourist town – lively entertainment. In 1601 Spanish troops landed here to help the Irish in a revolt. They were besieged and the northern Irish chiefs marched to relieve them but were defeated by the English; the failure at Kinsale marked the end of Irish independence.

The **Old Head of Kinsale** is a cliff, 16km/10mi south of Kinsale, near which the *Lusitania* was torpedoed in 1915. A commercial field of natural gas lies off Kinsale Head: it feeds a power station and a fertilizer plant, and provides heating for Cork city.

Macroom L13

Co. Cork (pop. 2200) A market town for the Irish-speaking region to the west of it, Macroom straddles the picturesque Cork/Killarney road, widening out from the Cork end of town to the square and castle gateway at the Killarney end. Woollens from **Dripsey** Woollen Mills (16km/10mi east) are on sale here. The scenic road from Macroom to Glengarriff lies through the **Keimaneigh Pass**, a gorge with overhanging cliffs. Gougane Barra Forest Park is just beyond the pass.

Mitchelstown H17

Co. Cork (pop. 3000) A large market square for a small town, busy with local produce. The town lives off the creamery, producing butter and cheese. Mitchelstown Caves, including the largest underground cavern in the British Isles, are 12km/9mi to the east, just off the Cahir road.

Skibbereen P10

Co. Cork (pop. 2200) The centre of the south-west Cork peninsula or Carbery Coast. In this region, the ravine around **Leap** (north of Glandore) and the coast road from **Ross Carbery** to **Glandore** are striking to see. Roaringwater Bay, belying its name, is quietly attractive with the little fishing harbour of **Skull** (French lobster boats) and the village of **Ballydehob** (gala in August) set in some wild pockets of country; see the coast scenery between Mizen Head and Three Castle Head. In the bay, **Sherkin Island** is reached by motorboat from Baltimore (every two hours from 1200), while Irish-speaking **Clear Island** has a ferry from Baltimore (45 minute trip; 3 times a day in July and August, otherwise at 1400).

Sneem M6

Co. Kerry (pop. 300) A village noted for its prettiness (two village greens), in the middle of still prettier country – wild mountain to the north and a beautiful valley to the west. **Staigue Fort** (reached from the resort of Castlecove, 4km/2½mi west), is the best-preserved stone fort in Ireland – 27m/89ft in diameter. Further west the Pass of Coomakista offers expansive views across the sea to the Skelligs.

Parknasilla, 5km/3mi south east of Sneem, is a pretty estate devoted to holiday-makers.

Tralee H8

Co. Kerry (pop. 13,000) The largest town in Kerry, combined business centre and tourist resort. A square-patterned town, lively and cheerful – bunting across the streets for much of the year. Centre for festivals; the biggest is the Rose of Tralee International Festival in September – a week of street-dancing and song which is supposed to end when the Rose of Tralee is crowned (any girl of Irish blood). The song *Rose of Tralee* is by William Mulchinock (1820–64); it is of course played during the festival. *Siamsa* is the national theatre of folk memory (see p. 29) performed at the Ashe Memorial Hall, Denny Street. At the end of Denny Street, the Town Park has green acres for recuperation. Day Street is a quiet backwater of Georgian houses; Castle Street is a parade of pubs and restaurants.

Tralee is connected to the sea by a canal; old tower windmill by the bridge. **Fenit** and **Ardfert** are two agreeable little villages in the neighbourhood associated with St Brendan; born AD 484, he sailed from Fenit to discover America (probably landing in Florida), and returned to found St Brendan's Cathedral (now with Hiberno-Romanesque doorway, Early English nave) at Ardfert. Banna Strand (3km/2mi west of Ardfert) is where the Irish patriot Sir Roger Casement landed in 1916, but he was soon captured at McKenna's Fort.

Waterville M4

Co. Kerry (pop. 500) Halfway point in the Ring of Kerry, set in rich, flat farmland encircled by mountains, overlooking the curved sandy beach of Ballinskelligs Bay. This hamlet has become home to many foreign residents and has a reputation as the most expensive place in Ireland. **Ballinskelligs** village on the opposite side of the bay is Irish-speaking. Lough Currane at the back of Waterville is rich in archaeological remains – St Finan's 6th-century oratory on Church Island, a drowned castle, the Baslicon Dolmen (grave of a daughter of Milesius, a prehistoric invader) and horseshoe-shaped Beenbane Fort at its western shore.

Youghal L20

Co. Cork (pop. 5500) Pronounced *Yawl.* A town of mediaeval foundation; some of the walls still stand or have been reconstructed. Now a busy holiday resort at the mouth of the River Blackwater. Winding streets, old shopfronts, steep steps overlooking a jumble of slate roofs and churches towards the sea, good beaches round the bay. It is claimed that the first potatoes in Europe were planted here by Sir Walter Raleigh.

Dingle Peninsula

THE MID WEST

This is the land of wide-open spaces, warm and fertile but empty. The centre of County Clare is far-viewed moorland, looking across farm and bog to the ocean. The seaboard is a mixture of jagged rocks and great cliffs like the Cliffs of Moher, and little farms reddened with fuchsias enjoying the sea-warmed air. North of the moors, the Burren is a tract of limestone stripped of all soil, where little grows and nothing dare die, for it can't be buried. The southern peninsula of Clare is more the 'traditional' Ireland of the deserted cabin. In east Clare the land is broken up into low hills, rich in woodland, overlooking Lough Derg.

Lough Derg is an inland sea, 30 miles long and up to five miles wide (48km; 8km), an expansion of the River Shannon which flows on after the lake to its broad estuary. East of the lake the low mountains of North Tipperary are barer than the Clare hills; interspersed with fertile farmland. The farming is repeated in County Limerick, heart of the Golden Vale, a great stretch of rich dairy farmland. But this farmland, despite its richness and fertility, looks as empty of people as the moors and bogs.

Clare and Limerick are a land of castles – some counts say 450, others make a total of 950; most of them are the remains of fortified farm dwellings, but there are still plenty of square Irish castles open to visitors. A few castles have been specially preserved forming the castle circuit – banquets and rather synthetic Irish entertainments for the benefit of travellers arriving at Shannon Airport. This is also a region rich in native Irish music and storytelling. You won't find these by enquiry at the tourist office, only by following your nose. Tipperary is strong in Gaelic games.

Festivals End of March, Limerick Festival is for Irish dancing and Gaelic drama; in late July, Miltown Malbay has a summer school which concentrates on Gaelic piping, mixed up with a contest to choose 'Clare's Darling Girl'.

Adare K8

Co. Limerick Noted as a pretty village, the thatched cottages date from the 19th century. The old Trinitarian Abbey incorporates the R.C. parish church, and the Augustinian Priory houses the C. of I. church. Ruins of Desmond Castle, a strongly fortified keep built on the site of a ring fort.

Castle Matrix (at Rathkeale, 11km/7mi west) offers mediaeval banquets. Raleigh supposedly grew the first potatoes in Ireland here, but see Youghal p. 77.

Ballyvaughan E6

Co. Clare An attractive village. **Ailwee Cave** (3km/2mi south east) dates back to two million BC; stalagmites and stalactites – open April to October, 1000 to 1830.

Bruree L9

Co. Limerick A village centre for pre-Celtic and Celtic forts, spread along the River Maigue; for three 14th-century de Lacy castles; and for the de Valera Museum (see below).

Castleconnell I10

Co. Limerick A pretty village on the Shannon (waterskiing); walk along the river banks to the Falls of Doonass (rapids). Pleasant walks in the Clare Glens (8km/5mi east) – waterfalls, and woodland of oak and ash.

Ennis H7

Co. Clare (pop. 10,000) An old town, not a mere through-road. Narrow streets converge on the busy marketplace (monument to Dan O'Connell), and beyond are the remains of the Franciscan Friary (sculptures). O'Connell and Eamon de Valera were both parliamentary representatives for Ennis.

At **Craggaunowen**, just beyond Quin (12km/8mi south east of Ennis) there's a reconstruction of a crannog, a lake dwelling of the Bronze Age. **Lough Gur**, 20km/12mi south of Limerick, has an original crannog, surrounded by stone circles, forts and dolmens.

Kilfenora F6

Co. Clare Here is a display centre, explaining the history, geology, plant and animal life of the Burren region. (Open daily, Easter to October.)

Kilkee I3

Co. Clare (pop. 1300) A resort on the Clare coast, with a curving, sandy beach, and an outcrop of rock (Duggerna Reef) which keeps the water calm. Cliffs with caves just outside. Full range of seaside amusements, including skindiving.

Doonbeg (9km/6mi east of Kilkee) is a natural centre for traditional Irish music.

Traditional Ireland still survives along the Atlantic seaboard south west of Kilkee to **Loop Head** (lighthouse, not open to public) – low stone cottages, the thatch turning green where they are empty, or replaced by corrugated iron where they are still used; narrow, stone-walled strips of land extending from the sea to the hills; the crash of waves on the cliffs of the north coast. Soft Gaelic speech, and trim hedges round trim houses, near **Carrigaholt**. At **Kilbaha**, 'Have one for the road in the nearest bar to New York'.

Killaloe/Ballina H10

Co. Clare (pop. 1000) A twin town, Killaloe in Co. Clare is joined by a graceful arched bridge over the River Shannon to its suburb village of Ballina in Co. Tipperary. Fishing, sailing and cruising centre; beautiful situation on the exit of the Shannon from Lough Derg. Visit St Flannan's Cathedral (Romanesque); nearby is the shaft of a cross bearing runic and ogham inscriptions.

Day cruises on the lake start from Killaloe. Both shores at the southern end of Lough Derg are gently wooded. On the west side **Mountshannon** and **Scarriff** with its little harbour are two pretty villages. A fort called Beal Boru, from which Brian Boru took his name, is just south of Scarriff. From the east shore, beyond Ballina, rise the Arra Mountains, where the bones of the Leinstermen are buried.

Kilrush J4

Co. Clare (pop. 1000) A market town above the sea, it has a small harbour but

Cliffs of Moher

just south is Cappagh Pier for larger boats. Kilrush is the nearest town for the **Killimer** ferry, which connects with **Tarbert** on the south side of the Shannon estuary and avoids the long drive to the first bridge at Limerick, 40 miles away (64km). The ferry leaves every hour on the hour from north to south, from 0700 (1000, Sunday) to 2100; half an hour later from south to north. At Moneypoint an electricity generating station promises to transform the area.

Lahinch G4

Co. Clare (pop. 500) A seaside resort, with a bleak amusement centre. Inland, on a cascading river, **Ennistymon** is surrounded by woods.

Lahinch is the starting point for a visit to the **Cliffs of Moher**, a five mile stretch of cliffs which at their highest are nearly 213m/700ft sheer above the sea. O'Brien's Tower, at the summit, was built in 1835 as an observation post.

Limerick J10

Co. Limerick (pop. 68,000) A major industrial city, the fourth largest in Ireland. The main street, O'Connell Street, has an array of slab-sided shops and offices. South of here a rectangular grid of modern streets has little of interest for the visitor. But the eventful history of Limerick can be seen in some of its buildings.

The ninth-century Danish settlement was taken by the Irish under Brian Boru around 1000 and became capital of his successors, the O'Briens. Parts of their palace of the mid 1100s still stand, for it was used as the base of St Mary's Cathedral, which is down by the river. The town was taken on several occasions by the Normans, until in 1210 King John visited it and ordered a castle to be built 'to watch towards Thomond', *ie* much of Cos. Tipperary, Limerick and Clare. The castle is still there by Thomond Bridge (open in summer, Irish *seisiun* twice weekly). From then on the city was strongly English, protected from the marauding Irish by stout walls, the remains of which are in Lilia Street with gateways near St John's Hospital. In the revolt of 1641 Limerick joined the confederate cause and had to be taken by Cromwell's men, then in 1690 it became the last base of the Catholic forces against William of Orange, after the Battle of the Boyne (page 56).

While William sat outside the walls, awaiting his artillery, the Irish commander, Patrick Sarsfield slipped out, intercepting and destroying the artillery after a 96km/60mi detour. 'Patrick Sarsfield's Ride' leads through lost, remote country-

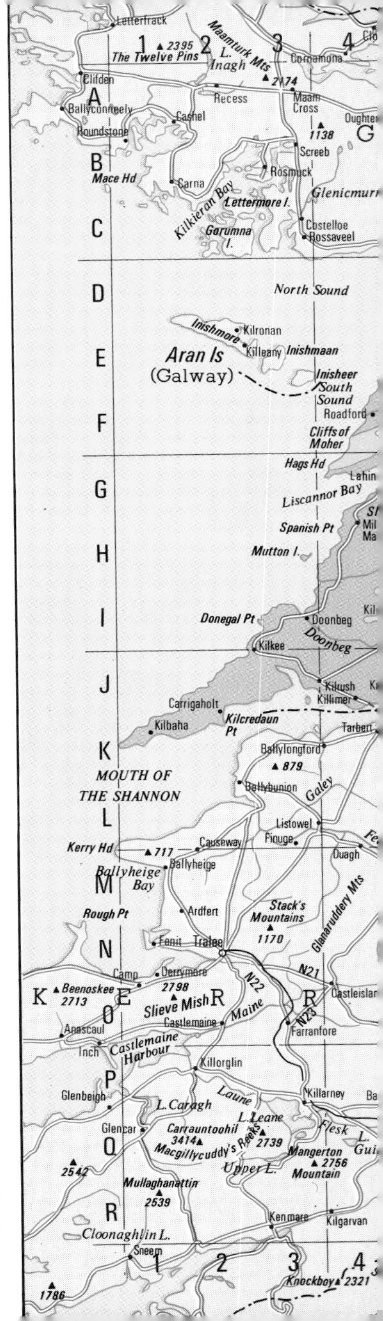

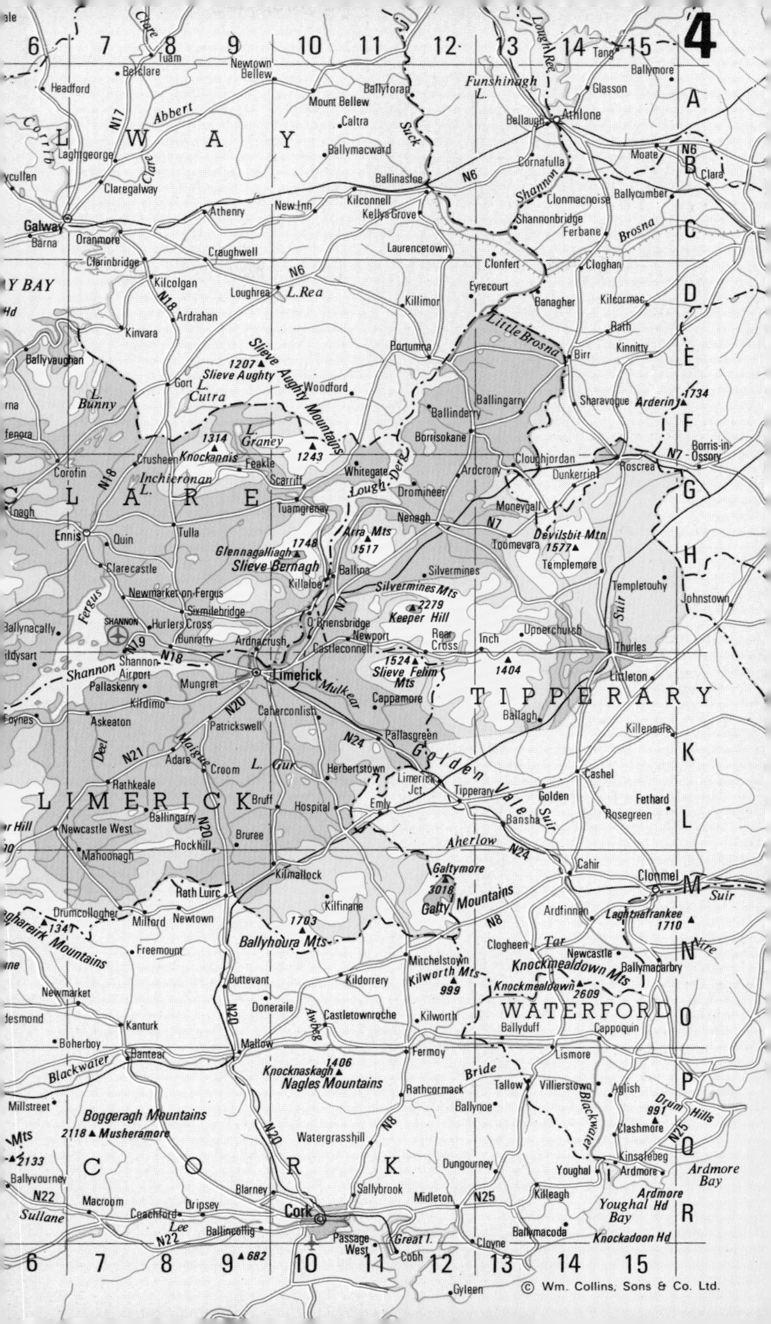
4
6 7 8 9 10 11 12 13 14 15
Clare
Tuam
Belclare
Newtown Bellew
Lough Ree
Tang
Ballymore
Headford
Ballyforan
Funshinagh L.
Glasson
Mount Bellew
A
Corrib
N17
Abbert
Caltra
Suck
Bellaugh
Athlone
L W A Y
Laghtgeorge
Ballymacward
Moate
N6
B
Clara
Clare
Cornafulla
Claregalway
Ballinasloe
N6
Shannon
Ballycumber
New Inn
Kilconnell
Clonmacnoise
Galway
Athenry
Kellys Grove
Shannonbridge
Barna
Oranmore
Ferbane
C
Brosna
Laurencetown
Craughwell
Clarinbridge
Clonfert
Cloghan
N6
Kilcolgan
Eyrecourt
D
Y BAY
Loughrea
L.Rea
Banagher
Kilcormac
N18
Killimor
Ardrahan
Little Brosna
Rath
Kinvara
Portumna
Kinnitty
Slieve Aughty Mountains
Birr
E
Ballyvaughan
1207
Slieve Aughty
Woodford
Gort
L. Cutra
1734
L. Bunny
Ballingarry
Sharavogue
Arderin
Ballinderry
F
1314
L. Graney
Borrisokane
Knockannis
1243
Borris-in-Ossory
Corofin
Crusheen
Cloughjordan
N7
Feakle
Whitegate
Ardcrony
Roscrea
N18
Inchieronan L.
Scarriff
Lough Derg
Dunkerrin
Dromineer
G
C L A R E
Tuamgreney
Moneygall
Ennis
Nenagh
N7
Quin
Tulla
Arra Mts
Devilsbit Mtn
1748
Toomevara
Glennagalliagh
1517
1577
Clarecastle
Slieve Bernagh
H
Ballina
Templemore
Killaloe
Silvermines
Templetouhy
Fergus
Newmarket-on-Fergus
Silvermines Mts
N7
Johnstown
Sixmilebridge
2279
Suir
SHANNON
Keeper Hill
Hurlers Cross
O'Briensbridge
Ballynacally
N19
Bunratty
Ardnacrush
Newport
Rear Cross
Inch
Upperchurch
Castleconnell
Thurles
Shannon Airport
N18
1524
Shannon
Limerick
Slieve Felim Mts
1404
Littleton
Pallaskenry
Mungret
Mulkear
T I P P E R A R Y
Kildimo
Cappamore
Foynes
N20
Caherconlish
Ballagh
Askeaton
Patrickswell
Killenaule
Pallasgreen
Deel
N24
N21
Maigue
Golden Vale
K
Adare
L. Gur
Croom
Herbertstown
Cashel
Limerick Jct.
Rathkeale
Tipperary
Golden
L I M E R I C K
Bruff
Fethard
Hospital
Emly
Ballingarry
N20
Bansha
Suir
Rosegreen
L
Newcastle West
Bruree
Aherlow
Rockhill
N24
Mahoonagh
Cahir
Galtymore
Kilmallock
Clonmel
3018
M
Suir
Galty Mountains
Rath Luirc
Kilfinane
Ardfinnan
Drumcollogher
Milford
Newtown
N8
Laghtnafrankee
1710
1703
Ballyhoura Mts
Clogheen
Tar
Nire
Freemount
N
Newcastle
Mitchelstown
Knockmealdown Mts
Ballymacarbry
Buttevant
Kildorrery
Kilworth Mts
999
Knockmealdown
2609
Newmarket
N20
Doneraile
Awbeg
W A T E R F O R D
Castletownroche
Kilworth
O
Kanturk
Ballyduff
Cappoquin
Boherboy
Mallow
Banteer
Fermoy
Lismore
Blackwater
1406
Knocknaskagh
Bride
Nagles Mountains
P
Rathcormack
Tallow
Villierstown
Aglish
Millstreet
Blackwater
Ballynoe
991
Drum Hills
Boggeragh Mountains
2118
Musheramore
Clashmore
N20
N8
N25
Mts
Q
Watergrasshill
Kinsalebeg
2133
C O R K
Dungourney
Ardmore
Youghal
Ardmore Bay
Ballyvourney
Blarney
Sallybrook
N22
Macroom
Dripsey
Midleton
N25
Killeagh
Ardmore Hd
Youghal Bay
R
Sullane
Coachford
Cork
Lee
Ballincollig
Passage West
Great I.
N22
Cloyne
Ballymacoda
Knockadoon Hd
Cobh
682
6 7 8 9 10 11 12 13 14 15
Gyleen

Georgian Limerick

side and can still be followed – there is a tour starting from the city, but it is easier to pick up the signposted trail from Killaloe.

The next lot of artillery was not intercepted and the marks of the bombardment are visible in King John's Castle. The city surrendered, on a promise of religious freedom for the Catholics, but that part of the treaty was not ratified by the English parliament, so Limerick became known as the 'City of the Broken Treaty'. The Treaty Stone, used for the signing in 1691, stands on a pedestal at the end of Thomond Bridge, facing the castle.

Limerick grew as a Georgian city, and a few buildings are left, *eg* in John Square and Perry Square. For a short tour of Limerick, walk from Sarsfield Bridge along the strand past the weir, over Thomond Bridge and the canal bridge, and then see O'Callaghan Strand from the quays on the left bank.

Lisdoonvarna F5

Co. Clare (pop. 500) A spa; nearly all hotels and spa centre. Good centre for seeing the Burren.

Nenagh G12

Co. Tipperary (pop. 5000) The chief town of north Tipperary; modern shops in streets round the main crossroads. Centre of a fertile plain, but just south are the bare, flat, empty Silvermines Mountains. On their southern slopes (near Rear Cross) is the 'Land of Tombs', a Neolithic cemetery (2000 BC).

Newcastle West L7

Co. Limerick (pop. 2500) A market town situated on the River Deel; the large square keeps the place alive. Starting point of the co-operative creamery movement. In the centre of the town, Desmond Castle has a well-preserved banqueting hall and the remains of the Great Hall of the Knights Templar.

Shannon J7

Co. Clare On a flat promontory on the broadest part of the River Shannon, Shannon Airport is the gateway to Ireland for transatlantic visitors. Around the airport there has grown up a considerable industrial estate, drawing workers from Ennis and Limerick, busy with lightweight, modern products – electrical and electronic. Shannon town has grown to service the airport and local industry – street after street of identical, little, modern houses, ending abruptly in the marshy grass that was there before the airport came. Bed and Breakfast signs all over Shannon town, and at the airport a major hotel and excellent restaurant, and an 18-hole golf course.

The Shannon region is geared to the tourist impatient for a taste of the 'real' Ireland of popular imagination. The Rent-an-Irish-Cottage scheme, based on the airport, provides modern accommodation in an old, romantic style up to 50km/30mi from Shannon. Several castles provide stylish banquets accompanied by Irish entertainment: **Knappogue** (at Kinvara, Co. Galway) and **Dromoland** (Newmarket-on-Fergus), **Castle Matrix** (Rathkeale) and **Ballyportry** (Corofin) are on the castle circuit, but the most famous is **Bunratty Castle**. Here, for an interesting fee, visitors are served a 'mediaeval' feast by serving wenches who break off to sing 'traditional' songs. All carefully authentic, as Disneyland is authentic, and good fun if that's what you like.

By the side of Bunratty Castle is the Folk Museum, a much more genuine affair. Here are collected representative cottages and farmhouses, as well as everyday implements and other reminders of the past, to show you how life really was lived in this part of Ireland and how styles developed. The *cheili* held here on summer evenings, for paying visitors, is a fair attempt to reproduce an old-time party.

Thurles I15

Co. Tipperary (pop. 10,000) Pronounced *Ther-less.* A major market town (spacious main street) in the centre of a rich agricultural region – cattle and sugar beet. Here is the sportsground of the Gaelic Athletic Association, founded in Thurles in 1884.

Bunratty Castle and a mediaeval banquet in progress

Reconstruction of traditional Irish cottages at Bunratty Folk Park

THE WEST

It maybe someday I'll go back to Ireland
If it's only at the closing of my day
Just to see again the moon rise over Claddagh
And to watch the sun go down on Galway Bay.

To see again the ripple on the trout stream
And the women in the meadow saving hay
To sit beside a turf fire in the cabin
To watch the bare foot gosoons at their play.

The winds that blow across the bogs of Ireland
Are perfumed by the heather as they blow
The people in the upland digging praties
Speak a language that the strangers do not know.

The Ireland of Colahan's song, composed for exiles who would never return, is Connacht, heartland of Ireland's Western World, its essence being counties Galway and Mayo. After crushing the Irish revolt of 1641, Cromwell confiscated the estates of the landowners who could not prove they had supported parliament in the war, and even those Catholics who were left with land had to exchange it for the poor thin soil of Connacht. By 1700 Galway and Mayo were the only counties where as much as 25% of the land was owned by Catholics. The gentry were thus reduced to a depressed peasant rabble, saved from starvation only by the ease with which potatoes grew even in Connacht. Their life was desperate even when the crops did not fail. When the potatoes were blighted in the Great Famine of 1845–49 their descendants sailed away by the thousand from Galway Bay, in the coffin ships that took them to the promised land, America. (The coffin ships were cargo boats that arrived with timber and departed with humans as ballast. Passenger liners used for later emigrants have also become 'coffin ships' in Nationalist legend.)

The exiles sent money back home to support the Land League, founded in Co. Mayo in 1879, which fought the land war compelling landlords to reduce rents and

Connemara Pony Show, Clifden

Lough Ahalia, Connemara

stop evictions. The name of Captain Boycott, a land agent in Mayo who was the first to be 'boycotted' in the land war, is remembered now the war is just history.

Not all this region is so poor as the far west which is the chief attraction for visitors. The line of Loughs Conn, Mask and Corrib marks the divide between the agricultural plain and the sparse mountains. East of this line is farmland and bog, clay-covered limestone, level or low hills rising in the south to the Slieve Aughty Mountains. Cattle country and tillage alternating with sheep pastures – an extension of the great Midland plain of Ireland.

Between the lakes and the ocean is the core of Ireland's Western World, a land of bare purple mountain, green bog, rock-strewn streams, the occasional bent tree, and deserted cottages – a land made not for human habitation but to be admired for its barren beauty. This region is summed up in the name Connemara, the epitome of wild, desolate beauty.

Connemara is in fact only a small part of the West, though the name is used loosely for the whole region. The northern seaboard of Mayo is a bleak, empty moorland but with splendid cliffs, notably Benwee Head beyond the little harbour of Portacloy. The west coast of Mayo, with the Corraun Peninsula and Achill Island, and inland Mt Nephin, looking eastward to Lough Conn, are more attractive to the eye. South of Clew Bay, the Murrisk Peninsula of Mayo, is like Connemara but less intense. Connemara itself revolves round the Twelve Pins (Bens), twelve peaks which loom over the fishing villages round the coast and the hills and streams inland. Clifden town is the 'capital' of Connemara, and the hamlet of Recess roughly its centre. Joyce's Country, between Lough Mask and Lough Corrib, and around Maam Cross, is a softer, gentler version of the area. South of Recess, moving towards Galway, is Iar Connacht, a strange lost region, low and flat, covered by patches of lake, soft marsh and firm bog, the sea and the land intersecting each other as far as you can see to the mist-obscured horizon. The diffuse light and striking landscape are more attractive to many people than the acknowledged beauties of Connemara. This area is fairly well populated, and there are herds of two cows and even four cows. Much of it is Irish-speaking, and there are still some older folk who speak English with difficulty. Unlike other parts of the Gaeltacht, road signs are not bilingual but are in Irish only, so it pays to learn the Irish names – it is only too easy to get lost in this wilderness, where the roads wander round in search of firm land.

Galway is famous for oysters (the best beds are at Clarinbridge), and other goodies from the sea are there almost for the asking – salmon especially. Trout comes from nearly all the streams, and Castlebar ham is famous throughout Ireland. Traditional handwoven tweeds can be bought from tourist shops, or more cheaply if you spend the time to get back to source.

Connemara marble, green or white, may be found all over the West in the raw state, and worked pieces can be bought in Clifden and in Moycullen at the Connemara Marble Factory.

Festivals End June, Castlebar Walk; end July (last Sunday) pre-dawn mass on Croagh Patrick; mid August, blessing the waters in Galway; August, Connemara Pony Show at Clifden; September, Sea Angling Festival in Galway, and the Galway Oyster Festival; early October, Castlebar Song Contest.

Achill Island F3

Co. Mayo Joined to the mainland by a road bridge, the island is full of peace and colour. There are moors and bogs, but of a lighter green in contrast to the purple of the rest of the region. Sandy bays, backed by the odd thatched cabin, tiled house, or cluster of houses, overlooked by mountains. In places the mountains come right to the sea to form cliffs, *eg* the Menawn Cliffs (245m/800ft). The chief village is **Achill Sound**, which is the only shopping place for self-caterers. **Keel** is a resort-village on a broad bay facing the Menawn Cliffs to the south (mostly grass-covered but sheer in places); **Dooagh** is a scattered village behind a small sandy bay 18km/11mi west of Keel; **Dugort** is a resort on the north coast, with boat trips to caves in the Cliffs of Slievemore and walking expeditions to the top of **Slievemore** and along the cliff top to Slievemore village, deserted for 100 years.

The highest mountain, with superb views, is **Croaghaun** (668m/2192ft) with a sheer drop to the sea; reached from Keem Bay. Seals around all the bays; basking sharks (harmless) at Keem Bay; salmon netting in Dooagh Bay; tuna fish occasionally; freshwater fishing in the many small rivers and lakelets.

The whole island is almost deserted but for visitors.

Aran Islands O4

Co. Galway The heartland of Gaelic Irishness, these three islands just over the horizon from Galway city could formerly be reached only by dangerous ship-landing, and the smallest only by currach (the small roundish boat made from wooden lathes covered by tarred canvas which is still the characteristic fishing boat of the region). Now there is an airstrip on each island with daily flights from Carnmore (6km/4mi east of Galway city). By sea, there is a regular service (daily in summer, twice weekly in winter) from Galway to Inishmore, and a daily boat

5
6
7
8
9
10
11
12
13
14
15
A
B
C
D
E
F
G
H
J
K
L
M
N
O
P
Q
R
Mullaghmore
Inishmurray
Cliffoney
Lough Melvin
Garrison
REP. OF IRE.
N.I.
N15
1720
Dartry Mts
Glenade L.
Benbulbin
1730
1515
Downpatrick Hd
Roskeeragh Pt
Sligo Bay
Glencar L.
Lenadoon Pt
Easky
Rosses Point
1247
Ballycastle
Maamakeogh
Killala Bay
Dromore West
Sligo
N16
Beltra
Dromahair
L.Gill
Inishcrone
Knockalongy
N4
Bellhavel L.
Dowra
Killala
Oweniny
Cloonaghmore
Coolaney
Collooney
Drumkeeran
Crockets Town
Ballina
Deel
Slieve Gamph or The Ox Mountains
S L I G O
Unshin
L. Allen
Crossmolina
Lough Conn
Riverstown
Moy
Ballymote
Ballyfarnan
L. Arrow
1927
Nephin Beg
2646
Nephin
1188
Tobercurry
Kesh
Keadew
Shannon
Drumshanbo
2295
Birreencorragh
Curry
L.Key
Beg Range
L.Cullin
Curlew Mts
Foxford
Boyle
L. Drumharlow
L. Beltra
1412
Swinford
Charlestown
L.Gara
N5
Drumsna
M A Y O
Newport
Bellavary
Ballaghaderreen
Cavetown L.
Kilkelly
Castlebar
Kiltimagh
Urlaur L.
Frenchpark
Castlebar L.
Manulla
N17
Elphin
Westport
Mannin L.
Cloonagh L.
Bellanagare
Balla
Knock
Strokestown
L. Forbes
Ballyhaunis
L. O'Flyn
Tulsk
Mayo
Castlerea
Eriff
Claremorris
Brickeens
Ballinlough
Ballintober
1294
Partry
Robe
L.Carra
Cloonfad
Ballindine
Partry Mountain
Hollymount
Ballymoe
Lough Mask
Ballinrobe
Dunmore
Suck
Roscommon
R O S C O M M O N
Glenamaddy
Kilmaine
Knockcroghery
Neale
Clonbern
Creggs
Clare
Lough Ree
Clonbur
Cong
Athleague
Shrule
Cornamona
Tuam
Ballygar
Belclare
Newtown Bellew
Funshinagh L.
Headford
Ballyforan
Lough Corrib
Mount Bellew
Maam Cross
Athlone
Oughterard
Abbert
Caltra
Bellaugh
1138
G A L W A Y
Screeb
Ross L.
Laghtgeorge
Ballymacward
Cornafulla
Moycullen
Ballinasloe
N6
Glenicmurrin L.
Claregalway
Kilconnell
Kellys Grove
New Inn
Athenry
Costelloe
Galway
Shannonbridge
Rossaveel
Spiddle
Barna
Oranmore
Laurencetown
Craughwell
Clarinbridge
Clonfert
GALWAY BAY
Kilcolgan
Eyrecourt
Loughrea
L.Rea
N18
Killimor
Banagher
Black Hd
Ardrahan
Kinvara
Slieve Elva
338
Ballyvaughan
Portumna
Slieve Aughty Mountains
1207
Slieve Aughty
Inisheer
South Sound
Gort
L. Cutra
Woodford
L. Bunny
Lisdoonvarna
Ballingarry
Roadford
Ballinderry
Cliffs of Moher
Kilfenora
1314
L. Graney
Borrisokane
Knockannis
1243
Ennistymon
Crusheen
Feakle
Cloughjordan
Corofin
Lahinch
Inchicronan L.
Scarriff
Whitegate
Ardcrony
Cullenagh
Lough Derg
Dromineer
Slieve Callan
1284
Inagh
C L A R E
Tuamgreany
Moneygall
Miltown Malbay
Nenagh
Ennis
Quin
Tulla
Arra Mts
1517
N7
Toomevara
Glennagalliagh
1748
1577
Clarecastle
Newmarket-on-Fergus
Silvermines Mts

Achill Island

from Rossaveel (42km/26mi west of Galway city) which touches each of the islands.

The islands are **Inishmore** (3090 hectares/7635 acres, pop. 864), **Inishmaan** (911 hectares/2252 acres, pop. 319), and **Inisheer** (566 hectares/1400 acres, pop. 313). The islands are for the most part bare limestone; in areas with some soil cultivation is made possible by clearing the stones to make dry-stone walls (prominent on Inisheer), otherwise sand is mixed with dried seaweed to form a soil which, spread on the rocks, permits cultivation. This sparse farming is supplemented by fishing; the currach is used for inshore fishing and there are also modern trawlers. The traditional costume of the Aran islanders is entirely home-spun and hand-woven – patterned white sweater, brightly coloured girdle, white canvas coat, hide shoes with no heel; this costume is still worn by some, especially on Inishmaan. None of the islanders use English when speaking to each other.

The islands are full of antiquities – ruins of prehistoric forts and early Christian churches. Most impressive is the fort of Aengus on Inishmore; semicircular and made of stone, it is at the edge of a 90m/300ft cliff. If antiquities are your interest, you must get the detailed guide from Galway Tourist Office. Otherwise the sights of the islands are cliffs, seascapes and bathing beaches.

The life of the islands was made famous by Synge's plays *Riders to the Sea* and the *Aran Islands*, but it was already vanishing in 1934 when the famous film *Man of Aran* was made.

Ballina D8

Co. Mayo (pop. 6000) A little town, largest in Mayo, on the estuary of the River Moy; good shops around the pedestrian precinct and full of angling shops, angling men and angling pubs.

Belmullet C3

Co. Mayo A little fishing village and resort on the narrow neck of land that joins the Mullet Peninsula to the mainland. The seaward side of the peninsula is bare rock, the Atlantic gales stripping off any vegetation, while the east side has gentler fields (golf) leading down to sandy bays on landlocked Blacksod Bay.

The road from Belmullet to **Killala** is for the lover of wild cliffs, desolate moorland and immense open spaces. Benwee Head (253m/829ft) is the highest cliff of the region, and either side of **Portacloy** is a succession of cliffs and headlands, fjords and little creeks. At **Porturlin** 12km/8mi east of Portacloy, the Arches are a rock formation in the sea with cliffs towering above; entered by rowboat. From the cliffs you can see the Stacks of Broadhaven, seven pillars of rock rising 90m/300ft from the sea. Inland, the Barony of Erris is bleak, uninhabited but superb heather-clad moorland.

Castlebar G7

Co. Mayo (pop. 6000) County town of Mayo. The Mall is a grass-covered green surrounded by comfortable houses (formerly the private cricket pitch of Lord Lucan), and sets the tone for the town. The Irish Land League was founded here in 1879. The Town Hall is the former Linen Hall where flax markets were held. The linen industry has declined but there is a new industrial estate. Golf, tennis and squash facilities. Castlebar International Four-Day's Walk, end of June; and Castlebar International Song Contest, early October.

Clare Island H3

Co. Mayo Five miles from east to west and three miles long (8km by 5km). Clare Island in Clew Bay offers peace, remoteness and cliff scenery. Almost the whole southern coast is 30m/100ft-high cliffs, while Knockmore Mountain in the west descends sharply from 460m/1500ft to cliffs which rise a sheer 90m/300ft from the sea. Reached by boat from **Roonagh Quay**, 5km/3mi west of Louisburgh.

Clifden K3

Co. Galway The 'capital' of Connemara, and a convenient centre from which to explore the region. Clifden itself is a compact group of sharp-gabled houses in grey stone which blends in with the blue-grey mountains behind, like snowless Alps overlooking the green Atlantic. The Connemara Pony Show is held here in August – the ponies were once found wild in the mountains, but today they are specially bred.

Connemara marble is still mined; the white marble comes from **Streamstown**, 3km/2mi north of Clifden.

The region is cut by deep valleys with rushing streams and some bog. Visit the Aasleagh Falls outside **Leenaun** and **Recess**, an 'oasis in the wild countryside'. Access from here to the quarries of green Connemara marble at **Cashel**, another lovely village (Gen. de Gaulle stayed here). **Maam Cross** is just a road junction; the sign says 'Shopping centre of Connemara' but only tourist goods are available and a hotel.

Cong K7

Co. Mayo One of the centres for Lough Corrib, it stands on the neck of land between Lough Corrib and Lough Mask. Both lakes offer good trout fishing; fairly shallow and studded with islands. They are connected by an underground river which can be reached from Cong. Many caves around Cong, also prehistoric antiquities and monastic sites. Other villages which are centres for these lakes are **Oughterard** (boat rental and castles);

Clifden

Clonbur (boat rental, castles, good base for the lovely but minute Lough Coolin); **Cornamona** (Irish-speaking); and on the east shore (less scenic) **Headford** which is more of a market town.

Galway M8

Co. Galway (pop. 35,000) A city with a long history, which shows in the winding layout of the streets and in the general atmosphere of comfortable ease that comes with age. A university town with a cosmopolitan feel, enhanced by a busy cultural life – a resident professional theatre company, a main square that you can sit in in comfort, art galleries (not short of paintings of Connemara) and historical societies. Late-night shopping on Friday creates a bad rush hour.

The town was essentially a Norman creation and became, in this remote north-western fastness, almost an independent city-state, while outside the walls appeared the Irish fishing village. In the later Middle Ages a lively trade with Spain developed and the Spanish Arch, one of four arches protecting the quay where Spanish ships unloaded their cargo, remains to remind visitors of the past. The city grew under the rule of 14 families of Norman descent, most famous of which was the Lynch family. Mayor Lynch had to sentence his son to death for the murder of a Spanish visitor, and when the official executioner refused to carry out the sentence, Lynch hanged his son himself; from this came the American custom of 'lynching'. The deed is commemorated by a plaque in a Gothic doorway opposite the Church of St Nicholas.

Columbus allegedly prayed in the Church of St Nicholas before setting out for the New World – another part of the Spanish connection; the traditional Saturday market is still held in front of the church.

Centre of Galway is Eyre Square, now landscaped as a memorial garden to John F. Kennedy, who addressed the people of Galway from here in 1963. At the Bank of Ireland branch in Eyre Square you can see the Galway Sword, a fine piece made in the early 1600s from local silver, and the Galway Mace made in 1710 in Irish silver.

The **Claddagh** was the Gaelic fishing village on the Corrib estuary, opposite the quays of Galway harbour. Old photographs show the lines of long, low, whitewashed, thatched cottages, like the mud cabins in the poorest parts of the West. These were demolished in 1934 and replaced by a housing estate. The Claddagh ring is a band of metal with each end shaped as a hand, the two hands holding a heart surmounted by a crown. It was the traditional wedding ring of the area, and is currently in vogue with the young of Galway, married or not. The Claddagh community still elect their own 'king' who reigns during the Claddagh Summer Festival.

Other events include the Oyster Festival in September; horse racing (Galway Horse Show, July, and Galway Plate, August); summer courses for foreign students July to September at the University College; watching the salmon climb the fish ladder into the Corrib from Salmon Weir Bridge beside the cathedral; International Sea Angling Festival in

The O'Conaire Statue, Eyre Square, Galway

September; Irish theatre July to August; Irish music, dancing, storytelling in late autumn.

Salthill is a suburb of Galway (to the west) and is a seaside resort; mainly Victorian buildings but there is also a modern Leisureland which is extensive and just what the name suggests.

Athenry is a separate town with a history as long as Galway's but it has now become almost an extension of the city. A fortified Norman town, it declined in the 1500s but has preserved its mediaeval shape and feel.

Gort P10

Co. Galway A rather dull market town in itself, centre of an interesting geological region. South of Gort (2km/1mi), the Punchbowl is a 150ft-deep crater (46m) in the limestone, with an underground river at the bottom from Lough Cutra. There are many other disappearing rivers in the region, *eg* the Beagh River. Several castles to visit in the surrounding countryside. The ruins of Coole House stand 3km/2mi to the north; tree autographed by many famous visitors, garden and yew walk. Coole Lake and Forest Park.

Killala C8

Co. Mayo Site of a landing by French forces in 1798. St Patrick founded the bishopric of Killala; St Patrick's Stone (with the crossed circle found on all high crosses) which there is reason to believe was carved by the saint himself, lies neglected under shrubbery at **Kilmore Moy**, between Ballina and Killala.

Kinvara O10

Co. Galway A fishing village, and a good base for visiting the surrounding countryside. Sixteenth-century Dunguaire Castle (3km/2mi north, looking over Galway Bay) has been restored and is used for mediaeval banquets.

Knock H9

Co. Mayo A small village, 11km/7mi north from **Claremorris**, where an apparition of the Virgin Mary, St Joseph and John the Evangelist was seen in 1879. A new basilica has been built at this shrine, and there is a park and a museum in addition to a rest-house and hostels.

Letterfrack J3

Co. Galway One of the most popular villages of Connemara; shopping centre for local products. To the north, **Renvyle** has good beaches nearby.

Loughrea N12

Co. Galway (pop. 3000) On the shore of Lough Rea (don't confuse with the much bigger Lough Ree in Midland Region), this is a minor industrial town; mining nearby at Tynagh (lead and zinc). Business centre and former administrative centre. High Victorian cathedral. Base of the 'Galway Blazers' Hunt – so called because they burnt down the stables of a Tipperary hunt during an evening's friendly jollity.

Portumna O14

Co. Galway A market town on Lough Derg; fishing and cruiser rental. West of Portumna the Forest Park has many lovely walks; well-marked Nature Trail.

Rosmuck M5

Co. Galway Hardly a village at all, typical of the places in south Connemara. This is an extraordinary region – flat and low, bog alternating with lake, then moorland, then the inlets of the sea. Wild, desolate and for many visitors fascinating. From a distance, you can't tell land from sea. It's usually raining or at least a bit misty, with a diffuse light and occasional shafts of sunlight.

Off the road from **Screeb**, Pearse's Cottage is well signposted (Teach Pharsaig). It is a place of pilgrimage for lovers of the language – this is where Patrick Pearse, blood-minded spirit of the Easter Rising, came to learn the Irish language.

Roundstone L3

Co. Galway A quiet holiday village on the coast of Connemara. The Roundstone Project is a scheme to introduce small-scale craft industry into the area to halt depopulation; it includes careful design and landscaping of modern housing so that the village merges into the surroundings.

Tuam K10

Co. Galway Another minor industrial base (sugar refinery), with a Catholic and a Protestant cathedral.

Westport H6

Co. Mayo (pop. 3000) An elegant little town on Clew Bay (sea fishing). The Mall is a graceful thoroughfare along the river. Westport House, home of the Marquess of Sligo, is open April to September; zoo park.

Starting point for **Croagh Patrick**, a lone, bare conical hill rising 765m/2510ft above Clew Bay; Ireland's Holy Mountain, where the Saint spent the forty days of Lent in AD 441. There is a national pilgrimage on the last Sunday in July. Hagiologists make the ascent barefoot. Splendid views from the summit.

THE MID NORTH

The border runs across this region, dividing Fermanagh in Northern Ireland from the northern part of County Leitrim and its neighbour County Sligo in the Republic. But scenically the region is one unit. Its heart is a tract of limestone blocks standing above the land like cliffs, for example O'Rourke's Table near Dromahair and Benbulbin near Sligo town. North Leitrim, east Sligo, and west Fermanagh are mountainous, the mountains overlooking lakes which have steeply shelving shores covered by forest.

Greatest of the lakes in this region is Lough Erne, 'the Amazon without the mosquitoes' – the Upper Lake a mass of islands, the Lower Lake a huge open waterway. This Fermanagh lakeland is a centre for boating and cruising holidays, the Norfolk Broads on a large, empty scale. Between Lower Lough Erne and the border is a limestone plateau, a mixture of forest and deeply rural country. East of Lough Erne, and in the Ox Mountains west of Sligo, is farmland, less scenically striking with its fair share of bog.

The southern part of County Leitrim is an area of little hills and lakes like the adjoining Midland region, and has been included in that region, p. 120.

From North Leitrim came the source of all Ireland's ills – Dervorgilla, wife of Tiernan O'Rourke, King of Breffni. She ran away with Dermot, King of Leinster, who was then deposed. He sought the help of the Normans to recover his kingdom, and when he died their leader took the title King of Leinster. And so Henry II of England who did not mind Irish kings in Ireland but would allow no other Norman to call himself king, invaded the country, thus starting the English involvement with Ireland.

Sligo and Leitrim absorbed the Norman and subsequent invasions, and converted the invaders to Irishmen with the exception of the Earl of Leitrim. He gained the name the 'Wicked Earl', the most rapacious and heartless of 19th-century evicting landlords. He was assassinated, thus helping to discourage other like-minded landlords. Fermanagh took a different course. It was one of the areas chosen for 'plantation' – displacement of native Irish landowners in the 17th century and replacement by Protestant settlers. The plantation succeeded in the towns, especially Enniskillen, which resisted the Irish counterattacks in 1641 and 1689, but hardly took root in the country.

The region is best known for its legends and literature. Here the earlier inhabitants, the Firbolg (pre-Gaelic invaders), were nearly wiped out by the Celtic gods, the Tuathe De Danann around 1500 BC. At Knocknarea Hill (near Strandhill, west of Sligo town) is the reputed tomb of Queen Maeve, a pre-Christian Queen of Connacht. It was her men, according to one legend, who went cattle-stealing near Dundalk (p. 57) giving rise to the most famous epic poem in old Irish, the *Cattle Raid of Cooley*. Queen Maeve turns up in English legend as Queen Mab, or Titania.

It was the legends of this district which started the poet Yeats on his literary career, writing of 'the cairn-heaped grassy hill/Where passionate Maeve is stony still'. The fame of Yeats, leader of the Anglo-Irish literary movement of the late 19th century and possibly Ireland's greatest poet, has led to all this part of Sligo being called the Yeats' Country. The land which he knew and embodied in his poems is still there, even for the visitor with no liking for romantic poetry. And those who love Yeats' poems will love them more when they see the soil from which the poems sprang.

William Butler Yeats was born in Dublin in 1865 into a Sligo family at the lower levels of the Protestant Ascendancy. At an early age he learnt the local legends, and later published poems with a Celtic influence. Then he fell in with Douglas Hyde, another Sligo member of the Anglo-Irish, who founded the Gaelic League in 1893; Hyde wanted to deanglicize Irish life and replace English as the everyday speech by Gaelic. As a result of this association, Yeats set out to create in English, a true Irish literature. He fell in love with Maud Gonne and used her to play the lead in *Countess Cathleen*, the first play put on by the Irish Literary Theatre (more famous under its later name of the Abbey Theatre).

During a stay in London he took an interest in the occult, theosophy and mystical Buddhism, and once back home he wove these into local folklore – Celtic sagas and Irish fairy tales. He met the Gore-Booth sisters at Lissadell House; both were lovely in the pale slim taste of Edwardian England. Constance Gore-Booth married a Polish count, and as the Countess Markievicz played a leading role in the Easter Rising.

All these people are in Yeats' poems and plays, and the countryside around Sligo is full of the places he mentions – Glencar Waterfall, Lissadell House, the lake isle of Innisfree. At most of the sites there is now a neat little plaque recording a few lines from the relevant poem. The region is popular with painters too because the mood changes so rapidly – this is the 'Land of Heart's Desire'.

Ballymote G6

Co. Sligo A small business town in a flat agricultural plain; from Ballymote you can see the hills of Keshcorran rising abruptly from the plain about 8km/5mi away. On the west side of these hills, at **Kesh** (or Keash), are the entrances to limestone caves where Cormac MacArt, King of Munster, was reared by a she-wolf and from which Dermot (of Diarmait and Grainne) set out on the famous boar hunt which ended at Benbulbin and is immortalized in one of Yeats' poems. From the summit of Kesh you look across to the Bricklieve Mountains; at **Castlebaldwin** is a collection of passage graves dating from around 2000 BC. According to legend, around 1300 BC the final defeat of the Firbolgs took place at **Kilmactranny**, near the east shore of Lough Arrow.

Belcoo E10

Co. Fermanagh (pop. 200) This hamlet lies between Lower and Upper Lough Macnean, at the border crossing between the Republic and Northern Ireland on the Sligo/Enniskillin road. Of all the border crossings, the transition from Irish to British is most sudden here, though the bones of the countryside are unchanged. On one side, wild hedges and picturesque (but empty), single-storied cabins; on the other

Kesh Bay, Lough Erne

The forests above Lough Macnean

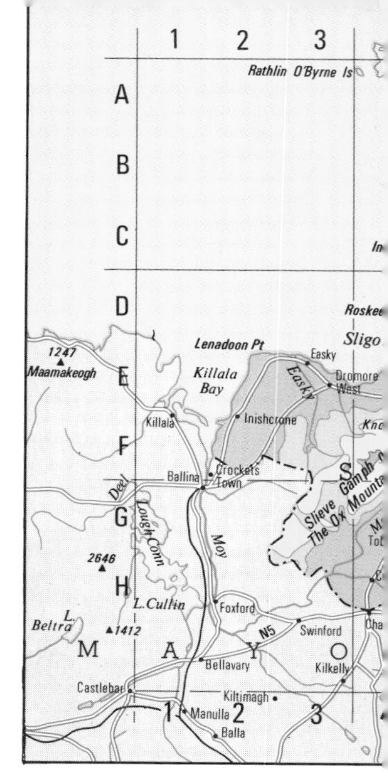

side weed-free fences and gaunt two-storied terrace houses, relieved by roses.

Belcoo is the starting point for the forests and mountains overlooking Lough Macnean. The **Ballintempo Forest** and the **Big Dog Forest** are for walking in utter solitude. Between them is a plateau riddled with caves, offering occasional views across the lake. Lough Macnean itself is a quiet fishing-and-boating lake set in the mountains; rowboats can be rented from some of the shore-side houses.

Belleek C8

Co. Fermanagh A grey village crossroads where Lough Erne empties towards the sea. Famous for porcelain; originally made with local feldspar, production continues with imported clays. The pottery can be visited and samples of Belleek bought direct from the factory shop. There is a bigger selection in Belfast but a good choice available in Enniskillin. The porcelain is characterized by a delicate, lacy effect.

Benbulbin D6

Co. Sligo A block of carboniferous limestone with a cliff face on its wester edge rising 527m/1730ft above the surrounding terraced countryside. An outstanding landmark on the approach to Sligo from the west. The top is a flat plateau, covered by red bog. The edges, by the cliff face and on the scree-covered lower slopes, are still home to arctic plants – sandworts and mountain sorrel – which have clung on here despite the changed climate.

Boho D10

Co. Fermanagh Pronounced *Bo* or *Boo.* A pretty village in a limestone valley, surrounded by moors full of caves. Most of the caves are for experienced cavers only; **Noon's Hole**, on the plateau 5km/3mi north west of Boho is Ireland's deepest cave.

Derrygonnelly C10

Co. Fermanagh A quiet little place with a village green and market house; a base for visiting the **Lough Navar Forest** recreation area (north west) – wild forest but with adequately marked nature trails. The Viewpoint (300m/985ft) gives splendid views across Lough Erne to the Atlantic

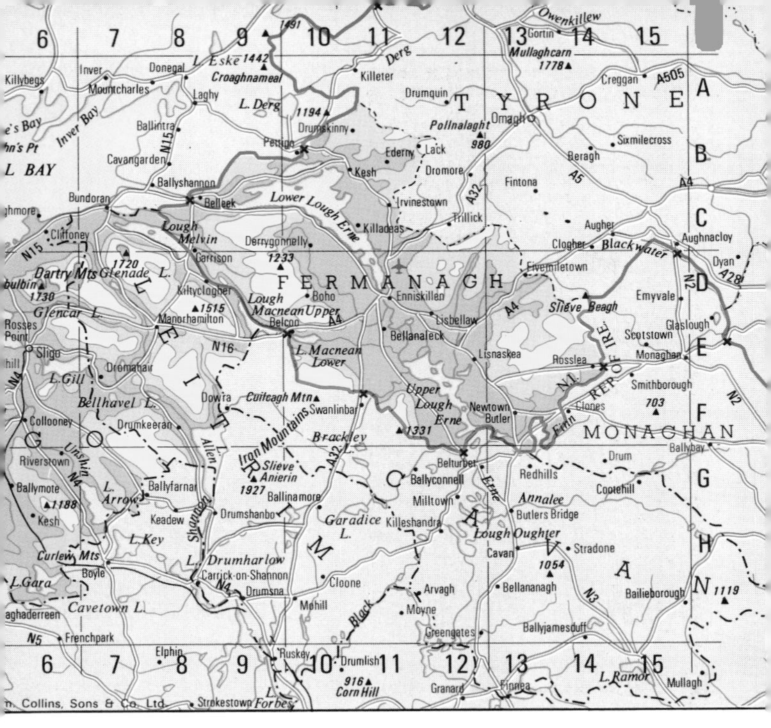

and the distant mountains of Donegal. Opposite the entrance to the park is **Corral Glen** with ancient woodlands, waterfall and a path to Carrick Lough.

Dromahair E7

Co. Leitrim A peaceful village with wide streets, on a little hill; houses without shops. It was from the castle here that Dervorgilla eloped. **O'Rourke's Table** nearby is a steep-sided limestone plateau covered by soft ferns and softer mosses.

Enniskillen D11

Co. Fermanagh (pop. 7000) The county town of Fermanagh and the boating and angling centre for Lough Erne. The main street of Enniskillen, rising and falling on a low hill, is a control zone, where you cannot leave a car unattended. And yet the town remains alive, at least by Northern Ireland standards. The town is surrounded by the branches of the River Erne, connecting the upper to the lower lake; the main road bypassing the town runs alongside one branch. Here is Enniskillen Castle, home of the Inniskilling Fusiliers which now houses the county as well as the regimental museum. On the other branch is the boat-rental centre, for Lough Erne is the largest holiday waterway in the British Isles; sports centre by the jetties — ideal for children on a rainy day.

Florence Court (1764) is a beautiful stately home and garden. 14km/9mi south west of Enniskillen (open to the public). Nearby is the **Marble Arch**, a labyrinth of caves in the Cuilcagh Mountains. There is an hour-long underground boat trip through the formations of stalactites and this is open throughout the year. The area is a paradise for speleologists, with vast chambers like the Giant's Hall — 60m long and 30m high (200ft and 100ft) — bottomless crevices and underground lakes. However, the lower entrance to the caves is worth a visit and can be reached after a riverside walk up the Marble Arch Glen, which is a near-tropical riot of creepers and ferns.

Erne Lough F12/C10

Co. Fermanagh Upper and lower loughs. The Upper Lake is 18km/11mi long, but it seems like a succession of small lakes. It is in fact a continuous waterway, an expan-

Devenish

sion of the River Erne, broken up by islands (a few of which are connected by road bridges). Officially there are 150 islands; if you are trying to navigate there could be 500. From land, the lake is often quite hard to find. On the upper lake, boats can be rented at **Bellanaleck**, 7km/4mi from Enniskillen, and at Belturbet across the border in County Cavan.

The upper lake is connected to the lower by the River Erne. The Lower Lake is a grand open stretch of water, 8km/5mi across at its widest point. There are cruises round the lake from Enniskillen, taking 2—3 hours to visit the main points of interest. However, the main attraction of Lough Erne is being able to cruise for long spells of time in your rented cruiser. (Details from Erne Charter Boat Assn., Enniskillen — see p. 42.) There are nine islands on the lower lake, all near the shore; the most famous is **Devenish Island**, with remnants of a 6th-century monastery and the best-preserved round tower in Ireland, 25m/80ft high.

Other islands are **Inishmacsaint**, with a high cross and ruins of a monastery; **Davy's Island** and **White Island** in Castle Archdale Bay, happy hunting grounds for archaeologists. Boats may be rented at **Killadeas**, which is also a water-skiing centre, and at **Kesh**.

Castle Archdale Forest has a caravan (trailer) and camp site and a nature reserve on the adjacent islands.

Glencar Lake D6

Co. Sligo/Leitrim Lake and waterfalls. A side turning off the Sligo/Manorhamilton road runs along the north shore of the lake. South of the wooded valley in which the lake lies, the mountains rise over 300m/985ft, while to the north they rise, more distantly, to 600m/1970ft; looking along the lake is a flat, parcelled-up valley facing the sea at **Drumcliff**. The waterfall at the east end of the lake inspired Yeats' poem *The Stolen Child.*

Inishcrone E2

Co. Sligo Also called Enniscrone. A rather sparse resort, with a few guesthouses along the low-cliffed front and a long beach overlooking Killala Bay. Very fully-equipped children's play centre. **Easky** (13km/8mi north east) is a fishing village with a rushing trout stream in the middle.

Lisnaskea E12

Co. Fermanagh (pop. 1300) The second-largest town of Fermanagh, this grey stone village is spread along a winding street. It is a focus of life for boaters on Upper Lough Erne, and a starting point for some of the attractively wooded hills of east Fermanagh – Doon Forest, Lisnaskea Forest and Carnmore Viewpoint.

Manorhamilton D8

Co. Leitrim (pop. 800) Spread out along the four arms of a crossroads, the hill rising steeply above gives character and charm to an otherwise bare little town. It is the meeting place of a number of very attractive valleys. The road west leads to Glencar Lake (see above); due north (through a small pass) leads to Lough Melvin and the scenic road, flanked by mountains, which follows the south shore of Lough Melvin almost to the coast; north west is another scenic road (through the pretty village of **Lurganboy**, just outside Manorhamilton) passing little Lough Glenade which is in a deep glen with the mountains high above; eastwards a flatter road leads to the best of all the lakes in this region, Lough Macnean. It is best visited from Belcoo (see above) but a diversion to **Kiltyclogher** village, from which you can get to the upper end of Lough Macnean, leads through another very scenic road.

Sligo E6

Co. Sligo (pop. 1500) Centre of the lovely Yeats' country and the largest town in the north west, Sligo exudes the confidence of a city. It lies mainly on the south bank of the River Garavogue; short riverside walk along Kennedy Parade by the old Dominican Abbey.

Shopping, food and entertainment centre. (Most shops closed on Monday.) Many Gaelic cultural activities, but these are concentrated in the visitors' season. Yeats International Summer School and Yeats English Language School. Drama Circle is turning into a minor repertory company. County Museum has special section on Yeats, and paintings by his brother Jack are in the Sligo Art Gallery next door.

Coney Island in Sligo Bay is still inhabited and can be reached across the sands when the tide is out – the route is marked by pillars. It gave its name to the pleasure ground of New York.

From Sligo walk along the river through a wooded estate to **Lough Gill** which is very prettily set in the hills. On this lake is the tiny island of **Innisfree**, inspiration of one of Yeats' best-loved poems:

I will arise and go now, and go to Innisfree,
And a small cabin build there, of clay and wattles made:
Nine bean-rows will I have there, a hive for the honey-bee,
And live alone in the bee-loud glade.

There are cruises on Lough Gill which take 2½ hours – a Rhine cruise in miniature. On these you can no more escape Yeats' poetry, than you can escape Heine's *Lorelei* on a Rhine cruise.

Drumcliff (9km/6mi north) is where Yeats is buried. Nearby is **Lissadell House**, home of Eva and Constance Gore-Booth; it sits in fine woods overlooking the bay. Open to the public May to September; published opening times are 1430 to 1715, but the practical times are more generous. (Closed on Sundays.)

Strandhill is a resort 8km/5mi west of Sligo; good for Irish music to a modern beat. **Rosses Point**, another resort on the other side of the bay, is good for yachting.

Yeats' grave, Drumcliff

THE NORTH WEST

When King James VI of Scotland came to the English throne in 1603, the Gaelic rulers of north-west Ireland hoped that the new king with his talk of toleration for Catholics might be less oppressive than Queen Elizabeth. But James had inherited not only the crown of Elizabeth but also her absolutism. The Gaels lost heart. In 1607 the Earl of *Tir Eoghain* (Tyrone) and his ally the Earl of *Tir Chonaill* (Donegal) fled to join the Irish exiles in France. Their lands, which they had ruled as chiefs but not owned as proprietors, were confiscated and the best parts parcelled out amongst Protestant settlers – mainly Lowland Scots, but also some English in the new county of London Derry.

While the planters were building their memorial in the towns, like the walls of Derry and the Diamond in Donegal, the Irish were writing their own memorial. *The Annals of the Four Masters* is a history of Ireland compiled over the years 1632–36 by four Franciscan monks in the friary which now stands in ruins outside Donegal town, a sad picture of Gaelic society up to the Flight of the Earls.

The poor farming country of west Donegal and the Sperrin Mountains was not attractive in the plantation land-grab, and was left wholly to the Irish; today these areas are the most attractive for tourists. The seaboard of Donegal must be the scenic high point of all Ireland. Here is the most strikingly rugged coast with the highest cliffs, the most extensive, empty beaches and barest, stoniest uplands. Away from the grandeur, there is a softer landscape of muted grey-green; a patchwork of small fields interspersed with heathery moor, outcrops of rock, ice-scoured lakes and inlets of the sea. It is built of granite, ridges and valleys running from north east to south west, a continuation of the Highlands of Scotland.

Much of this western tip is still Irish-speaking. The area lives by a few sheep, a bit of fishing, some cattle, and now the summer visitors. There is also uranium, and if the ore is worth mining, there will be a new Donegal on these ancient rocks.

The Sperrin Mountains divide the soft river valleys of County Derry from the farmed hills of County Tyrone. Although rising to over 680m/2200ft, they are mostly bog or moorland cut by peat-red streams; promoted as 'horizons of solitude'. Their most attractive part is probably the walking country along the ridge south of the Glenelly valley. In the Sperrin foothills are sleeping villages, with gently wooded lanes especially at their western end and a number of forests at their eastern end.

Between the Sperrins and Lough Neagh is flat, bare farmland, while west of the Sperrins, beyond the Foyle valley and the border that cuts off Derry from much of its natural hinterland in the Republic, is the undulating country of east Donegal – a mixture of pasture and tillage, and moor.

There are two nicely contrasting open-air museums in the region to show you how the past informs the present. At Glencolumbkille old Donegal cottages of different periods are assembled, together with household implements and pictures, presenting the conditions which were endured in the past and which endure in folk memory – remains of the same type of cottage can be seen all over west Donegal. Outside Omagh in County Tyrone there are reproductions of the log cabins which originated here during the plantation of Ulster and survived in America as the homesteads of the Scotch-Irish who went from Ulster to be pioneers on the western frontier.

Ardara — I3

Co. Donegal A rather bare village, with a wide, town-like, main street. Lively night-life. Lying in a flat, cow-covered valley, there is a boggy plateau on one side and two bays, Loughros More and Loughros Beg, like two silted estuaries, on the other. But the drive to **Gweebarra Bay** is more scenic, and the little villages on this bay – **Narin**, **Portnoo** and tiny **Rossbeg** – combine olde-worlde Irishness with an awareness that they are holiday resorts.

Ballyronan — J14

Co. Londonderry A quiet little harbour on

Lough Neagh, where nothing much happens. There's a little jetty at which the pleasure steamer occasionally calls, a few pubs, a few boats, a few fishermen. The surrounding countryside is almost flat – the straight roads rising and falling fifty feet every half mile.

Ballyshannon L4

Co. Donegal(pop. 2000) Grey-cream town straddling a hill, a bit like a continental village; seaside resort. Folk festival at the beginning of August.

Bloody Foreland E3

Co. Donegal A headland near **Gweedore**, strongly promoted for its red colouring and panoramic views; it is not very high, mainly grey and usually mist-obscured.

Buncrana E9

Co. Donegal (pop. 3000) The principal town of the **Inishowen Peninsula**, Buncrana is a straightforward seaside resort. It faces west across Lough Swilly with an extensive beach to the south (backed by hills). Not tawdry.

The peninsula has a scenic drive round the coast (160km/100mi – the Inis Eoghain Hundred); wild and rugged. At the western side the steep Urris Hills are separated by the **Gap of Mamore** (a favourite outing from Buncrana) from the Mamore Hills, with the Dunaff Cliffs beyond. On the east, around the heights of **Inishowen Head** there is a rocky coastline of cliffs with views across Lough Foyle and towards the Giant's Causeway; the most attractive inland scene from here is the four-mile-long **Glen of Agiveney** (6km). **Malin Head** at the tip of the peninsula is the most northerly part of the Irish mainland. The small island of Inishtrahull, visible from Malin Head, is 'Ultima thule', known to the ancient world as one of the farthest outposts of northern barbarism.

Noteworthy beaches at **Pollan Strand** (north of Ballyliffen); between Buncrana and **Fahan**; **Shrove Strand** below Inishowen Head; **Greencastle**.

Bundoran L3

Co. Donegal A seaside resort, with penny arcades, bingo and 'gift shoppes', but also ordinary shops that make no point of the fact that they are thatched; plenty of colourful paint. Huge beach to the south, ending in cliffs; good rocks for crabbing. Many caves, cliff walks and country rambles.

Mullaghmore (9km/6mi west) is a tiny resort, with a harbour, amusements, and cows on the sandbanks. The seagulls fly backwards.

Bunglass J2

Co. Donegal The Bunglass cliffs (312m/1024ft) near Carrick are considerably lower than their better-known neighbours, the Slieve League cliffs, but you can get to the top of them by car. The road up from Bunglass offers repeated views of clefts in the rock; strong winds at the top.

Slieve League

Bunglass itself, although signposted from a distance, is just two or three houses.

Burtonport G3

Co. Donegal A little fishing village, with a concrete quay sticking out where lobster or herring is landed. On the red rocks all round the harbour you may find your own lobster. Untouristed.

Carrick J2

Co. Donegal A quiet village, with a quiet annual fête, a couple of stores, and several pubs. Best starting point for the **Slieve League** cliffs, which stand 602m/1972ft above the sea. The only way to the top is on foot (always windy). See Bunglass, above.

Cookstown J13

Co. Tyrone A long main street and very little else; an early planned village. The surrounding country is an undulating plain.

Creeslough E6

Co. Donegal An unremarkable small village but centre for some of the best Donegal scenery. The **Ards Forest Park** has the trees and deer enclosure of other forest parks, but after picnicking in the forest you can stretch out on the beach, for it lies along an arm of the sea (Sheep Haven Bay). There is a variety of rock shapes on the shore, and marine plants are mixed up with near-tropical growth. The Ards Peninsula, which can be visited with permission of the Capuchin monks, has some of the best soft scenery in Donegal.

Dunfanaghy is a minor resort – tea-shops rather than arcades.

Horn Head is a cliff rising 180m/600ft sheer from the sea, with a vista of islands and headlands along the coast. **Muckish Mountain** behind it is true mountain, with bare rocks above the vegetation; parts of it are for climbers only, though most is accessible to walkers. (Excursions from the Adventure Centre in Creeslough, which takes children for a week at a time.)

Glen Lough is an attractive lake with wooded slopes overlooking it on one side and a disjointed plain on the other; high above, on a mountain pass, **Lough Salt** offers huge views over the empty land.

Donegal J4

Co. Donegal Foreign visitors who have all heard of the beauties of Donegal County flock first to Donegal town, and are not disappointed. It is only a big village, in no way the largest in the county, but friendly and geared to cater for tourists. Life is centred round the Diamond, a market-place at the top of the town with an obelisk to commemorate the men who compiled

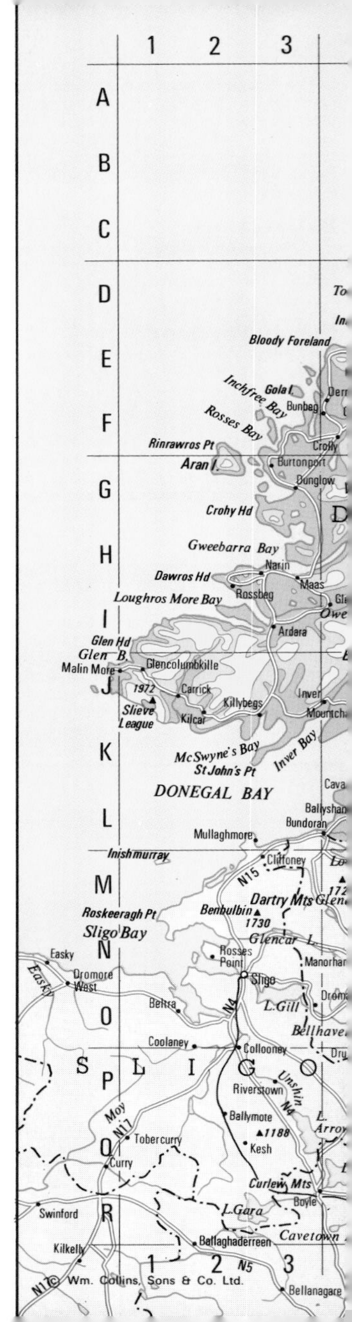

6 7 8 9 10 11 12 13 14 15
A B C D E F G H I J K L M N O P Q R
Inishtrahull
Malin Hd
Glengad Hd.
Culdaff
Bay
Dunaff
Hd
Malin
Fanad Hd
Mulroy Bay
Culdaff
Sheep Haven
Melmore Pt
Ballyliffen
Clonmany
Carndonagh
Benbane Hd
Giant's Causeway
Doagh
Beg
Inishowen Hd
Downings
Portsalon
Inishowen Peninsula
2019
Slieve Snaght
Moville
Greencastle
Portrush
Bushmills
Ballycastle
Lough Swilly
Castlerock
Portstewart
Derrykeevan
Carrowkeel
Glen
L.
Buncrana
Lough
Carrowkeel
Bush
Coleraine
Ballybogy
Rathmullan
Fahan
Scalp Mt.
1589
Foyle
Macasquin
Keel
L.
Inch
I.
Muff
Limavady
A37
Ballymoney
L. Beagh
L. Fern
Rathmelton
Bridgend
Eglinton
A2
Ballykelly
Aghadowey
A26
Finvoy
Dunloy
N13
Londonderry
Roe
Gartan L.
Newtown
Cunningham
LONDONDERRY
Garvagh
Letterkenny
Manorcunningham
A29
Kilrea
Bann
Swilly
EGAL
Dungiven
A5
Claudy
A6
Carn
1205
N14
Foyle
Cark Mtn
Park
Portglenone
Dunnamanagh
Mullaghmore
Deele
Sawel
2240
1825
Maghera
Main
Lifford
Strabane
A6
Stranorlar
Castlefin
Draperstown
L.Beg
Finn
N15
Sion Mills
Sperrin Mountains
Castledawson
A26
Ballybofey
Glenelly
Fearn Hill
Plumbridge
Magherafelt
Toomebridge
L. Mourne
755
Owenkillew
Slieve
Gallion
Mourne
M22
1491
Barnesmore
Castlederg
Newtownstewart
Gortin
Ballyronan
1735
1442
Moneymore
Derg
Mullaghcarn
Killeter
1778
J
nameal
Creggan
A505
LOUGH
NEAGH
Drumquin
Cookstown
L. Derg
TYRONE
Pomeroy
Ballinderry
1194
Omagh
Stewartstown
Drumskinny
Pollnalaght
A29
Pettigo
980
Sixmilecross
Ederny
Lark
Beragh
Coalisland
Kesh
Dromore
Dungannon
Maghery
A32
A5
Fintona
A4
Bann
Lower Lough Erne
Irvinestown
Trillick
Ballygawley
M1
Killadeas
Lurgan
Derrygonnelly
Augher
Moy
Charlemont
Craigavon
Portadown
1233
Clogher
Blackwater
Aughnacloy
Blackwater
Gilford
Fivemiletown
Dyan
A3
FERMANAGH
A28
Lough
Boho
N2
Armagh
Tanderagee
Macnean Upper
Enniskillen
A4
Slieve Beagh
Emyvale
Caledon
Belcoo
A4
Lisbellaw
IRE
ARMAGH
Scarva
Bellanaleck
Glaslough
A3
L. Macnean
Lower
Scotstown
N12
Markethill
Lisnaskea
Rosslea
Monaghan
OF
Keady
Poyntzpass
N.I.
REP.
Smithborough
Cuilcagh Mtn
Swanlinbar
Upper
Lough
Erne
Newtown
Butler
703
N2
Carnagh
Newtown
Hamilton
Belleek
Newry
Camlough
Mountains
Brackley
L.
1331
Finn
MONAGHAN
Castleblayney
Slieve
Anierin
Belturbet
Drum
Ballybay
Muckno
L.
Slieve
Gullion
Ballyconnell
Redhills
Crossmaglen
Forkill
Omeath
Ballinamore
Erne
Cootehill
Milltown
Annalee
Shantonagh
Drumbilla
Fane
Garadice
L.
Killeshandra
Butlers Bridge
Dundalk
Lough Oughter
Shercock
Sillan L.
Cavan
Stradone
Carrickmacross
Shannon
1054
Knockbridge
Cloone
CAVAN
Arvagh
Bellananagh
Mohill
N3
Bailieborough
1119
N2
LOUTH
Moyne
Kingscourt
L.
Gowna
Ruskey
Kilnaleck
Virginia
Drumcondra
Ardee
Dee
N1
Dunleer
6 7 8 9 10 11 12 13 14 15

Burtonport

The Annals of the Four Masters; here are the shops and people. At the bottom of the hill is the small harbour; see the anchor (1790) salvaged from a French ship.

Good countryside around. **Lough Eske** is pretty, its shores edged with trees and in the background gaunt mountains; waterfalls nearby. Cliffs above Lough Belshade and purple vistas along the **Barnesmore Gap** (on the road to Ballybofey). Eglish Glen in the Blue Stack Mountains is a local beauty spot.

Downings D7

Co. Donegal The so-called principal 'resort' of the Rosguill Peninsula, Downings is a scattering of white-painted summer houses around a grey stone nucleus with a little harbour. Beach and caravans (trailers). On the peninsula follow the Atlantic Drive – bay after bay after bay; the old cabins empty, new ones next to them; shepherds speaking Gaelic to the sheep and English to each other.

Dungannon L13

Co. Tyrone (pop. 8000) The centre of the town is a market street sloping up the hill to a dead end at the site of an Irish castle (former seat of the O'Neills). The flight of Hugh O'Neill, Earl of Tyrone, in 1607 marks the end of the Gaelic order in Ireland. In the 19th century a police barracks was built on the site, the plans of which were originally drawn for a fort on the Khyber Pass. When the building was finished someone noticed that a mistake had been made and stopped the building of an Irish police station in India. The barracks are still there at the bus terminus, but screened by the inevitable chicken wire. Security in Dungannon is strict, and sometimes you can't get in at all.

The town grew up on the wealth from linen, but today the chief factories make Moygashel fabric and Tyrone crystal. As compensation for the graceless greyness of the town, the surroundings are a delight – undulating country of trees and streams and low stone walls along country lanes, and 18th-century farmhouses nestling at the foot of the hills. **Castlecaulfield** to the west, and **Caledon** with the Creeve Lough Forest, and **Moy** to the south are three villages within easy reach of Dungannon which offer the deep peace of the country to offset the tension of the town.

Dungiven G12

Co. Londonderry A small market town attractively situated at the junction of three rivers and surrounded by hills; the road south east, towards **Maghera**, leads through the Glenshane Pass overlooking the river Roe.

Dunglow G3

Co. Donegal a two-streeted village; somehow all roads seem to lead into it and no road leads out, so the traffic jams when a wedding coincides with a sale are quite memorable.

Dunglow is the centre of a district called **The Rosses**, a flat, unproductive stretch, with streams, boulder-bedded rivers, beaches and deserted houses.

Eglinton F11

Co. Londonderry A pretty village only 8km/5mi from tense Derry, but relaxed.

Beauty spots south of the village include **Muff Glen** and **Ness Country Park** (mainly deciduous) with a waterfall on the Burntollet River.

Errigal F4

Co. Donegal A massive dome of quartzite, the mountain stands 752m/2466ft above the adjoining valley; walking for the energetic; reached from **Dunlewy**. Nearby is Glenveagh Deer Forest and the deep ravine of **Lough Beagh**.

Falcarragh E5

Co. Donegal A scattered village, heart of the Irish-speaking area. There are many Irish colleges round here; a college is a local public building – school, community centre, village hall – which is taken over in summer for teaching their 'native language' to the Anglophone Irish. There is an interesting one in Falcarragh – it is a sporting centre, where kids come mainly to learn canoeing, mountaineering and rock-climbing, but where all the instruction and meal-time chat is in Gaelic.

Glencolumbkille J1

Co. Donegal A goal for visitors to Donegal because of its collection of Irish cottages from different periods – a terribly poor cabin of 1750, a dark smoke-infested hut of 1820 and an almost affluent cottage (until you compare it with today's standards) of 1890. Each contains household utensils of its period. These cottages were preserved as examples of their type and rebuilt here in a group, like the old clachan, to remind the Irish of their past. Beyond this group of houses is a holiday village of thatched cottages in traditional style but with modern amenities; available for rent. The beach is small by Donegal standards but superb; reached down steps in the rock and swooping round the cliffs. Glencolumbkille is the heart of a Gaelic-speaking area. Original home of St Colmkille (Columba).

Glenties I4

Co. Donegal A neat little village, kept trimly in awe of the mountains looming nearby. The immediate surroundings are wooded, but the scenic route towards **Lough Finn** rises to moor-covered mountains, mostly bare, with empty, tumbling cottages here and there. At long, narrow Lough Finn steep hills on one side face the road on the other. The legend of Lough Finn is one of the most poignant Irish legends. Fergoman was trapped by a wild sow and his sister Finna, hearing his cries, swam across the lake to aid him. But she had swum from his side of the lake towards the cliffs, which echoed his shouts, and arriving there she heard his voice again from the other side. She swam back, only to be deceived again by the echo, and so she crossed and re-crossed, until she drowned. Fergoman died of tusk wounds. The sow still roams the moors.

Gortin J10

Co. Tyrone Forest Park; a circuit cut through a forest of conifers.

Grianan of Aileach F9

A stone fort 16km/10mi south of Buncrana, dating from about 1700 BC. Its fame was such that it is described by

Grianan of Aileach

Ptolemy (AD 140); residence of the O'Neills, Kings of Ulster from AD 450 to 1150; restored to its present condition in 1870. (Grianan means palace; Aileach was the kingdom of the North.)

Killeter J7

Co. Tyrone This has the reputation as the most remote village in Northern Ireland. Here you may really feel past the back of beyond, but you can go still further. Over the border in Donegal is an island in **Lough Derg**, a centre of pilgrimage (June to mid-August) at the cave where St Patrick fasted. (If the direct road is closed, a detour through Pettigo is worthwhile.)

Killybegs J2

Co. Donegal One of the main fishing ports of Ireland; the jetty sees trawlers from

Bishop's Gate, Londonderry

Bulgaria, Russia, Iceland and Spain – even from Ireland. Fish landed here is carried away by refrigerated truck. Fish shops (frozen cod and battered chicken) along the front. Killybegs Carpet Factory, the products of which adorn Dublin Castle, is open to view.

Londonderry G10

Co. Londonderry (pop. 55,000) You must walk round the walls of Derry on a first visit to the Maiden City – for interest's sake and to get some idea of life there today. The siege of 300 years ago is being re-enacted in the present troubles, but they flare up only occasionally, and there is another, more attractive side to the town of Derry.

First, the **Walls**: There are organized tours of the walls leaving from the tourist information centre four times a day. The walls were built in 1614 after the monastic settlement called Derry and all the surrounding lands from Donegal to the River Bann were confiscated by King James and granted to Protestant colonists financed by the city guilds of London. (Thus the new town was named London-Derry; the old, short form is used for convenience and in official publications of the Republic, while the full, longer form Londonderry is used to demonstrate loyalty and in official publications of the Northern Ireland government). They are six metres thick (20ft) and up to six metres high, and it is still possible to walk all the way round on top of the walls. Many old cannon face outwards from the walls – installed to repel Catholics, they are an attraction today and occasional playground for small children of any religion.

The walls were needed shortly after they were completed when Protestant refugees flocked to the city during the Catholic rising of 1641; in 1649 the first siege lasted for 20 weeks. The Great Siege of Derry began on December 7, 1688 when thirteen Protestant apprentices closed the gates on the Catholic forces of James II; with the arrival of James himself there began 105 days of disease and starvation which was ended by the breakthrough of three supply ships. The date of the relief, August 12 (new calendar), is still celebrated every year by a march round the walls headed by an organization called the Apprentice Boys of Derry. The slogan of the siege was 'No Surrender', which remains the slogan of northern Protestants.

The heart of the city lies within these walls, on a steep hill on a bend in the west bank of the River Foyle. Here are the more chic shops, centred round the Diamond (central market square), and the tourist's sights – St Columb's Cathedral (the best example of 'planters' Gothic', from which curfew is rung at 0900 and 2100), the College, the Courthouse modelled on the Erechtheion, and the art gallery.

Just outside the walls, below the main gate, Shipquay Gate, on an embankment which was marsh at the time of the siege, are the bus station and the Guildhall. The **Guildhall**, Derry's City Hall built in 1895, in a style and with decorated windows that recall the connection with London, has a splendid timbered banqueting hall used sometimes as a music room.

North of the Guildhall the river begins to widen out into the Foyle estuary, and here the small docks are quietly busy. Parallel to the river is Strand Road, where the modern shops are lively with cafés and people and some entertainments. Beyond Strand Road the old Georgian streets of Derry slope up towards the park. Gaunt red brick warehouses are scattered within and outside the city walls, left over from the 19th century when Londonderry flourished on linen; some are empty now, others struggle on in the shirt trade.

The present life, the faded elegance, the faded harshness, are all relieved by the view across the river to the green parks and fields of the east bank. That bank of the river, the untroubled Waterside, is much less densely built, and is a tract of sedate, comfortable fairly modern housing in a park-like setting.

All this part of Derry is very pleasant to be in. It is shared by Catholics and Protestants, but is predominantly Protestant. Security measures are evident, of course – the Guildhall is in a wire cage – but they don't dominate and depress.

However, behind the river and close to the walls is the wholly Catholic part of the city. Huge signs, 'You are now entering Free Derry', advertise the crossing into the Bogside and Creggan estates. Bogside is a land of concrete flats, grey, paper-scattered, windblown, barricaded; Creggan is terrace after terrace of houses, massed menacingly on the hill like grey regiments.

You can stay in Derry, put the troubles out of mind, and use it as a centre from which to visit some of the finest of Ireland's scenery. To the west, the beaches and peninsulas of north Donegal are within easy reach. close at hand are the rustic idyll of **Eglinton** village, quiet despite the nearby airport, and the waterfalls splashing into the Burntollet River in the **Ness Country Park**. The **Roe Valley Country Park**, 32km/20mi to the east, marks the start of a range of open-topped hills leading up to the bluffs of Binevenagh with more forest, overlooking the 12km/7miling beach of Magilligan Strand (gliding and sand-yachting).

Derry does not only celebrate the 12th of July. St Columba lives again at the Feis Dhoire Cholmcille in Easter week, and the Derry Feis in April is a gathering for the Gaelic traditions of the area.

Newtownstewart J9

Co. Tyrone Outside Strabane, it looks just like a Yorkshire hill town but it is not a joyous place to live. Open, with people about, and such a contrast to Strabane as to be memorable. Passed on the way to the Sperrins.

Omagh K10

Co. Tyrone (pop. 12,000) Pronounced *Oma.* A mixture of market town, busy and tractor-blocked when the farmers bring in their cattle, and depressed industrial town; comfortable houses with manicured front lawns on the outskirts, redevelop-

Pennsylvanian farmhouse, Ulster/American Folk Park, near Omagh

Sperrin Mountains

ment towards the centre, empty warehouses along the river, and a security-conscious town centre (easy access from car park) on the hill leading up to the asymmetrical church.

Tyrone Agricultural Festival in May; Omagh Agricultural Show first week in July.

Three miles north of Omagh (5km), on the road to Derry, is the **Ulster/American Folk Park**, built with funds provided by the Mellon family of Pittsburgh. Here are reproduced the farm buildings of old Ulster from which the Scotch-Irish went to settle America, and the stockades and log cabins and waggons they built on the American frontier.

Park H11

Co. Londonderry Just a pub where some of the roads from the Sperrins try to find each other. Nice country atmosphere.

Plumbridge I10

Co. Tyrone 'Gateway to the Sperrins'. A crossroads; wide main street; no sign of the troubles apart from police barracks.

Rathmullan E8

Co. Donegal Chief town on the Fanad Peninsula. The peninsula has a splendid coast road (13km/8mi) from the viewing point of **Fanad Head** along **Lough Swilly** past the cliffs of **Doagh Beg**. The lough offers flat stretches of sea mixed up with flat outgrowths of land, and a short distance behind, green mountains rising to bare, rocky moor.

Strabane H9

Co. Tyrone (pop. 10,000) Pronounced *Straban*. A market town, security not too apparent. The local textile industry has been moribund for years, and unemployment combined with bombings give parts of the town a derelict air. Cattle market by the old canal; main square with mixture of old and nondescript houses; walks along the river looking towards the arched bridge over the Foyle which connects with **Lifford** in Donegal. Gray's Printing Works, in narrow Main Street, still has its 18th-century shop front and is where John Dunlop learned the printing trade before going off to America; he later printed the Declaration of Independence.

South of Strabane, towards Omagh, the side road through the Sperrin foothills leads through much prettier country than the main road along the river.

THE NORTH EAST

The Giant's Causeway and the present troubles must be the two best-known features of north-east Ireland – both the work of pent-up pressure forcing their way through cracks in the surface. The troubles are largely confined to areas which, as it happens, are of little charm, while the Causeway is only one of the many attractions of the region. In summer a bus runs between the National Trust's car park at the information centre at the entrance to the Causeway down to the head of the Grand Causeway itself.

The Causeway is the most impressive natural sight in the North East, even in the British Isles – it has been called the 'Eighth wonder of the world'. An exaggeration perhaps, but from photographs you cannot guess the effect of seeing those regular pillars of rock standing out from the cliff face and up from the sea. Until you get there (half-mile walk down from the car park) you may not realize the extent of the Causeway – the Causeway Coast stretches for 13km/8mi of grassy cliff from the Grand Causeway. It is part of the north Antrim coast, a stretch of cliffs and bays, partly holiday resort but mainly unspoilt countryside. South of Torr Head the Antrim Coast Road is cut into the chalk cliffs to form the most striking coastal drive in Ireland, with turnings into the Glens of Antrim – half tamed, half wild; scooped out of the moorland plateau.

Further south, the Mountains of Mourne are a walled-in wilderness for walkers – they come down to the sea along the Mourne coastal path. Strangford Lough is an arm of the sea (boating and fishing), with the Ards Peninsula on one side, a quiet retreat of fishing villages, and on the other the Lecale Peninsula, rich in antiquities associated with St Patrick.

These are the standard tourist attractions of the North East, but the rest of the countryside, away from the towns, has a lot to offer. Over-disciplined, perhaps, but soft and gardened – pleasant rather than romantic. The land is farmed with a blend of love and efficiency, with an eye to landscape and to neatness. The villages and smaller towns are trim and cared-for, like part of one large park. Take Dromore, for example, a little waterfall, lawns by the river and colour all round, or Hillsborough with its continuing elegance, or Castlewellan, or lost Dromara. These smaller places have not only kept the peace of a past age, the troubles appear to pass them by.

The larger towns, like Portadown, Lisburn and Ballymena, are just industrial towns, modernized in patches to make life more agreeable but with little to attract visitors; in them you cannot but be aware of strife or the threat of strife. Whatever charm there may be in industrial Belfast or the urban sprawl of the Lagan valley, it is obscured by the scars and suspicions of the present troubles.

The pattern of trouble and calm coincides roughly with the original pattern of settlement – where the religions are mixed there is not only a tradition of sectarian strife but the minority provides a sea of sympathy in which activists can swim. Counties Antrim and Down were largely populated by Scots centuries ago, while much of Armagh received mixed Scottish-English settlers, and you can see this in the style of the churches and some of the houses even today.

The connection between north-east Ireland and Scotland goes back a long way – at least to AD 500. It may be that even earlier than that Gaelic-speaking Celts crossed to Ireland from Scotland, leaving behind their kinsmen, the Picts. At all events, in the sixth century parties of Irish known at the time as Scoti, crossed the narrow channel from Antrim to the western Highlands and set up a kingdom which straddled both sides of the channel. The eastern part of this kingdom became Scotland; its rulers took over neighbouring Pictland, and in time all of modern Scotland. The present British royal family is descended from those ancient Ulster kings. Throughout the Middle Ages Scots from the Western Isles crossed back into Antrim and their chiefs, the MacDonnells, joined in a three-cornered fight between the earlier Irish, returned Irish, and English. Later, Scots from the Lowlands

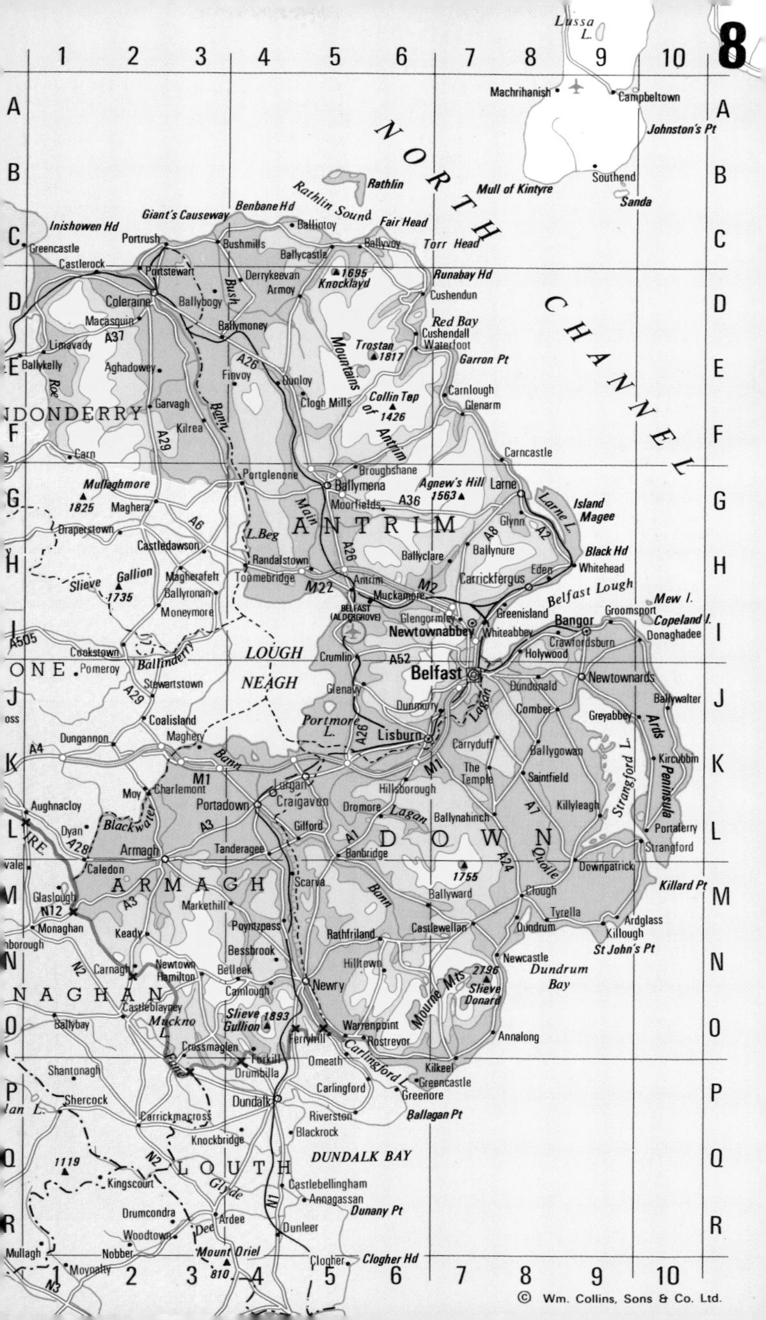
NORTH CHANNEL
Lussa L.
Machrihanish
Campbeltown
Johnston's Pt
Southend
Mull of Kintyre
Sanda
Rathlin
Rathlin Sound
Fair Head
Torr Head
Benbane Hd
Giant's Causeway
Inishowen Hd
Greencastle
Portrush
Bushmills
Ballintoy
Ballycastle
Ballyvoy
Castlerock
Portstewart
Derrykeevan
1695
Knocklayd
Runabay Hd
Armoy
Coleraine
Ballybogy
Bush
Cushendun
Macasquin
Ballymoney
Red Bay
Cushendall
Waterfoot
Limavady
A37
Trostan
1817
Mountains
Garron Pt
Ballykelly
Aghadowey
A26
Finvoy
Dunloy
Roe
Carnlough
Collin Top
1426
of
Antrim
Cloghmills
Glenarm
LONDONDERRY
Garvagh
Bann
Kilrea
A29
Carn
Carncastle
Broughshane
Portglenone
Ballymena
Agnew's Hill
1563
Larne
Mullaghmore
1825
Maghera
Moorfields
A36
Main
Larne L.
Island Magee
Draperstown
A6
ANTRIM
Glynn
A8
A2
L. Beg
Castledawson
Ballyclare
Ballynure
Black Hd
Randalstown
Whitehead
Eden
Gallion
1735
Slieve
Magherafelt
Toomebridge
M22
Antrim
M2
Carrickfergus
Belfast Lough
Ballyronan
Muckamore
Mew I.
BELFAST (ALDERGROVE)
Greenisland
Groomsport
Moneymore
Glengormley
Bangor
Copeland I.
Newtownabbey
Whiteabbey
Donaghadee
A505
Crawfordsburn
Cookstown
LOUGH
Holywood
Pomeroy
Ballinderry
Crumlin
A52
TYRONE
NEAGH
Belfast
Newtownards
Stewartstown
Glenavy
Dundonald
A29
Ballywalter
Dunmurry
Comber
Lagan
Coalisland
Portmore L.
A26
Greyabbey
Ards
Dungannon
Maghery
Lisburn
Carryduff
Ballygowan
Kircubbin
A4
Bann
M1
M1
Strangford L.
Peninsula
The Temple
Saintfield
Moy
Charlemont
Lurgan
Craigavon
Hillsborough
Aughnacloy
Portadown
Dromore
Killyleagh
Lagan
Blackwater
Gilford
Ballynahinch
A1
Dyan
A3
A1
DOWN
Portaferry
EIRE
A28
Tanderagee
Strangford
Armagh
Banbridge
Quoile
Caledon
A24
Downpatrick
1755
ARMAGH
Scarva
Killard Pt
Glaslough
Bann
Ballyward
Clough
A3
N12
Markethill
Tyrella
Poyntzpass
Castlewellan
Ardglass
Monaghan
Keady
Rathfriland
Dundrum
Killough
Bessbrook
St John's Pt
Newtown Hamilton
Hilltown
Newcastle
Carnagh
N2
Belleek
Dundrum Bay
2796
Newry
Slieve Donard
MONAGHAN
Camlough
Mourne Mts
Castleblayney
Slieve Gullion
1893
Muckno L.
Ballybay
Ferryhill
Warrenpoint
Annalong
Rostrevor
Crossmaglen
Forkill
Omeath
Carlingford L.
Kilkeel
Shantonagh
Fane
Drumbilla
Greencastle
Carlingford
Greenore
Shercock
Dundalk
Ballagan Pt
Carrickmacross
Riverstown
Blackrock
Knockbridge
DUNDALK BAY
1119
N2
LOUTH
Kingscourt
Glyde
Castlebellingham
N1
Annagassan
Dunany Pt
Drumcondra
Ardee
Dee
Dunleer
Woodtown
Mullagh
Nobber
Mount Oriel
810
Clogher
Clogher Hd
Moynalty
N3

started to move into north Down and south Antrim in such numbers that by 1585 the English authorities counted these as Scottish shires. When the folk back home turned Presbyterian, the settlers in the north east did the same, so that when King James decided to plant the rest of Ulster with loyal Protestants, the lands east of the River Bann were already settled. The MacDonnells and their people were pushed back into the glens, which even today remain the home of Gaelic tradition and folklore. In the 19th century Belfast grew and industrialized faster than any other British city, drawing in skilled labour from Clydeside and Tyneside, and Catholic Irish to fill the unskilled jobs. And so the scene was set for today's troubles.

Away from the troubles there's an Ireland here with a calm character all of its own. Most of the area of the North East presents a picture of ordered rural enjoyment of life. After some time further south you may appreciate the order; after a few days of that order you may look again for some bubbling relaxation.

Antrim H5

Co. Antrim (pop. 8500) A broad high street, not depressed by strife, and industrial redevelopment at the lower end of the town, maintains an air of prosperity. Steamer outings on **Lough Neagh**, marina at Sixmilewater, recreation centre for a rainy day, wooded avenues in the park, miniature steam railway along the lake shores.

Ardglass M9

Co. Down (pop. 1000) A fishing village, quietly busy, peaceful. **Killough** nearby is a little more resort-like, shaded streets; looks as though it has seen greater days.

Armagh L2

Co. Armagh (pop. 12,000) The holy city of Ireland, its old cathedral founded by St Patrick himself. Was a dignified town, a blend of English cathedral city, 18th-century elegance and Irish gaiety, the sidewalks paved in red marble. This has been obscured by bombings and tight security, but the control zone has been turned to advantage as a smiling pedestrian precinct. There are two cathedrals to St Patrick on low hills 1km/ ½mi apart, one Protestant, the other Catholic. On the north-eastern outskirts of Armagh, beyond tracts of low red-brick housing, is the Astronomical Centre; the planetarium gives daily shows and the observatory has a telescope for public use. North west is apple-growing country, in May white with blossom; **Gosford Forest Park** (near Markethill) and **Carnagh Forest** (near Keady — Gaelic centre) are for tree lovers; **Blackwater Valley** (river park opposite Benburb) for quiet fishing and aquatics.

Ballintoy C5

Co. Antrim Extremely picturesque little harbour at the foot of a winding hill on the Causeway Coast. Teas.

Ballycastle C5

Co. Antrim (pop. 3000) A market town by the sea, where the Oul Lammas Fair is held at the end of August. Boats to Rathlin Island. **Ballycastle Forest**, with scenic drive, to the south, while westwards a cliff-top walk leads (past caravan/trailer sites) to the **Carrick-a-Rede** rope bridge 8km/5mi away. 9km/6mi east of Ballycastle are the 200m/655ft high cliffs of **Fair Head**, looking across to Scotland 23km/14mi away.

Ballymena G5

Co. Antrim (pop. 16,500) A modernized market town, some textile industry, shopping centre for clothing and cattle, flower-growing centre. Ballymenans claim to be like Aberdonians — shrewd or stingy according to your point of view, but anyway the epitome of the hard-headed northern businessman. St Patrick was a slave on **Mt Slemish**, 12km/7mi west of Ballymena, before his escape to France.

St Patrick's Catholic Cathedral, Armagh

Lammas Fair, Ballycastle

Ballymoney **D3**
Co. Antrim (pop. 4000) A late Georgian market town, in lowland pastoral country; on the edge of the largest tract of bog in Northern Ireland; **Safari Park** at Dervock 8km/5mi north.

Bangor **I9**
Co. Down (pop. 35,000) The largest holiday resort in Northern Ireland. Modern facilities. Small harbour, short and long beaches, every entertainment, market day Wednesday. Coastal path to **Holywood** through Crawfordsburn Country Park.

Belfast **J7**
Co. Antrim partly in Co. Down (pop. 360,000, or for the whole conurbation 600,000) Belfast is the second largest city in Ireland, and by far its largest centre of industry. It is the capital of Northern Ireland, but unlike Dublin which grew up and was beautified as a capital, Belfast developed purely for production and still looks much like any industrial town of northern Britain. The first impression one gets of Belfast is the result of the conflict that has filled the streets and the headlines since the end of the 1960s – the heavy atmosphere of barricades, armed troops, armoured police and destruction – but there is more to Belfast than industry and strife. Its charms may hardly be enough to cause a holidaymaker to select Belfast out of all Ireland, but there's light and air as well as brooding darkness.

City Layout
The very centre of the city is **City Hall**, a soberly self-assertive pile of Portland stone put up by the city fathers at the turn of the century when they paused from work to notice that their little village had become a major town. There are tours of the City Hall on Wednesday mornings,

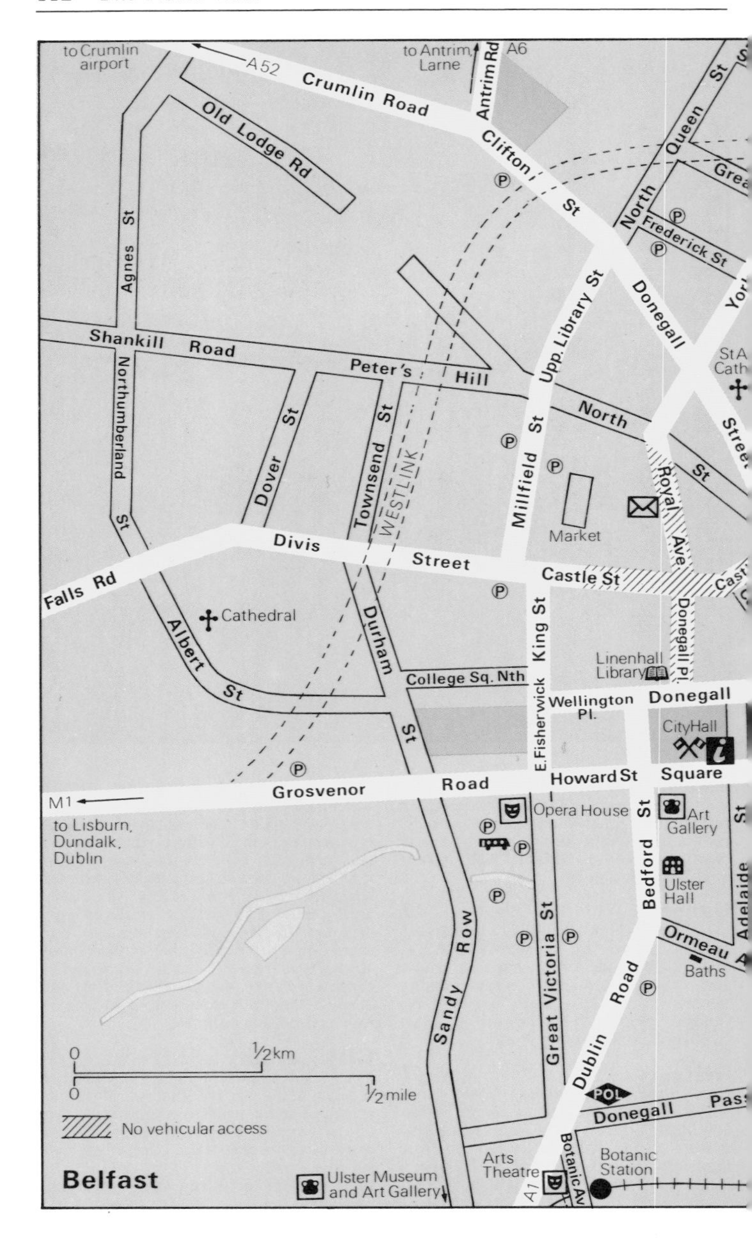
to Crumlin airport
A52
Crumlin Road
to Antrim, Larne
Antrim Rd
A6
Old Lodge Rd
Clifton St
North Queen St
Frederick St
Agnes St
Shankill Road
Upp. Library St
Donegall
Northumberland St
Peter's Hill
North St
Dover St
Townsend St
WESTLINK
Millfield St
Royal Ave
Market
Falls Rd
Divis Street
Castle St
King St
Cathedral
Albert St
Durham St
College Sq. Nth
Donegall Pl.
Linenhall Library
Wellington Pl.
Donegall Square
City Hall
E. Fisherwick
Grosvenor Road
Howard St
M1
to Lisburn, Dundalk, Dublin
Opera House
Bedford St
Art Gallery
Ulster Hall
Adelaide St
Sandy Row
Great Victoria St
Ormeau
Baths
Dublin Road
POL
Donegall Pass
0
½ km
½ mile
No vehicular access
Arts Theatre
Botanic Av
Botanic Station
A1
Belfast
Ulster Museum and Art Gallery

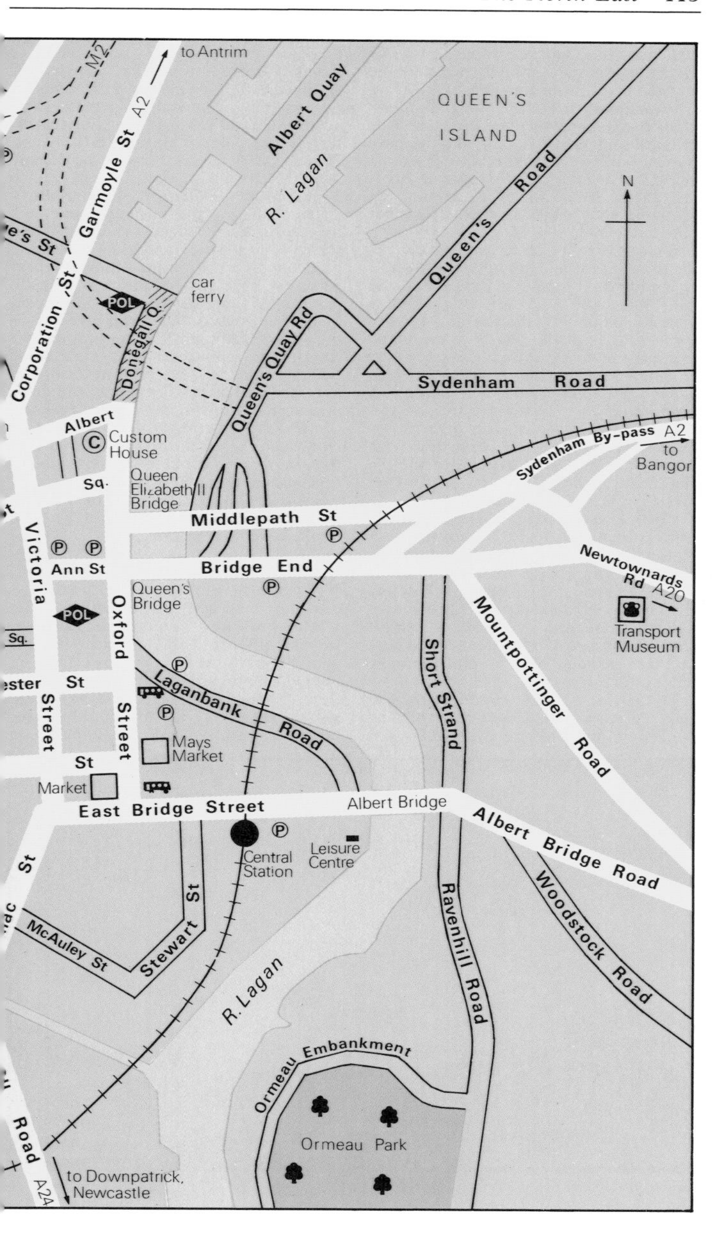
to Antrim
M2
A2
Albert Quay
QUEEN'S
ISLAND
R. Lagan
Queen's Road
N
Garmoyle St
Corporation St
POL
car
ferry
Donegall Q.
Queen's Quay Rd
Sydenham Road
Albert
Custom
House
Sq.
Queen
Elizabeth II
Bridge
Queen's Quay
Sydenham By-pass
A2
to
Bangor
Middlepath St
Victoria
Ann St
Bridge End
Newtownards
Rd
A20
Transport
Museum
Queen's
Bridge
POL
Oxford
Sq.
Street
St
Laganbank
Road
Short Strand
Mountpottinger
Road
Street
Mays
Market
St
Market
East Bridge Street
Albert Bridge
Albert Bridge Road
Central
Station
Leisure
Centre
St
McAuley St
Stewart St
Ravenhill Road
Woodstock Road
R. Lagan
Ormeau Embankment
Ormeau Park
Road
A24
to Downpatrick,
Newcastle

advance booking, tel 220202 ext 216. The Hall stands in Donegall Square, and this square and the adjacent side streets are the starting point for in-town bus services.

Immediately north of Donegall Square is the main shopping area. Buses, service vehicles and delivery vans are the only transport allowed into this area. It is not a bad place to collect your Irish souvenirs, for goods from all over Ireland are available and prices are a shade keener than elsewhere.

West of the city centre lies the core of the zone of conflict – roughly the triangle of land between the Old Park Road, the Falls Road and Andersonstown. This is inhabited mainly by the poorer Catholics with enclaves of the poorer Protestants; cramped red-brick 19th-century terraces or more modern blocks of grey flats, scarred by road blocks and burnt-out, abandoned or boarded up houses, plastered with slogans. This area is now reached from the city centre by the Westlink, a new road that has made the change from the M1 and M2 motorways much simpler and quicker.

North of the centre is suburbia, mainly Presbyterian with a scattering of Methodist, Catholic and Anglican churches, where there are quiet streets of pebble dash and roses. The ring of hills and cliffs that runs round the north and west of Belfast untouched by buildings can be seen from nearly every street round here so there is none of the claustrophobic sense of urban sprawl.

To the east is the heartland of working class Protestantism. First, Harland and Wolff's shipyard where the *Titanic* was built and now building oil tankers when there is work, and the aircraft factory. Beyond the factories lie the houses cramped at first and getting more spacious as you move outwards. There is little demolition and few signs of the security forces; the painted slogans call for the Pope to suffer the same fate as the slogans of west Belfast wish on the Queen.

The south of Belfast, the university district, which is the most agreeable part for visitors has changed a good deal over the past few years and now has some excellent places to eat and a number of art galleries. This part of the city is easily reached by arrivals at the Gt Victoria Street Bus Station. Near the city centre, in the region of Botanic Railway Station, are restaurants and a small concentration of bed and breakfast places – necessary to note, for Belfast has few hotels and these are like miniature fortresses. (For ease and comfort, it is better to go outside Belfast – Holywood, Dunmurry or of course Bangor.) Further out is an untroubled, spacious suburbia housing the university, the Ulster Museum set in the Botanic Gardens and a couple of theatres. Boating on the River Lagan.

Sights

Well worth a visit if you're in Belfast, even justifying a special trip to Belfast, is the **Ulster Folk and Transport Museum**, which is at **Cultra**, on the road to Bangor and 15 mins by car from the city centre (by bus from Oxford Street Station or by train from Botanic or Central Station). Here are specimens of a dozen old Ulster farmhouses and collections of implements

Stormont, Belfast

and pictures to recall the vanished life that made Ulster. It is interesting to compare this display with the Bunratty Folk Museum, p. 82. (Open 1100 to 1900 May to September, 1100 to 1700 October to April, from 1400 Sundays.)

The northern suburbs of Belfast have one of the most spectacular parks of any city. It is formed by the grounds of **Belfast Castle**, **Hazelwood** and **Bellvue**. Set in the parkland of Hazelwood is **Belfast Zoo**. This parkland is overlooked by the fine steep cliffs of **Cave Hill** on the road north, towards Antrim; and the grounds of **Stormont**, seat of government and of the Northern Ireland parliament when there is one, are open on the road east, towards the Ards Peninsula. The smaller, inner parks show the sort of life Belfastians would like to lead if there were no conflict; the **Botanic Gardens** are grass and flowers and non-sectarian bands, and house the Ulster Museum and Art Gallery; **Dixon Park** is full of roses and if you want to escape the 12th July parades (Battle of the Boyne) the Belfast International Rose Trials are here; **Barnett's Demesne** is woodland; **Wilson Park** is by the river; **Ormeau Park** also by the river and **Musgrave Park** with its heather garden are most agreeable. Further out, **Crawfordsburn Country Park** has trees by the sea, **Belvoir Park Forest** takes caravans (trailers), and **Jordanstown Lough Shore Park** has both.

There are at least eight golf courses in the immediate vicinity of Belfast. Four cinemas, three theatres (rather erratic); the grand **Opera House** has been restored to its 19th-century opulence, and re-opened in 1980; there is a residential professional orchestra and there are two semi-resident orchestras encouraged by the Belfast Philharmonic Society, and several halls used for music; **Queen's University** is most alive for its Art Festival in November but throughout the year has intellectual rather than artistic culture to offer. The Royal Ulster Agricultural Society's show, in May at **Balmoral**, is the northern version of the Royal Dublin Show.

Away from the trouble centres, you can feel throughout Belfast a pleasant life aching, like flowers in the desert, to burst into life at the first drops of peace. And you can admire the way people are coping with, or ignoring, the troubles, planning for a better future and believing in it.

Transport

Northern Ireland has an excellent network of regular bus services and there are particularly good bus links between towns not served by the railway. There are tours every day of the week leaving from the Great Victoria Street bus station. Cheap day return journeys leave from Oxford Street bus station. Contact Ulsterbus on Belfast 220011 for more information. Car parking is not allowed on any street in the centre of the city and this is not just a parking restriction but a security measure. There are plenty of large car parks within easy walking distance of the shops with a new multi-storey car park opposite the Tourist Centre.

Spade mill, Cultra

There are three types of taxi: shiny black boxes, like London taxicabs which wait at the city's half dozen or so ranks, many near the City Hall. There are also ordinary saloon cars with a 'taxi' sign on the roof which are replacing the black boxes; and pirate taxis, which are old black boxes, decidedly not shiny. The pirates are not licensed as taxicabs, mostly not licensed to be on the road at all, and many of them are uninsured. They provide a minibus service in West and North Belfast carrying six or eight passengers; they stop if you call unless already overflowing, and you pay the driver what seems fair – it's the quickest way to conversation in an otherwise reticent city, if you don't mind having your ears pinned back.

York Road Railway Station is for Larne (ferries to Scotland) while Belfast Central, connected to Botanic Station, is for other destinations.

Bushmills C4

Co. Antrim (pop. 1200) A grey stone village at a crossroads, home of old Bushmills whiskey. The distillery receives visitors in the afternoon (advance notice requested; closed in August). Bushmills is the nearest town for the **Giant's Causeway**, 5km/3mi, north. The Causeway Coast as a whole extends westward from Fair Head for nearly 30km/19mi, but the most spectacular columns of the Giant's Causeway are concentrated below causeway head. Here there is a car park, restaurant, and exhibition centre; detailed guide and explanation of the causeway available.

Carrickfergus H8

Co. Antrim (pop. 15,000) Formerly the main port of north-east Ireland, now essentially a holiday resort on Belfast Lough, with a small textile industry for variety. The best-preserved Norman castle in Ireland is here, overlooking the little stone harbour; guided tours.

Castlewellan M7

Co. Down (pop. 2000) An agreeable big village – two tree-shaded squares, market on Monday, fair on the second Monday in the month. **Castlewellan Forest Park** is one of the largest, 465 hectares/1150 acres; tree walks, red squirrels, lakes and mountain, and a mature aboretum.

Coleraine D2

Co. Londonderry (pop. 15,000) Quite a large town – a market town and manufacturing centre, with a new university just outside – but with the streets and shops of an expanding village. The town centre could resume its old-world, settled air when the security net is lifted. Banks of the river are open in the middle of the town. The university, spreading functionally and modern over a green field site, is gritting its teeth to be non-denominational.

Crossmaglen O3

Co. Armagh (pop. 1000) A lively, isolated village in the heart of the 'bandit country' of south Armagh. Huge village square, big enough for a town market, adequate parking for the tanks and armoured cars of various types of visitor.

Cushendall and Cushendun D7

Co. Antrim (pop. 700 and 200) The seaside ends of the **Glens of Antrim**, with secluded facilities for visitors. The grave of the Celtic poet Ossian is just above Cushendall. There are nine glens in all, curving down to the sea from the moorland plateau of the Antrim Mountains. Each is broken up into small fields for sheep farming, a pastoral idyll below the bogs and moors, with five forests and forest parks. Cushendall is considered the 'capital of the glens', but **Glenarm** can claim to be the prettiest of the glen villages, and **Glenariff** which terminates at Waterfoot (see below) is generally accepted as the prettiest of the glens. The most striking parts of the coast road are between Cushendall and Glenarm.

Downpatrick M9

Co. Down (pop. 7500) A lively little town; cattle market. Most people come for the cathedral – in its grounds is the reputed

Cushendall

Carrickfergus Castle

Giant's Causeway

Portaferry

grave of St Patrick; the granite block marking the grave is modern.

Larne G8

Co. Antrim (pop. 20,000) Terminus of the passenger, car and freight ferry from Stranraer and Cairnryan in Scotland (70 mins.) Shopping centre, some electrical industry. Starting point of the Antrim coast road.

Newcastle N8

Co. Down (pop. 5000) Seaside resort, with a 5km/3mi curving sandy beach on one side and the **Mountains of Mourne**, where they come down to the sea, on the other. **Newcastle Forest** (in Donard Park) in the immediate vicinity, and **Tollymore Forest Park** (woodland, river and mountain) 4km/2mi inland. Two hours' walk to the summit of Slieve Donard (852m/2796ft), reputed to offer views to Donegal, Wicklow, Scotland and the Isle of Man. Mourne coastal path south of Newcastle; scenic, caves, but few parking places.

Strangford harbour

Newry N5

Co. Down (pop. 11,000) A saddening industrial town made sadder by the troubles; centre is now a paved pedestrian precinct; bedraggled canal with gaunt warehouses; friendly people determined to make the best of it; the roads out, into rolling countryside, are lined with semi-detached trim houses with roses.

To the south west is **Slieve Gullion** (577m/1893ft). There is a winding forest drive almost to the top; paths continue to the summit.

Portaferry L10

Co. Down (pop. 1600) Last village of the Ards Peninsula, connected to little **Strangford** village by a drive-on drive-off ferry. Lovely idle wait. Before the ferry nobody came here, and even now the peninsula is not crowded. Along the coast either side of the ferry are little fishing villages that seem to have been transplanted bodily from the west coast of Scotland — quiet but wakeful. Strangford Lough itself is a small inland sea, popular for boating and skate fishing.

Portrush and Portstewart C/D2

Co. Antrim and Co. Londonderry (pop. 5000 each) Two halves of a holiday resort, separated by a caravan (trailer) site. Portstewart is the posh end, Portrush the more popular with entertainments and revivalist meetings. Four golf courses.

Rathlin Island B6

Co. Antrim (pop. 150) Completely ringed by cliffs, with little stone jetties, white-washed houses stone-walled fields and stone-strewn uplands beyond; cattle, sea-birds along the cliffs, the last place in Ireland where Scots Gaelic was spoken (until the 1920s). Reached in fine weather by motorboat from Ballycastle.

It was in a cave on Rathlin that Robert the Bruce took inspiration from the spider that tried and tried again, until it succeeded.

Warrenpoint O5

Co. Down(pop. 4500) A holiday resort and minor port at the head of Carlingford Lough. The spacious square is in turns market, amusement centre, car park. Quite untroubled atmosphere. Ferry for passengers to **Omeath** in the Republic (no cars). Inland from Warrenpoint, **Rostrevor Park** is all trees, with a caravan (trailer) site tucked away; from there the road leads up to the Spelga Dam, which is as far into the Mourne Mountains as you can get by car.

The heart of the **Mountains of Mourne** (between the dam, the little village of Attical and Newcastle) is enclosed by a 7ft-high stone wall (2m), and is called the Wilderness. the only way across is on foot; heathery plateau rising to bare, granite mountain, probably the best walking country anywhere in Ireland.

Waterfoot E6

Co. Antrim A large village by the sea at the end of the most attractive of the glens of Antrim, Glenariff – precipitous mountains enveloping a fertile valley, with waterfalls and forest park. A very Irish Catholic village.

Antrim Coast from Lurigethan

THE MIDLANDS

'Lakeland' is the name given to this region by the Tourist Board, but, though there are indeed lakes, this is for lack of any other common feature. Even to Irish people, it's the mysterious Midlands – unknown, unremarkable, a bit of a joke as a symbol of insular, claustrophobic provincialism; a shy, reserved landscape with a shy, welcoming people. If the West of Ireland is most Gaelic in character, the South East English, and the North East Scottish, it is the Midlands that are most Irish with their fusion of different influences.

The lakes are mostly north of Mullingar, with the greatest concentration in County Cavan; the largest of them all, Lough Ree, is just north of Athlone. There are rivers, streams and limestone lakes, ranging from little wet holes in the ground up to great expanses of water (16,200 hectares/40,000 acres) – mostly coarse fishing, but a fair amount of brown trout. In the south, in Counties Laois and Offaly, there is more bog; huge tracts of bare peat cut open to dry out and feed the peat-fired power stations. Here too are the Slieve Bloom Mountains; bare hills or deep forest, opening up as an amenity for the inhabitants of the Midlands to exchange their closed-in fields and meadows for a broader prospect.

More than the lakes and bogs and hills and forest parks, this is a limestone plain; rich cow-country in Westmeath, becoming sparser and poorer towards Roscommon and Leitrim. Wind-blown Leitrim is one of the least productive counties – here it takes 2 hectares/5 acres to support one cow – but it is being transformed by draining, made possible by grants given under EEC improvement schemes. The land is full of quietly sleeping country houses, which may also revive with the growing prosperity. They seem to manage to be tucked away, to see without being seen, so you could think the countryside quite deserted. Deserted, that is, until you come into the towns – always full, always lively with visiting countrymen. The towns are of very mixed origins, but have all converged into a dull uniformity of architecture and large-village individuality in interest. The northern towns – Monaghan, Clones, Castleblayney – show their origin in the Ulster plantation of the early 17th century. Most of the towns grew into their present shape in the early 18th century; for the most part the great, remembered events of history passed this region by, and only Athlone is a historical landmark – something you may feel in the town itself.

The region's gentle quietness is reflected in the work of the writers whose inspiration came from here – they were all Anglo-Irish, for in the Midlands the different races blended in with each other, if not harmoniously, at least with less dissent and slaughter than elsewhere. Oliver Goldsmith, before he went off to fame and the jibes of Dr Johnson in England, grew up around Athlone; Maria Edgeworth, an unsubtle Jane Austen, spent her life near Longford; Anthony Trollope developed his love of rural life while inspector of Post around Banagher; Mullingar was home to James Joyce and, suitably disguised, turns up in *Ulysses*; a distorted picture of Irish life, making its own truth, appears in the songs of Percy French, inspector of drains in Cavan.

Festivals Mid-April, Cavan International Song Contest; May 1 Abbeyleix Festival; April, All-Ireland Amateur Drama Contest, Athlone; mid-July, Fiddler of Oriel Festival in Monaghan; late July, Erne Festival, Belturbet; late June, fair at Emyvale, Co. Monaghan; mid-July, One Earth Music Festival, Scotstown, Co. Monaghan; late August, Birr Vintage Week; early September, Clones Farming Show; September 9, pilgrimage to Clonmacnoise.

Abbeyleix Q10

Co. Laois (pop. 1000) An attractive little town stretching along the Dublin/Cork road, with trees and lawns by the roadside. **Durrow**, 9km/6mi to the south east, is a similar village, with a small village green each side of the road. (The *Book of Durrow*, second only to the *Book of Kells* and also now in Trinity College Library, came however from Durrow Monastery outside Tullamore.)

Athlone K7

Co. Westmeath (pop. 10,000) A substantial ancient/modern town on the River Shannon; some narrow winding streets, tucked away behind a lively main shopping street; kept busy from the factories and industrial estate, which are out of sight by the railway bridge or in the Altown direction. Favourite stop-off for cabin cruisers on the Shannon, and for boat rental.

Lough Ree, 3km/2mi north, is an expansion of the Shannon, 15 miles long and up to 6 miles wide (24km, 9km), with many islands and gently sloping, wooded shores. 19km/12mi south of Athlone (9km/6mi by river) is **Clonmacnoise**, a monastic site by the banks of the Shannon; the Cross of the Scriptures is one of the most-photographed Celtic crosses, but in addition there are the haunting ruins of a cathedral, eight churches, two round towers and two other high crosses. The hamlet of **Lissoy**, 15km/10mi north west of Athlone, is where Goldsmith lived as a boy and returned as a man – the heart of Goldsmith Country. 'Let not his frailties be remembered, he was a very great man'.

Clonmacnoise

Athlone at night

Belturbet D9

Co. Cavan (pop. 1000) Spread along the right bank of the River Erne, this is a large village and market centre, a favourite base for the coarse fishing which abounds in the area, and a starting point for cabin cruisers on Lough Erne.

Birr O7

Co. Offaly (pop. 3500) Birr has the grey stone houses of an Irish Midlands town, but is laid out around a dignified Irish-Georgian square – an early attempt at town planning. Birr Castle houses the remains of the telescope which, when built by the Earl of Rosse in 1843, was the world's largest. The telescope and the landscaped demesne of the castle are open in summer 0900 to 1300 and 1400 to 1800. Birr is a fishing centre, and good base for the **Slieve Bloom Mountains**. These are a ridge of low hills, covered by heather but increasingly being forested, which are excellent for escape into open country; difficult access by car. For the motorist, the best view is at the Cut, on the road south from Clonaslee to Roscrea; on foot the valley of the Barrow has several waterfalls, while the valleys up to the Glendine Gap, bare in the west and thickly forested in the east, are home to antlered deer. **Kinnitty** in the Blooms, promoted as a strikingly pretty village, is grey and bare but relieved by architectural details if you have an eye for them.

Carrickmacross E14

Co. Monaghan (pop. 2100) A wide street of dull houses and a few shops. Formerly noted for lace; still obtainable from the nearby convent. Many caves nearby. The **Dun-a-Ri Forest Park** to the south west is an attractive mixture of conifers with young hardwoods pushing through.

Carrick-on-Shannon F6

Co. Leitrim (pop. 2000) The town itself curves and rises over a hill, and is full of life; its main attraction for visitors is the marina, down on the river, where cabin cruisers can be rented. **Lough Key Forest Park** is about 12km/7mi from Carrick on the Sligo road, with mature hardwoods and cedars and interesting bog plants; overlooks still Lough Key whose islands are home to ruined castle or monastery. Good reception facilities.

Cavan E10

Co. Cavan (pop. 3500) Percy French wrote such well-known ballads as *The Mountains of Mourne* and *Phil the Phluter's Ball* after he left Cavan (where he served for some years as inspector of drains), but the town itself did not inspire

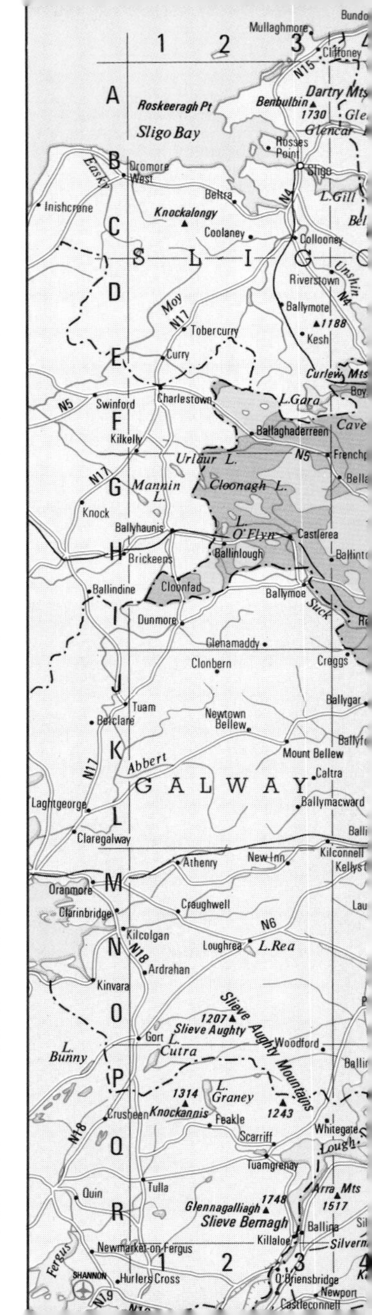

9
FERMANAGH
ARMAGH
MONAGHAN
CAVAN
LEITRIM
LONGFORD
LOUTH
MEATH
OFFALY
KILDARE
LAOIS
Lower Lough Erne
Upper Lough Erne
Enniskillen
Lough Macnean Upper
L. Macnean Lower
Cuilcagh Mtn
Iron Mountains
Slieve Anierin
Slieve Beagh
Lough Oughter
Cavan
Monaghan
Armagh
Athlone
Mullingar
Longford
Tullamore
Port Laoise
Carlow
Navan
Kells
Trim
Naas
Kildare
Grand Canal
Bog of Allen
Slieve Bloom Mts
Lough Ree
Shannon
Boyne
Liffey
Barrow
Lugnaquillia Mtn
Slieve Na Calliagh
© Wm. Collins, Sons & Co. Ltd.

St Mel's Cathedral, Longford

him to verse. The cathedral surely would have done. Built in 1942, it is described as eclectic – four Corinthian columns to support Romanesque cupolas topped by a virile Gothic spire – with a beautiful interior. The Cavan crystal works are open to visitors. **Killykeen Forest Park**, to the west, is mainly mature spruces and the 'islands' in its lake are crannogs.

Clones C11

Co. Monaghan A very 'northern' looking town – a sloping main square with a high cross, and nearby a round tower. Encircled by the River Finn – signposted everywhere, but very elusive.

Longford H8

Co. Longford A bare town in a bare plain. The cathedral was an earlier, simpler version of Cavan Cathedral mentioned above – four Ionic columns to support a Roman arch. Tullynally Castle, residence of Lord Longford at **Castlepollard**, is open in summer 1430 to 1800. Longford was the centre of a literary circle.

Monaghan B13

Co. Monaghan (pop. 5500) As the Shannon flows through Ireland widening out here and there into a broad lake, the main road meanders through Monaghan, broadening into a square, the Diamond, a crossroads – each with its stone memorial. But life is not restricted to this main road, many side roads are just as busy with small shops and workshops, for Monaghan is a stop on several express bus routes and the centre for an active industrial estate. At night the pubs and dances are busy, people coming from Clones and Castleblayney, and even across the border from Armagh. **Rossmore Forest Park** just south of Monaghan.

Mullingar J10

Co. Westmeath (pop. 7000) Market town for an area given over to cattle; its long main street, busy with small shops and with a square on one side surrounded by hotels and bars, could still be waiting for the cows to be driven in.

Port Laoise P10

Co. Laois (pop. 4000) The main road bypasses the town, which is a high street widening peacefully down from a roundabout, to connect with the small industrial estate towards the jail. Housing development on the low hills around the town.

Roscommon I4

Co. Roscommon (pop. 1300) Very small for a county town, but feels more than just a shopping centre; it lies on a hill with a collection of 18th-century municipal buildings (it was formerly a wool town) including a typical court house in the square at the top. Visit the 13th-century abbey and castle.

Tullamore **M9**
Co. Offaly (pop. 7000) A market centre and substantial crossroads; the town spreads along the various roads into the centre. A number of dignified older buildings, but lost in Victorian redevelopment. At the north end of the town, the Irish Mist distillery is close by the locks of the Grand Union Canal which formerly terminated here.

Abbeyleix

INDEX

All main entries are printed in heavy type. Map references are also printed in heavy type. The map page number precedes the grid reference.